VARIOUS
POSITIONS

VARIOUS
POSITIONS
A LIFE OF
LEONARD
COHEN
IRA B. NADEL

PANTHEON BOOKS   NEW YORK

All rights reserved under International and
Pan-American Copyright Conventions. Published in
the United States by Pantheon Books, a division of
Random House, Inc., New York, and simultaneously
in Canada by Random House of Canada Limited, Toronto.

Pages 323-325 constitute a continuation of the copyright page.

Library of Congress Cataloging-in Publication Data

Nadel, Ira Bruce.
   Various positions : a life of Leonard Cohen / Ira B. Nadel.
      p. cm.

Includes index.
ISBN 0-679-44235-9

1. Cohen, Leonard, 1934–   – Biography.
2. Poets, Canadian – 20th century – Biography.
3. Lyricists – Canada – Biography.
4. Singers – Canada – Biography.
I. Title.

PR9199.3.C57Z8   1996
811'.54-dc20   [B]   96-12098   CIP

Random House Web Address: http://www.randomhouse.com/

Printed in the United States of America

First Edition

9 8 7 6 5 4 3 2 1

For Dara & Ryan

I wish I could say everything there was to say in one word. I hate all the things that can happen between the beginning of a sentence and the end.

– Leonard Cohen, *The Favorite Game*

What is a poet? A poet is an unhappy being whose heart is torn by secret sufferings, but whose lips are so strangely formed that when the sighs and the cries escape them, they sound like beautiful music.

– Kierkegaard, *Either/Or*

CONTENTS

INTRODUCTION

THE ENIGMA of Leonard Cohen: a well-tailored bohemian, an infamous lover who lives alone, a singer whose voice resides in the basement of song, a Jew who practices Zen. Attempting to unravel this mystery has taken me to Los Angeles, New York, Nashville, Montreal, and the island of Hydra, retracing his steps. Cohen has been patient throughout this process, even when I posed a question the publisher insisted I ask: could this be called an authorized biography? Cohen paused and then thoughtfully said, "tolerated," adding an instant later, "benignly tolerated." Such understatement disguises the remarkable assistance he and those close to him have provided for my work. In some small way, this account is an acknowledgment of their trust.

Cohen has been called "part wolf and part angel"; "the grocer of despair"; the "poet laureate of pessimism"; and, more colloquially, the "prince of bummers." His early albums supported this view, morbidly described as "music to slit your wrists by." After listening to Leonard Cohen, one woman exclaimed, "Thank God Sylvia Plath never tried to sing!" His later work shifted this view and his most recent albums have been called celebratory and, in a moment of rashness, optimistic. But his stylish, self-regarding abjection is present in virtually all that he writes, exhibiting a "moody amorousness," a narcissistic eroticism that has only enhanced his appeal. Cohen has always felt gloomy but, as he has said, his gloom is probably no more intense than anyone else's. "There is a confusion between depression and seriousness. I happen to like the *mode* of seriousness. It's peaceful and relaxing to me to be serious." Nietzsche sums up the paradox: "In punishment there is so much that is *festive*."

Cohen had early success, a *poet maudit* whose gloomy anthems helped define a lingering literary adolescence. But his success has always been a qualified one; his records were critically lauded but sold unspectacularly, his books were controversial though largely unread. In the mid-eighties his work underwent a commercial resurgence as younger artists recognized their debt to him. A 1991 tribute album entitled *I'm Your Fan* featured a series of alternative bands, and the 1995 tribute album *Tower of Song* followed.

The title of this book, *Various Positions*, originates in Cohen's favorite album, released in 1984, but it is also a philosophical statement, reflecting a dictum offered by Cohen's Zen master, Joshu Sasaki Roshi: "A Zen man has no attachments." To fix a position, to hold a singular point of view for a lifetime, is antithetical to Zen because there are no absolutes in the Zen world. The only absolute is change; all is transition. The only thing that lasts and the only reality in Zen is the pure and unattached self, which one must constantly seek to uncover. To do so, however, requires discipline.

Whether writing three pages a day, as Cohen's London landlady insisted he do in 1959, or laboring over song lyrics, which often take him years to complete, discipline is the source of Cohen's success. Everything he writes must be worked over until it yields the truth. "Last thought best thought," he has said, inverting the weight usually given to a first, spontaneous thought. "I am formal, uptight, agonized most of the time," he told an interviewer in 1993. "I have to do a lot of undressing before I can get to the truth; I'm not a spontaneous, visceral kind of chap."

As part of the process of artistic discovery, Cohen preserves his work in all of its stages. His collection of notes, papers, journals, drafts, memoirs, and letters form a lasting record of his work. Such an archive, he explains, is "at the very center of the thing. I see the work floating on the material." The published songs or poems are "just the Beacon, the designation—somehow the signal for an investigation of the entire work. . . . The archive is the mountain, and the published work the volcano."

He views his archive as the unhewn rock cited in the Bible: "the thing you place on the altar, the ark, whatever the thing is that's hammered, that's ornamented, that's careful, but the platform has got to be unhewn rock, and it's got to be there, and it's got to be solid." His progress is noted in the increments of a miniaturist, each draft inching toward its goal. Through the work, Cohen's life is seen, its small victories and continual setbacks. For better or worse, Cohen has retained every record of himself.

"Keeping things was the only thing I had a sense of," Cohen has said:

I didn't have a sense of who I was, or where I was going, or what the world was like, what women were like. The only thing I had a sense of is that I'm going to document *this* little life. . . . I never said I was a great poet; never once did I suggest I was anything more than a minor poet and a songster and whatever it is. Let some other people make the designations. I only said that I got it here. It's all here. . . . I did do what I set out to do which was to document my trip without any judgment on it. But my trip is here. There is no question about it.

Art holds a unity that history does not, and for Cohen, there is no separation between music and writing. This embodies the Judaic tradition of the unity of the Written Law with the Oral Law; they are inseparable, the Oral Law sometimes interpreted as the soul of the Written Law. Their revelations are contemporaneous.

In his life, Cohen has sought to witness, touch, and experience beauty at close quarters. The irony of this desire, however, is that once he touches it, it evaporates. The many he has loved, he has left. When he has obtained beauty, he has abandoned it, feeling that it entrapped him. As he writes in an unpublished novel, "what I admire in the morning I despise by sundown. I change between glutton and renunciation." This has meant numerous broken love affairs; but it has also meant the endurance of his aesthetic. Out of the depression and despair comes the will to create.

But Cohen has always exhibited an undercurrent of self-mocking humor. "I like to include a permission to laugh with most of my work," he remarked in 1992. "I've always thought I was a comic voice." But the humor doesn't undercut the essential seriousness of his work. "Each book represents for me a different kind of crisis," he explained early in his career. He has dealt with such crises ritualistically, initially through poetry and later with novels, psalms, and narrative songs. His small but faithful audience recognizes him as an almost pastoral figure, providing a form of spiritual guidance. His music is eclectic: a mix of Mediterranean rhythms, folk ballads, country and western, blues, jazz, and gospel, a flexible, mournful idiom that constantly reshapes itself.

At the core of Leonard Cohen's appeal is a poetics of survival, a means of confronting and transcending the darkness of the self. Aiding his own survival has been a twenty-five-year involvement with Zen Buddhism. Judaism initiated Cohen's spiritual quest, but Buddhism has provided direction. Its process of liberation through suffering "has led me to wherever I am." The importance of self-understanding in Zen has been its great attraction for him:

> I want no attachments. I want to begin again. I think I love you, but I love the idea of a clean slate more . . . the temptation of discipline makes me ruthless.

Cohen repeats this manifesto in his poems, songs, and fiction, and enacts it in his personal life. The passage summarizes Cohen's ongoing dilemma: how to be true to another as well as to himself.

Every biography is, of course, incomplete; it can only approximate moments that represent the life of its subject. But most of Cohen's artistic energy has gone toward approximating those moments, too, providing the biographer with some clues to the mystery of Leonard Cohen:

> Far from flying with the angels, he traces with the fidelity of a seismograph needle the state of the solid bloody landscape. . . . He can love the shapes of human beings, the fine and twisted shapes of the heart. It is good to have among us such men, such balancing monsters of love.

1

THE ROOT

OF THE CHORD

L EONARD COHEN buried the first thing he ever wrote. After his father died, he cut open one of his formal bow ties, sewed a message into it, then buried it in the snow in the small garden behind his Montreal home. For a nine-year-old boy, it was a powerful and symbolic gesture. In effect, Cohen conducted his own private burial, substituting prose for an outward expression of grief. The message also preserved a link with his father which was re-enacted each time he composed. Art and sacrament, ritual and writing, became fused.

The day of the funeral was also his sister's birthday, but no one mentioned it. Only later that night, when the two children tearfully confided to one another that they had glimpsed their father in the open coffin at the funeral service, was it noted. Cohen asked his sister not to cry because it was to be a day of celebration, but neither could escape the dominating image of the day: the face of their father, as stern in death as it had been in life.

His father's death in January 1944 was the central event of Cohen's youth and provided a rationale for his art. As he explained in *The Favorite Game*: "deprivation is the mother of poetry." It also sent him on a quest for a series of father/teachers, a quest he pursues to this day. Psychologically, the death of his father freed Cohen by allowing him to pursue his own interests unobstructed, but it also imprisoned him by forcing upon him the role of compromised patriarch, responsible for the welfare of the family, yet entirely dependent on his uncles.

"What was it like to have no father? It made you more grown up. You carved the chicken, you sat where he sat," the narrator answers in *The Favorite Game*. As with much of his work, Cohen transforms the psychological into the spiritual: "His father's death gave him a touch of mystery, contact with the unknown. He could speak with extra authority on God and Hell." The loss of his father left a lasting scar, one that Cohen defined in his first novel as "what happens when the word is made flesh." The note in the bow tie has been the talisman he has carried for a lifetime: "I've been digging in the garden for years, looking for it. Maybe that's all I'm doing, looking for the note."

LEONARD COHEN grew up in Westmount, the upper-middle-class Montreal neighborhood on the slope of Mount Royal. The semidetached, two-story brick house backs onto Murray Hill Park, an open space which connects the mansions to Côte-St-Antoine, where the Shaar Hashomayim Synagogue commands most of a city block. The park provides a view of the St. Lawrence River to the south and downtown Montreal to the east. From the enclosed second-story porch at the rear of the house, Cohen could see the city in the distance or spy on the lovers below him in the park. The park, he later wrote, "nourished all the sleepers in the surrounding houses. It was the green heart" that gave the playing children "heroic landscapes . . . the nurses and maids winding walks so they could imagine beauty."

Until 1950, Cohen had the small back bedroom that faced the park. When Cohen's mother Masha remarried in 1950 and a stepdaughter joined the family, Cohen gave up his small room and moved into what had once been the library. The room still contains his bed, dresser, two walls of crammed bookcases, and a desk facing the side window.

On the walls are a portrait of his father and photographs of Cohen and his sister Esther in their graduation robes from McGill. There is also one of Cohen praying in *tallit* (prayer shawl) and *tefillin* (symbolic representations of the commandments, actually leather straps attached to two small boxes containing portions of the Torah and worn at daily prayer) at the Wailing Wall in Jerusalem. Leather sets of Chaucer, Milton, Byron, Scott, Longfellow, Wordsworth, and Palgrave's *Golden Treasury* sit on the bookshelves. The books were given to his father for his bar mitzvah and inherited by the son. The *Daily Prayer Book* of the United Hebrew Congregations, given to his mother, rests on the top shelf of one bookcase, alongside *Ozar Taamei Hazal, Thesaurus of Talmudical Interpretations*, a seven-hundred-page volume compiled by Cohen's maternal grandfather, Rabbi Solomon Klinitsky-Klein.

There are poems by A.M. Klein, *Canadian Constitutional Law* by Bora Laskin, the *Writers Market 1957, The Criminal Code of Canada, 1953-54*, the collected poems of Marianne Moore, *Harmonium* by Wallace Stevens, the collected shorter poems of Auden, *A History of Sexual Customs* by Richard Lewinsohn, and *Torture of the Christian Martyrs* by A.R. Allinson, as well as Matthew Arnold's poems, Scott's *The Lady of the Lake*, Whitman's *Poems, Poems* by Robert Louis Stevenson, *Memoirs of Napoleon*, and, in white leather, Dante's *Divine Comedy*. Some of Cohen's diverse influences and budding ambitions are glimpsed, including his early interest in becoming a lawyer.

There is also a portrait of Cohen's father Nathan that reveals a well-dressed, serious looking man with slicked-back hair, a groomed moustache, and large, penetrating eyes. Known in the family as Nat, he affected Edwardian attire and in the picture wears an English suit with "all the English reticence that can be woven into the cloth." The portrait suggests nothing of his disability or poor health, the result of the war. He looks solid and middle class. But he had high blood pressure and would become flushed when angry, which was often. His sense of foreboding was great, and Edgar Cohen, Leonard Cohen's second cousin, twenty years his senior, recalled that once in synagogue, Nathan Cohen turned around and said to him, "My son, Leonard, I'll never see his bar mitzvah." He was right. Another time, when the youthful Cohen mistakenly recited the *Kaddish*, the prayer for the dead, instead of the *Kiddush*, the blessing over wine at the dinner table, his father did not interrupt him but with resignation murmured, "Let him go on; he will have to say it soon enough."

Nathan Cohen was trained as an engineer, but played an important role in the family's clothing manufacturing business. Cohen admired him, but within the Cohen family, Nathan was, in Cohen's words, "the persecuted brother, the near-poet, the innocent of machine toys, the sighing judge who listens but does not sentence." When he died, he threw the stable life of the family into turmoil: "He died ripe for myths and revenge, survived by a son who already believed in destiny-election. He died spitting blood, wondering why he wasn't president of the synagogue. One of the last things he said to his wife was: 'You should have married an Ambassador.'"

A photograph of Cohen's mother and father in a garden shows a smiling woman in an elegant dress, slightly taller than her husband. Husband and wife stare proudly at the camera, the mother with an inquisitive, suspicious glance, the father with a more imposing, slightly rigid demeanor. Nathan looks dapper with a cigar, boutonniere, and spats. They were married in 1927.

Cohen's mother was of Russian descent and exemplified the national character: by turns melancholic, emotional, romantic, and vital. Suzanne Elrod, the mother of Cohen's two children, remembers her as Cohen's "most dreamy spiritual influence." According to Masha's stepdaughter Roz Van Zaig, Masha "had the flair to be bohemian." She was quite musical and often sang European folksongs in Russian and Yiddish around the house. When her son learned to play the guitar, she sang with him in a magnificent contralto voice. She was dramatic and heavyset, with a flair for cooking. Masha's personality initially clashed with the quiet formality of the Cohens. Her English was poor and she always spoke in a deep voice with a Russian accent; some Cohens thought that

Nathan had married beneath him. She had trained as a nurse and her caring manner, essential for her physically ailing husband, soon made her acceptable to the larger family. Her zestful behavior, however, unsettled some of the more demure aunts and uncles.

THE ARRIVAL of Lazarus Cohen to rural Ontario in 1869 followed the arc of nineteenth-century Jewish immigration to Canada. He established himself in Maberly and after two years sent for his family who were still living in what was then Lithuania. By 1883, he had moved to Montreal, where his son had been going for religious training and where Jewish settlement was expanding. Lazarus was from a devout and scholarly family, a rabbi who reinvented himself as a businessman in the new world. His younger brother Hirsch was also a rabbi and later became the Chief Rabbi of Canada, celebrated for his powerful, rumbling, resonant voice, perhaps the source of Cohen's own unique sound. Lazarus proved to have a talent for business and in 1895, after he had moved to Montreal, became president of W.R. Cuthbert & Company, brass founders who, between 1896 and 1906, formed the first Jewish dredging firm in Canada. They had a fleet of dredges and a government contract to deepen almost every tributary of the St. Lawrence River between Lake Ontario and Quebec.

Lazarus was intensely involved in the Jewish community and in 1893 visited Palestine on behalf of a Jewish settlement group, the first direct contact by Canadian Jews with their homeland. He also became chairman of the Jewish Colonisation Committee of the Baron de Hirsch Institute, which had been organized to settle Jewish immigrants in Western Canada. In 1896 he became president of Shaar Hashomayim Congregation, a post he held until 1902. He wore a flowing white beard, favored cultured English to Yiddish, and spoke with a slight Scottish brogue, since he had first settled in the county of Glengarry before coming to Canada. He died on November 29, 1914, at age seventy, two weeks after he had been re-elected president of his synagogue. He was eulogized for being conversant with both the Talmud and English literature and for harmonizing the ancient traditions with modern culture.

In 1891 Lyon Cohen, eldest son of Lazarus, married Rachel Friedman and they had four children: Nathan, Horace, Lawrence, and Sylvia. Like his father, Lyon contributed to the foundation of Canadian Jewish life in Montreal. With Samuel William Jacobs, he began the first Jewish paper in Canada, *The Jewish Times*. In 1904, at only age thirty-five, he was elected president of Shaar Hashomayim, the largest and most prominent congregation in Canada. He was also a member of the Board of Governors of the Baron de Hirsch Institute of Montreal and became president of the institute in 1908. He transformed its building into the first active Jewish Community Centre of Montreal and established the first Hebrew Free Loan Society and the Mount Sinai Sanatorium in Ste-Agathe. In 1922 he became chairman of the Montreal Jewish Community Council, which he had helped to found. He was an "uptown" English-speaking Jew from Westmount, a stark contrast to the Yiddish-speaking "downtown Jews" of St-Lawrence and St-Urbain streets.

In 1900, Montreal was populated mostly by francophones but controlled largely by anglophones. Two thirds of the population was French, concentrated east of St. Lawrence Boulevard or "The Main," as it is called. The English lived on the west side of the city, in the mansions of the Golden Square Mile, in Westmount, and in the working class Irish ghetto, Griffintown. Jewish settlement was concentrated along The Main, the dividing line between English and French, the conciliatory geographic division of the two solitudes. St-Urbain was the enclave's western border, and it ran east to St. Denis, south to Craig and north to Duluth. Jewish immigration became significant only near the end of the nineteenth century; the number of Jews in Montreal more than quadrupled from roughly 16,400 in 1901 to 74,564 in 1911. Most remained traders, commission agents, or manufacturers.

Lazarus Cohen eschewed the traditional demographics and eventually settled in Westmount. The stone houses reflected those of Mayfair or Belgravia, incorporating Tudor, Gothic, and Rennaisance designs on the same block, occasionally in the same house. It was architecturally, geographically, and spiritually removed from francophone Montreal, from what would later be termed the French Fact.

In *The Favorite Game*, Cohen underscores the insularity of West-mount by contrasting it with the immigrant character of Montreal and the way the city constantly reminded its inhabitants of their past. The city, he writes, perpetuates a "past that happened somewhere else":

> This past is not preserved in the buildings or monuments, which fall easily to profit, but in the minds of her citizens. The clothes they wear, the jobs they perform are only the disguises of fashion. Each man speaks with his father's tongue.
>
> Just as there are no Canadians, there are no Montrealers. Ask a man who he is and he names a race . . . In Montreal there is no present tense, there is only the past claiming victories.

LYON COHEN strongly believed that a knowledge of Jewish history was necessary for self-respect, a belief passed on to his son Nathan and grandson Leonard. Knowledge of the Torah was indispensable, and performing *mitzvot* (good deeds) was essential. Aristocratic and urbane, conciliatory yet pragmatic, Lyon Cohen was a formidable presence in local Jewish life, particularly in the war effort.

Lyon devoted himself to the recruitment of Jewish men for the armed services and saw two of his own sons, Nathan and Horace, go off to fight in the Royal Montreal Regiment (the third, Lawrence, did not). He was president of a new, national relief body which sent aid to European Jews who had been victimized by the pogroms and he became chairman of the National Executive Committee of the Canadian Jewish Congress, inaugurated in March 1919 in Montreal. His home on Rosemount Avenue contained books of Jewish learning and proudly displayed a Star of David on the front. He frequently entertained Jewish leaders like Chaim Weizmann, Rabbi Stephen S. Wise, and Solomon Schecter. In addition to being scholarly, Lyon was a bit of a dandy; he used an expensive cane, always dressed in the finest suits, and lived comfortably with the assistance of servants.

In 1906 he organized the Freedman Company, a wholesale clothing manufacturer, and it became the major business of his sons Nathan and Horace (Lawrence would operate W.R. Cuthbert, a brass and plumbing foundry, taking over from their uncle, Abraham Cohen, who died prematurely at fifty-seven). In the late fifties, Lyon's grandson Leonard briefly worked at the foundry and in the shipping department of the Freedman Company. In 1919, Lyon organized and became president of the Canadian Export Clothiers Ltd.; later he became president of the Clothing Manufacturers Association of Montreal and a director of the Montreal Life Insurance Company. He was to be presented to the Pope during a European trip in 1924, but the day before the scheduled meeting he had a heart attack. He was taken to a sanatorium in Switzerland, where he recovered. He died on August 15, 1937 and one of the pall bearers at the funeral was liquor magnate Samuel Bronfman. Leonard Cohen was three years old.

Leonard's maternal grandfather, Rabbi Solomon Klinitsky-Klein, was a rabbinic scholar. He was known as *Sar ha Dikdook*, the Prince of Grammarians, for writing an encyclopedic guidebook to talmudic interpretations, *A Treasury of Rabbinic Interpretations*, and a dictionary of synonyms and homonyms, *Lexicon of Hebrew Homonyms*, praised by the poet A.M. Klein. Rabbi Klein was something of a confrontational teacher, noted for his disputations.

A disciple of Yitzhak Elchanan, a great rabbinic teacher, Rabbi Klein was born in Lithuania, and became the principal of a yeshiva in Kovno. He and his family escaped the pogroms in Russia and Eastern Europe, fleeing first to England and then emigrating to Canada in 1923. He first stayed in Halifax, and then moved to Montreal, where he had been corresponding with Lyon Cohen about resettlement. A friendship with the Cohen family led to the marriage in 1927 of his daughter Masha and Lyon's son Nathan.

Rabbi Klein made lengthy visits to Atlanta, Georgia, to be with his other daughter Manya, who had married into the Alexander family of Georgia. He found the trips stressful because there were few Jews in the South to share life with, although the Alexander family retained its orthodox practices, to the point of having their black servants wear skullcaps. Their large ante-bellum mansion on Peachtree Street became an unusual expression of Conservative Jewish life in Atlanta. It was presided over by Manya, who spoke English with a Russian accent highlighted by a southern drawl.

Rabbi Klein finally settled in New York where he became part of the crowd of European Jewish intellectuals centered at *The Forward*, the leading Yiddish paper in America, with contributors such as Isaac Bashevis Singer. But grammatical and talmudic studies absorbed Rabbi Klein, and he spent most of his time in study at the synagogue or in the library. He often visited his daughter Masha in Montreal and came to live with the family for about a year in the early fifties. Young Cohen would often sit with the "rebbe" and study the Book of Isaiah. Already quite elderly, the rabbi would read a passage with Cohen, explain it in a combination of English and Yiddish, nod off, then suddenly awake and repeat himself. "He'd read it again with all the freshness of the first reading and he'd begin the explanation over again, so sometimes the whole evening would be spent on one or two lines," Cohen recalled. "He swam in it so he could never leave it. He happened to be in a kind of confrontational, belligerent stance regarding the rabbinical vision."

Cohen sat and studied not because he was a devoted biblical scholar but "because I wanted the company of my grandfather. [And] I was interested in Isaiah for the poetry in English more than the poetry in Hebrew." The Book of Isaiah, with its combination of poetry and prose, punishment and redemption, remained a lasting influence on Cohen's work and forms one of several core texts for his literary and theological development. His reliance on images of fire for judgment and the metaphor of the path as the way to redemption derive from this central text. The prophetic tone of destruction in Isaiah, "the Lord is going to lay waste the earth / and devastate it" (24:1), manifests itself repeatedly throughout Cohen's work in personal and political terms. Isaiah also sets out an edict Cohen has followed: dispense with illusions, reject oppression, eliminate deceit.

Rabbi Klein had a sharp, Talmudic mind, the kind that could put a pin through the pages of a book and know every letter that it touched, Cohen recalled. Even when elderly and living with Masha and her family during a second period in the late fifties, Rabbi Klein exhibited a powerful, although not always concentrated, knowledge. He knew that he had published books in the past, and that Cohen had also published a work: *Let Us Compare Mythologies* (1956). But occasionally, when the rabbi met Cohen in the upstairs hall of the house, he would become confused and ask his grandson if *he* was the writer or not. When Cohen published the *Spice-Box of Earth* in 1961, he dedicated it to the memory of his grandfather and paternal grandmother. At the time of his death in Atlanta, Rabbi Klein was writing a dictionary without the use of reference books. Cohen inherited his *tefillin* as well as a reverence for prophetic Judaism. His grandfather became the first of a series of powerful teachers in his life who filled the role of his absent father.

LEONARD NORMAN COHEN was born on September 21, 1934, a Friday. In the Jewish religion it is said that those born on a Friday are marked for special piety. His chosen names reflected a family tradition of *L*'s, in Hebrew, the "Lamed," beginning with Lazarus and Lyon and continuing with Cohen's daughter Lorca. He was also thought to look more like his grandfather Lyon than his father Nathan. His Hebrew name, Eliezer, means "God is my help." Norman is the anglicized form of Nehemiah, the rebuilder. The names were significant because in Hebrew, words embody divine attributes.

Born in the year 5695 in the month of Tishri, according to the Hebrew calendar, Cohen entered a family that retained its Jewish traditions. His place in the synagogue was prominent (the family had the third row) as the grandson and great-grandson of two presidents, and early in his youth he participated in the daily prayers and weekly celebrations. Each Friday night the family observed Shabbat. "Religion structured our life," Cohen has remarked.

Nathan Cohen, with his brother Horace, ran the Freedman Company, by now a successful mid-priced men's clothing manufacturer. The company specialized in suits and topcoats, which were distributed throughout the country. At one time it was considered to be the largest men's clothing manufacturer in Canada. Most of the workers were French Canadian or Italian; the managers were mostly Jewish. Nathan, known as N.B., dealt with the factory, the workers, the machinery, and the suppliers. Horace, or H.R., ran the front office. He was the principal contact for the buyers and store owners and had all the qualities of a front man: charming, articulate, lazy, and pompous. He eventually became an Officer of the British Empire. Although Nathan's semi-invalid state limited his participation, he remained active in the company. But he resented being second-in-command to his younger brother, a resentment that may have been passed on to Cohen who later questioned his relationship with the family.

Beauty at Close Quarters, the title of the first-draft of *The Favorite Game*, elaborates this disenfranchisement. The hero's father was "a fat man who laughed easily with everybody but his brothers," the narrator writes, but explains that the "others" all "walked ahead of his father into public glory."

Nathan wasn't given to ostentation but the family had the perquisites of the upper-middle class, employing a maid, a chauffeur-gardener, and an Irish-Catholic nanny named Mary who was devoted to Cohen and had a special influence. She often took him to church, and Cohen grew up respecting rather than fearing the dominating presence of the Catholic church in Montreal. He would often go to her home to celebrate Christmas and recalled that he was brought up "part Catholic in a certain way." The church represented romance to Cohen and he saw "Christianity as the great missionary arm of Judaism. So I felt a certain patronizing interest in this version of the thing. I didn't have to believe in it."

The Cohen household reflected his father's formality rather than his mother's earthy personality. Nathan always dressed in a suit and occasionally wore a monocle and spats. Cohen rarely saw him without a suit jacket on. In Tarpon Springs, Florida, where his father vacationed, he was photographed in a suit against informal backdrops of fishing boats and sponge fishermen. Cohen, too, was expected to wear a suit to dinner, or at the very least, a sports jacket. His sister Esther would argue with her father about her habit of only partially unfolding her napkin; Nathan insisted that it be completely unfolded. He also became upset when the family's shoes and slippers were not carefully arranged under their respective beds. Decorum dictated the family, business, and communal life of the Cohens.

Although not a man of letters, Nathan recognized the value of books and gave his son an uncut set of leatherbound English poetry. His mother was not a great reader either, and Cohen recalls only a Russian volume of Gogol on her shelf. Nathan read aloud to his children, although he didn't have a gift for it. Cohen thought his father was reticent, withdrawn, and introspective. His enthusiasms were concert hall music—Sir Harry Lauder was a favorite, as well as Gilbert and Sullivan—and photography. An amateur filmmaker, Nathan Cohen documented the lives of his children on film. Some of the footage was excerpted in *Ladies and Gentlemen, . . . Mr. Leonard Cohen*, a 1965 National Film Board documentary on Cohen. The father's interest instilled in his son an early fascination with photography and the pleasure of being photographed. In the 1951 Westmount High School Yearbook, Cohen lists photography as his hobby, an interest represented in *The Favorite Game* and *Beautiful Losers*.

——————————

AS A CHILD, Cohen had a small Scottish terrier, nicknamed Tinkie for the tinkle of his license and identification tags. His parents surprised him with the dog as a gift, the scene described in *Beauty at Close Quarters*. His mother had actually named the dog Tovarishch, but his father disliked the reminder of the site of the Russo-German treaties. Tinkie disappeared in a snowstorm fifteen years later and was found dead under a neighbor's porch the next spring. The dog had been one of Cohen's closest childhood companions; Cohen still keeps a picture of Tinkie in his Los Angeles home. To this day he refuses to get another dog, although he had guppies, chicks, mice, turtles, and even a rescued pigeon during his childhood.

For his seventh birthday Cohen's father bought him a Chemcraft chemistry set and built a laboratory in the basement. With an alcohol lamp and chemicals, Cohen produced dyes, invisible inks, and other concoctions. His friends would join him in the basement, creating new colors and liquids.

Cohen's secure, comfortable childhood was unsettled by his father's poor health and premature death. A poignant scene in *Beauty at Close Quarters* narrates the impact of the illness as the father climbs the stairs in his home, pausing a minute or so at each step. With his son often by his side, the father "would continue the story he was telling and never stop to complain how difficult the ascent was. Very soon, however, he could spare no breath at all and they would climb in silence." In the funeral scene in *The Favorite Game*, Cohen recounts his anger at the loss of his father who died at the age of fifty-two, the solemnity of his uncles, the horror of an open coffin, and his mother's inability to face the tragedy. For his part, Cohen later recalled that "there was repression . . . I did not discover my feelings until my late thirties. I had to *adopt* the aspect of receptivity. I was very receptive to the Bible, authority. . . . Having no father I tried to capitalize [on his absence], resolve the Oedipal struggle, [create] good feelings."

Following his father's death, Cohen won a significant dispute with his mother over custody of Nathan's pistol, a military souvenir. Cohen had been fascinated by his father's military exploits and at one time Nathan had spoken of sending Cohen to a military college, an idea Cohen eagerly accepted. *The Favorite Game* describes the dispute over the gun, presented as an important talisman: a "huge .38 in a thick leather case . . . Lethal, angular, precise, it smoldered in the dark drawer with dangerous potential. The metal was always cold."

Cohen has always been fascinated by weapons, reflected in his novel *Beautiful Losers*. "I loved the magic of guns," the character F. declares. For several years Cohen himself kept a gun. In her lyrics to "Rainy Night House," Joni Mitchell describes how she and Cohen took a taxi to his mother's house in Westmount during her absence: "she went to Florida and left you with your father's gun alone." In "The Night Comes On," from Cohen's album *Various Positions* (1985), a wounded father tells his son:

Try to go on
Take my books, take my gun
And remember, my son, how they lied
And the night comes on
And it's very calm
I'd like to pretend that my father was wrong
But you don't want to lie to the young.

The gun remained in the house until vandals stole it in 1978, the night before Masha Cohen died. Its disappearance meant the loss of protection, Cohen once reflected. But its importance was clear, as the narrator explains in *The Favorite Game*: "The gun proved [the dying father] was once a warrior."

Cohen handled the pain of his father's death stoically. "I didn't feel a profound sense of loss, maybe because he was very ill throughout my entire childhood," he later said. In an unpublished poem that celebrates his father, written on the Greek island of Hydra, Cohen writes:

No one looks like my father
but me
In the world I alone
wear his face
And here I am in places
he never would have travelled
among men
who think I am myself. . . .

Following the death of Nathan Cohen, Masha's status in the family altered. Her financial situation changed and the loss of her husband and security threw her into uncertainty. Cohen found himself in an awkward position, relying on his uncles for employment and the family for income. This change in status was subtle but profound and it was felt by everyone. Masha's suffering was the most intense and obvious, manifested by mood swings and the occasional depression.

Thirteen years later Cohen dedicated his first book, *Let Us Compare Mythologies*, to his father, whose death he confronts in the poem "Rites." The work castigates the failure of his uncles to allow his father a peaceful death by unrealistically prophesying his recovery as he lay dying. Unsurprisingly, death is the topic of one of Cohen's essays from McGill. It emphasizes the scar that is "always left on one of the survivors—a scar that does not heal quickly."

At the time of his father's death, Cohen was attending Roslyn School, a nearby elementary school. Academically he did well but didn't distinguish himself. The school stressed extracurricular activities, including art classes and sports, and Cohen enjoyed both. Two afternoons a week and Sunday mornings, he attended the Hebrew School at the synagogue. Expectations of him, as a Cohen, were greater and the work harder, but as early as age six he was familiar with Hebrew and basic Judaism. Miss Gordon and Mr. Lerner, his teachers, were important influences, but neither of them, nor anyone else, ever sat him down and explained what God wanted from him. No theology was offered. In a sense it was atheistic, Cohen has said.

Regular Shabbat attendance with the family at Shaar Hashomayim reinforced his Judaism, and he vividly remembers sitting in the third row of the synagogue with:

> my uncle Horace and my cousin David and then me, and then Uncle Lawrence and then the cousins and then Uncle Sidney and the other cousins. There was a whole *string* of Cohens standing up there in the front line and singing our hearts out.

Still, it was a solemn occasion; one came to pray in a formal manner, with reverence but not feeling. Cohen's knowledge of Hebrew was limited to the liturgy: "I knew how to address the Almighty in Hebrew as long as it was exclusively concerned with redemption!"

In 1945 at age eleven, Cohen began an education of another sort when he first saw pictures from the concentration camps. This was the true beginning of his education as a Jew, he has said, and the realization that Jews are "the professionals in suffering." This view was later reinforced by his sister's trip to Israel in 1949 with a group of Jewish students. Cohen had become politicized by the suffering of the Jews at an early age.

In 1947 Cohen had his bar mitzvah, marking full acceptance into Judaism with his reading of the Torah. But the event was marred by his father's absence; the traditional prayer of release recited by the father (ending a father's responsiblity for his son) was missing from the ceremony. A celebration at the synagogue only partially alleviated the sadness of the event.

He began attending Westmount High in 1948, where he was elected to the Student Council. He later became its president and proved to be a convincing politician, persuasive, seductive, and showing a gift for organization. In *Beauty at Close Quarters*, he added a fictional reason for seeking the presidency: attraction to the beautiful outgoing president from whom he would have to receive hours of instruction. Cohen was also a member of the Board of Publishers, which oversaw the student paper and yearbook. He was a surprisingly avid athlete, involved in cycling, cross-country skiing, swimming, sailing, and was an unlikely member of the school hockey team. He was also chairman of Student Productions, the drama club, and soon had his first printed work appear: a homeroom Christmas skit for a holiday assembly, which was mimeographed and distributed to the cast. His "ambition," as described beneath his graduation photograph in the Westmount High School Yearbook for 1951, reads "World famous orator." His "pastime" was "Leading sing-songs at intermissions." But he also found time for girls: on the back of his 1950-51 Student Council card are the hastily written names and phone numbers of two female students.

Cohen's high school English teacher, Mr. Waring, encouraged his interest in literature, and writing began to play a larger part in Cohen's life. Increasingly, he sought solitude, rushing home to write rather than socialize with friends. Most of his early efforts were short poems, short stories, and effusive journal entries.

Yet he had a large group of buddies, which included his cousins and Mort Rosengarten. "FSOTC and Rosengarten, Too" was a popular rallying cry for him and his cousins: it meant "The Fighting Spirit of the Cohens and Rosengarten, Too." He enlarged his circle when he began university; it soon included Henry Zemel, Mike Doddman, Derrik Lyn, Robert Hershorn, Harold Pascal, and Lionel Tiger. One of his best friends at the time was Danny Usher, and the two of them would often walk around Murray Park in their raincoats reading and talking. They could always be identified: Danny tall and angular, Cohen short and intense.

At the same time, Cohen "swam in a Jewish world," studying the religion, remaining observant but debating its customs. His later departure from Judaic practice stemmed not from its tradition, which he loved, but from concern about its "methods and meditations" about which no one talked. Reflecting a lifetime interest in discipline and order and a desire to understand process, Cohen rationalized his interest in other spiritual investigations as wanting "to go into a system a little more thoroughly."

Music supplemented his Judaic and secular studies. Esther had started studying piano, and Cohen followed her, taking instruction from a Miss McDougall. Progress was slow, and he practiced in a desultory manner in a small basement room where the piano was kept. He preferred the spontaneity of playing melodies on a penny-whistle, which he always carried. He studied the clarinet and learned to play well enough to join the school band, but the guitar soon took over his musical interests.

As a high school student Cohen also became interested in hypnotism, which he discovered through the father of one of his first girlfriends. The father had tried to put Cohen under. He failed but Cohen was fascinated and he continued to study hypnotism, reading M. Young's *25 Lessons in Hypnotism, How to Become an Expert Operator* (1899). Cohen's only prop was a yellow pencil, slowly waved back and forth in front of his subject's eyes. It worked well enough to hypnotize the family maid and so Cohen undressed her, an adolescent fantasy come to life. He had less success bringing her out of the trance, though. Worried that his mother would come home, Cohen tried slapping the maid but it didn't have much effect. He referred to his book and was finally able to guide her out of the trance before he was discovered. During a summer spent as a counsellor at Camp Sunshine, a camp for disturbed children, Cohen also hypnotized one of the counsellors, revealing to the willing subject aspects of her life she herself had forgotten.

Cohen's interest in hypnotism was ongoing and had to do with its transcendant powers. In *Beauty at Close Quarters*, he writes: "he wanted to touch people like a magician, to change them or hurt them, leave his brand on them, to make them beautiful. He wanted to be the hypnotist who takes no chances of falling asleep himself. He wanted to kiss with one eye open."

To transform people, to make them "beautiful" while watching the process, was Cohen's ambition. Like his hero Breavman, he believed that "there [was] some tangent from the ordinary cycles of daily life, a formula not to change debris to gold, but to make debris beautiful." Cohen sought to be a "magic priest." Hypnotism was the earliest manifestation of this goal; poetry and music would become its later forms.

Cohen's fascination with the streets and the downtown nightlife also emerged during his adolescence. Around the age of thirteen or fourteen he began to sneak out of the house at night, walking around downtown and observing the junkies, prostitutes, cafe life, the buzz of the city. He would buy a sandwich at a cafeteria and listen to the jukebox, one of his great pleasures. He also hoped to meet girls.

He generally made these excursions alone, although occasionally his friend Mort Rosengarten would join him. Sometimes Cohen returned home to find his mother on the phone describing his coat to the police after checking his room and finding it empty. She would send Cohen to bed and rage outside the closed door, "calling on his dead father to witness his delinquency, calling on God to witness her ordeal in having to be both a father and mother to him." Part of what drove him downtown was a heroic vision of himself with "a history of injustices in his heart . . . followed by the sympathy of countless audiences," an idealistic description not very far from the situation of his early musical career.

In 1949, when he was fifteen, two important events occurred: he purchased a guitar and discovered Lorca. Moved by musical curiosity and the possibility that girls would be more interested in a guitar player than a clarinetist, pianist, or ukulele player, Cohen bought a second-hand guitar for twelve dollars from a pawn shop on Craig Street. Its steel strings made it "a ferocious instrument," Cohen has said. There was no guitar culture going on at the time, and it was generally thought that only Communists played the instrument. But Cohen discovered nylon strings and then flamenco when he met a nineteen-year-old Spanish immigrant playing for some young women in Murray Hill Park.

Dark, handsome, passionate, and lonely, the Spaniard embodied a culture as well as a musical talent and Cohen was impressed by both. After three lessons, Cohen learned a few chords and some flamenco. When the young man failed to show for the fourth lesson, Cohen called his boarding house and discovered that his teacher had committed suicide. He never learned his story but Cohen was grateful for his teaching, which became the basis of his musical composition and chord structure. He sang with Mort Rosengarten, who had learned to play the banjo, and his mother frequently joined them. "I'm a lot better than what I was described as for a long, long time," Cohen has remarked: "People said I only knew three chords when I knew five."

That year, Cohen also unexpectedly came upon *Selected Poems*, by Federico García Lorca, a writer about whom he knew nothing. Cohen has ironically said that Lorca "ruined" his life with his brooding vision and powerful verse. In a way, he later explained, Lorca:

> led me into the racket of poetry. He educated me. [Lorca] taught me to understand the dignity of sorrow through flamenco music, and to be deeply touched by the dance image of a Gypsy man and woman. Thanks to him, Spain entered my mind at fifteen, and later I became inflamed by the civil war leftist folk song movement.

In print and at concerts, Cohen has repeated the lines that first led to the destruction of his purity: *"Through the Arch of Elvira / I want to see you go, / so that I can learn your name / and break into tears,"* lines from Lorca's poem "The Divan at Tamarit." Lorca was a seminal influence on Cohen, as poet, performer, and artist. He was the first of a series of representative poets for Cohen. Louis Dudek, F.R. Scott, A.M. Klein, and Irving Layton would follow, but Lorca was his first poetic model.

Federico García Lorca was executed by Granadian Falangists on August 19, 1936, shortly after his return to Spain to aid in the Spanish Civil War. Cohen identified with Lorca's fanciful belief that he possessed the blood of gypsies and Jews and shared his elegiac tone and faith in a spiritual absolute. Three questions by Lorca anticipate themes that animate Cohen's work:

> *Am I to blame for being a Romantic and a dreamer in a life that is all materialism and stupidity?*
> *Am I to blame for having a heart, and for having been born among people interested only in comfort and in money?*
> *What stigma has passion placed on my brow?*

LEONARD COHEN began to write poetry seriously in 1950 at the age of sixteen, a year after he discovered Lorca. He recalls:

> I was sitting down at a card table on a sun porch one day when I decided to quit a job. I was working in a brass foundry [W.R. Cuthbert] at the time and one morning I thought, I just can't take this any more, and I went out to the sun porch and I started a poem. I had a marvelous sense of mastery and power, and freedom, and strength, when I was writing this poem.

Another explanation was his desire for women:

> I wanted them and couldn't have them. That's really how I started writing poetry. I wrote notes to women so as to have them. They began to show them around and soon people started calling it poetry. When it didn't work with women, I appealed to God.

Dionysus not Apollo reigned.

From his earliest efforts with poetry, Cohen was committed to the discipline, the task. In contrast to the casual activities of his friends, he was absorbed by his work. Cohen's stepsister remembers that he often worked late into the night. One product of those late nights is an essay entitled "Murray Park at 3 a.m." in which he recounts his "possession" of the park: "It is my domain because I love it best." He narrates the forms of his control, from fictitious assaults on the tennis players to his control of the floundering sailing vessels in the pond. The cement pools, sunken "in stone plazas of different levels joined by stone steps and bordered by clipped hedges, appear like the prospect to some mist-obscured exotic house of worship or love palace." And listening to his own footsteps walking home, he thinks, "You [an early love] brought me into the light. I was in the darkness."

Cohen's friends understood that his commitment to writing was genuine, and he recalled a game they played with an anthology of English poetry. His friends would open it at random, read him a line, and expect him to complete the poem.

Cohen and his friends were movie fans and often went to Ste-Catherine

Street movie houses on Saturday afternoons. But a Montreal bylaw prevented children under sixteen from entering alone. Cohen overcame this problem by altering streetcar passes to show an earlier birthdate. But the forged passes couldn't disguise the fact that he was simply too short to be sixteen. The tallest boy would buy the tickets then they would nervously walk down a long hall to the ticket usher where Cohen was often turned away. His success rate was only about twenty percent. A strict code of conduct was observed: every boy for himself. If one of them couldn't get in, the group wasn't expected to forfeit the movie in sympathy.

Cohen's height was enough of a problem that for his bar mitzvah he needed a footstool to see over the *bimah* or lecturn. After reading in *Reader's Digest* that pituitary injections of a hormone were guaranteed to make you taller, Cohen consulted the family doctor about getting the shots. The treatment was experimental and Cohen's doctor dissuaded him from trying it. He also tried stuffing Kleenex in his shoes, but the disadvantages soon became apparent and painful at a school dance and Cohen abandoned his search for height.

For several summers Cohen participated in the ritual of camp, beginning in 1944 at Camp Hiawatha in the Laurentians, where he met his life-long friend, Mort Rosengarten. A report of August 26, 1949, from Camp Wabi-Kon in northern Ontario cited Cohen's abilities as a leader, although it also noted his dislike of routine. At these and later camps, Cohen learned more about the guitar, and when he became a counsellor he frequently led singalongs when not instituting new games such as a haiku contest.

At Camp Sunshine, a Jewish Community Camp where he became a counsellor in 1950, Cohen met Jews unlike himself: they were extravagant and emotional and had an earnestness grounded in necessity, not fantasy. Their high schools were almost entirely Jewish, unlike Westmount High. Whereas Cohen's family liked "to think of themselves as Victorian gentlemen of Hebraic persuasion," the counsellors at camp recognized that they were Jews above all. Irving Morton, the director, was a twenty-seven-year-old intellectual, a socialist, and a folksinger. He had a large catalogue of folk songs that celebrated workers, from a Jewish collective in the Crimea, *Zhan Koye*, to the desperate struggle of miners.

He also believed in "creative camping": no regimentation, virtually no discipline, and no competition.

In 1950 at Camp Sunshine, Alfie Magerman, one of Cohen's closest friends, introduced him to *The People's Songbook*; his father, it turned out, was involved in union organization and the two sang from the book every morning. *The People's Songbook* represented a new folk culture of high moral and political content, "homemade songs of protest and affirmation." It was the time of the Weavers, who made their debut at the Village Vanguard in 1949, of Woody Guthrie, and of Josh White. Each song, whether a German anti-fascist song, a French partisan song, or "Viva la Quince Brigada," the historic song of the 15th or International Brigade of the Spanish Republican Army, reflected politics, patriotism, or protest. Israeli pioneer songs, Chinese resistance songs, a German solidarity song with words by Brecht (printed across the page from "The Star Spangled Banner"), all demonstrated to Cohen that songs could be about protest, freedom, and resistance. Cohen's "The Old Revolution," "The Partisan," and "The Traitor" all reflect what he learned from *The People's Songbook*. From that songbook, he said, he "developed a curious notion that the Nazis were overthrown by music."

He now understood that songs could convey social thought as well as personal hope, taking examples from Woody Guthrie, Brecht, and Earl Robinson (composer of "Joe Hill"). *The People's Songbook* introduced Cohen to the potential of folk music, confirmed when he heard Josh White perform at Ruby Foo's Chinese restaurant in 1949. Although Cohen found the burgeoning pop music world fascinating, hustling quarters around his house to sneak out at night and listen to jukeboxes, folk music was his first love. "Through my interest in folk music, I discovered what a lyric is and that led me to a more formal study of poetry."

Cohen thought of himself as a singer then, not a songwriter, although in 1951 he wrote his first song. He and another counsellor worked on a tune all summer and when it was done, they went to a local restaurant to celebrate. Unexpectedly, the very song they sweated over was heard from the jukebox. They had incorporated a pop song of the day, "Why, Oh Why," into their now dismal effort which they had to abandon. But Cohen soon made another attempt titled "Twelve O'Clock Chant," which he sings in the 1965 NFB film about him. The syncopation, lyrics, subject matter, and emotion expressed in the folk song underlie Cohen's later structures, melodies, and lyrics.

In 1950 Cohen's mother married Harry Ostrow, a Montreal pharmacist. Shortly after they were married, Ostrow was diagnosed with multiple sclerosis and there was some question as to whether or not he had hidden the knowledge of the disease from Masha before they were married. She had been a nurse with Nathan and that role was now being repeated. Masha had been trained as a nurse, but she didn't want it to become a way of life. A palpable tension developed between Cohen's mother and stepfather. Despite the presence of an older man in the household, Cohen still conducted the rituals for the festivals and high holidays. By 1957, Masha and Harry had separated, and Harry moved to Florida hoping that the climate would ease his illness.

After his father's death, Cohen felt detached from his family. He spent a great deal of time in his room reading and writing, developing a sense of his own private life at an early age. It was a time for exploration, experiment, and imaginary expeditions. The family indulged his solitary efforts and no one ever asked him how he felt about matters. If his grades slipped during these periods of familial disinterest, these was still a determination to do better: "There were no cries for help in those days. You just did it. You got the grades."

He maintained a good if distant relationship with his sister Esther, though. Four-and-a-half years older than Cohen, she had little contact with him growing up. Her friends were older and her interests different. There was little sense of co-education at home; their lives at synagogue, Hebrew school, music lessons, swimming lessons, and B'nai B'rith activities didn't intersect. However, Esther encouraged Cohen's efforts at writing and he shared his attempts at poetry and song with her. They became closer as they grew older, after Esther moved to New York and married Victor Cohen.

In his late teens, Cohen began a series of significant relationships with women. Yafa ("Bunny") Lerner was one of the first, a young woman from Montreal who was interested in dance. His first serious love interest was Freda Guttman, a seventeen-year-old art student whom Cohen met when he was sixteen. Freda attended McGill for one year and then transferred to the Rhode Island School of Design. For the next three or four years, she and Cohen continued to see each other, the relationship fuelled by both sexual and artistic excitement. Cohen read his new work to her, sang for her, and took her to parties. In the summer of 1955 he arranged for them to be counsellors together at a B'nai B'rith camp near Ottawa in the Gatineau hills. He and his girlfriend were unusual figures at the Jewish camp, he a poet and she an artist; one remembered anecdote was his preference for quoting Yeats while rowing campers about. He describes Freda in "The Fly," in his first book, *Let Us Compare Mythologies*, for which she provided the cover illustration and five interior sketches. When they broke up, Cohen wrote a short essay about Freda and the meaning of love, the first of many works dealing with women he has known.

In his essay, Cohen describes Freda as a slender and narrow-hipped woman with "especially beautiful thighs and that is why, I suppose, the word occurs so frequently in my verse." He was attracted to her mouth, her black hair, her long fingers, and to her movements: "She moved with her own kind of logic, more graceful than any woman I have ever seen." Sometimes, he writes, she was his closest comrade, but at other times her observations seemed trite. "A smothering sense of intimacy" soon enveloped him. He rejected this intimacy on the grounds that he did not love her, that he, in fact, knew "almost nothing about love." Such intimacy, he believed, "has something to do with mutual destruction." Cohen writes:

> I have never loved a woman for herself alone, but because I was caught up in time with her, between train arrivals and train departures and other commitments. I have loved because she was beautiful and we were two humans lying in the forest at the edge of a dark lake or because she was not beautiful and we were two humans walking between buildings who understood something about suffering. I have loved because so many loved her or because so many were indifferent to her, or to make her believe that she was a girl in a meadow upon whose aproned knees I laid my head or to make her believe that I was a saint and that she had been loved by a saint. I never told a woman I loved her and when I wrote the words "My love," I never meant it to mean "I love you."

This unusual paragraph, most likely written in 1956, forms an *Ars Amatoria* which outlines Cohen's attitude toward love, one that has remained consistent throughout his life. There is a studied schizophrenia, the seeking and rejecting of each love in turn.

"I have never thought of women as a medicine for loneliness." he writes,

> And I do not think that humans are so unique, one from the other, that there exists among the living only one special, perfect lover for each special, perfect beloved, to be pressed and fit together by Fate like jigsaw pieces. Each person we want to love takes us on a different path to love, and they change us and we change them as we all move together, and love offers as many alternate paths as any landscape.

Such views actually protect his easily broken heart. The title of a notebook from the mid-fifties, containing lyrical poems of desire and fear of loss, reads, "Leonard Cohen / Poems Written / While dying of love."

Cohen's fundamental position on love is that it is essential but redefines itself with each individual. One requires a variety of lovers to suit a variety of stages in one's life. "Love generally," he warns,

> but do not commit yourself to a particular love. You will become known as a sympathetic friend and a faithful lover because you never really permit these roles to seize your heart, you can practise and perfect them. But the heart is guarded, kept free and untarnished by any simple human affiliation so that it will reflect in glorious accuracy all the charts of the stars which the clouds one day will part to reveal. The important thing is not to approach anyone too close because tomorrow you may have become pure light.

Despite his resistance to love, or perhaps because of it, Cohen was a "charismatic" figure, Freda Guttman recalled. Although his origins were conservative, middle class and very Westmount, he drew people into his world of poetry and desire. His determination to be a poet and his early efforts at songwriting and singing were a source of fascination. He encouraged this image by showing up at parties with his guitar and offering a song whenever asked. As a Westmount bohemian, Cohen was something of an enigma but he has retained the trappings of both throughout his life. The bourgeois and bohemian co-exist in harmonious counterpoint. Unlike one of his closest friends at the time, Robert Hershorn, who was troubled by obligations to carry on his family's business, Cohen never seriously considered joining his uncles' businesses, although he was occasionally pressured to do so.

Cohen did not so much rebel against his Westmount life as follow an alternative path. He felt that his family, for all its prominence, lacked an ideology or dogma:

> life was purely made up of domestic habits and affiliations with the community. Aside from that, there were no pressures on the individual. I never knew of rebellions or conflicts because there was nothing to rebel against. I didn't have anything to renounce my family for. Because in a sense nothing was solid. I have no urge to struggle with this world, to take a position.

Freda Guttman recalls that Masha was obsessed with Cohen's well-being and frequently tried to make him feel guilty for being too independent. Proud of her cooking, she would often get up when Cohen came home at 2:00 a.m. with friends and cook for them. But Masha was prone to depression, the likely source of Cohen's own depressive states, and could be imperious. She once ordered Cohen not to leave the house with a cold: "I've nursed you back from the brink of the grave and *this* is how you treat me?" Guttman remembers her shouting. She and Cohen laughed at his mother's outbursts because this was how they expected a "Jewish mother" to act. Cohen defended himself with his wit and the secure knowledge that Masha loved him.

His friend Nancy Bacal, whom he first met in high school, said Cohen was "always feeling like his own person"; unlike others, he had a sense of direction, perceived by some as the need for control. But he also developed some unusual habits, one of them an obsession with his weight. His mother constantly pushed food on him and Cohen rebelled. "He seemed like a woman with food," Guttman said. Although he loved sweets, she recalls that he once refused to enter a Greek pastry shop in Montreal, as if the mere sight of any pastry would make him fat.

In his last year of high school, life became more complicated for Cohen. He chose to go on to McGill, the expected step for the Jewish middle-class youth of Westmount. But he felt the tensions between a bourgeois life defined by Westmount expectations and the emerging demands of an artist. Nancy Bacal explained that he was the only one she knew who could "contain and survive elements of pain in the dark. He was in touch with matters of the soul and heart." He would eventually resolve these tensions, drawing from the best of each world. But in university, the two sides of his personality began to clash.

2

L I F E   I N   A

G O L D E N   C O F F I N

LEONARD COHEN entered McGill University on September 21, 1951, his seventeenth birthday, and graduated on October 6, 1955, shortly after his twenty-first. Academically, his university career was undistinguished but he continued the extracurricular zeal of high school, becoming president of both the Debating Society and of his fraternity, ZBT. Initially, Cohen embodied the Westmount Jew destined for professional success, fulfilling a Westmount creed: "If you did things right, you would have all the riches life had to offer." But during his years at McGill, sporadically attending lectures, reading in the Gothic Redpath Library, writing poetry, Cohen distanced himself from that creed.

McGill was and still is the premier English-speaking university in Quebec. Situated on Sherbrooke Street in the center of Montreal, it commanded both an important social and physical position. It was the training ground for leading professionals, businessmen, doctors, economists, and professors, reflecting the interests of McGill's founder, the merchant and fur trader James McGill. Writers, artists, and musicians were of secondary importance. Stephen Leacock, humorist and writer, justified his attachment to McGill as an economist, not as an author. In the early fifties, McGill still maintained a careful eye on the number of Jews it admitted.

Cohen's average on the entrance exam was 74.1%. Ironically, his lowest mark was in English literature; math was his strongest subject. His actual undergraduate marks at McGill were less impressive: he graduated with an overall average of 56.4%. He studied arts his first year, commerce his second (with courses in accounting, commercial law, political science, and math), and then arts for years three and four, continuing with political science and adding zoology. English was his favorite subject. He attended lectures infrequently though and squeaked through McGill only with supplemental examinations. He explained that his completion of the program was "paying off old debts to my family and to my society."

Cohen introduced new ideas and radical policies to his fraternity. Drinking on the lawn and in the fraternity house was encouraged, leading to Cohen's impeachment. But he brought life to the institution, leading house meetings with his songs and guitar playing, and often unexpectedly promoting surprising moments such as the time a friend and female guest appeared at lunch sharing one overcoat which had difficulty staying closed. To his fraternity brothers Cohen brought "limitless space" and the gift of possibilities. He was a popular member.

Cohen was active in the Debating Union, first as secretary and later as president. In his first year at McGill, he won the Bovey Shield for Public Speaking, represented McGill in Burlington, Vermont, and at the end of the year received a Gold A award for Debating. In his second year he was corresponding secretary of the society, winning the Annual Raft Debate, and represented McGill at Osgoode Hall in Toronto. During his third year (1953–4), he was vice-president of the Union and was elected president in his fourth year. His presidential nomination speech began with Burke and moved on to a rejection of the "ineffectual shower curtains of political modesty."

Cohen participated in national and international debates, engaging diverse opponents that ranged from two Cambridge students to a team of convicts from the Norfolk Penitentiary outside Boston (with whom he debated the negative moral impact of TV on society). Cohen had been introduced to the convicts as a poet and he first clarified his position:

My colleague has promised you a poet, but I am afraid that you will be disappointed. I do not converse in rhyming couplets, nor do I wear a cape or walk brooding over the moor or drink wine from a polished human skull or stride frequently into the cosmic night. I am never discovered sitting amid Gothic ruins in moonlight clutching in my pale hand a dying medieval lily and sighing over virgins with bosoms heaving like the sea. In fact I wouldn't recognize a dying medieval lily if I fell over one, [and] hardly think I could do better with a virgin, and I'll drink out of anything that has a bottom to it.

Cohen lost to the inmates, who had not been defeated in twenty-four years. Impatient with the prolonged, ineffectual executive meetings of the Debating Union, Cohen moved to ban any further meetings. The Debating Union was a suitable apprenticeship for a budding lawyer, a career that Cohen was then considering.

Cohen also joined Hillel, the Jewish students' organization. He organized a Hillel band and participated in a Hillel play directed by Bernie Rothman. The cast included Yafa Lerner; Eddie Van Zaig (later to marry Roz Ostrow, Cohen's stepsister, also in the production); Freda Guttman, in charge of properties; Robert Hershorn, who was part of the stage crew; and "Lenny Cohen" as second guard. Law, the courts, and freedom were the focus of the work.

Before the start of his second year at McGill, Cohen and two friends formed the Buckskin Boys, a country and western band. The choice was not entirely a surprise since he had long admired country and western music, listening for hours to the musical narratives on radio stations from the states. They chose their name because all three band members had buckskin jackets, Cohen having inherited his from his father. The Buckskin Boys performed at square dances, in high schools, and in church basements, playing pop and country favorites. The group survived through the McGill years, and Cohen discovered that he liked to perform, although he admitted to being nervous on stage. Something of an instrumentalist at this time, he played backstage guitar for the dramatic society's production of *Twelfth Night*.

Walking along Sherbrooke Street late one afternoon in the fall of 1954, Cohen came upon a group of students celebrating a victory of the McGill football team. They were rocking several buses and the police had been summoned. While he was watching, Cohen was shoved by a policeman and told to move along. Cohen tried to explain that he was only watching, but the policeman grabbed Cohen's shoulder and told him to move. Cohen knocked the policeman's hand away and received an unexpected rabbit punch on the back of his neck. He regained consciousness in the "Black Maria," the police wagon, and was driven to station Number 10, charged, and released.

Several days later, Cohen appeared in juvenile court with a lawyer, his mother, and his sister. The charges included refusing to circulate, disturbing the peace, obstructing justice, blocking a public path, and resisting arrest. When they were read, Cohen's sister broke into hysterical laughter and had to be escorted from the court. Cohen received a suspended sentence. Several years later the episode resurfaced when Cohen applied for a job as a Pinkerton detective. He wasn't granted a second interview because Pinkerton's discovered that he had been charged with a criminal offense and had failed to note it on his application. He also applied for a position with the Hong Kong police force, which was advertising in the Montreal English language papers (only apparent requirement: a college degree). In 1957, he wrote to the U.S. Bureau of Indian Affairs inquiring about teaching jobs. They replied that jobs were scarce and thanked him for his inquiry.

Cohen's career interests vacillated widely during his university years, from law, to teaching, to police work. But three influential teachers, all writers, galvanized him: Louis Dudek, a poet/critic; Hugh MacLennan, a novelist; and F.R. Scott, a constitutional lawyer who was also a writer. Later, Cohen encountered a fourth literary mentor, Irving Layton, who became the most important. In the fall of 1954 Cohen took Dudek's poetry course which focused on the modernists, including Ezra Pound, with whom Dudek was corresponding.

Born in the east end of Montreal of Polish immigrant parents, Dudek was a poet and critic who held a Ph.D in literature from Columbia University. In the first weeks of the modern poetry course, Cohen showed Dudek some of his writing, which Dudek thought had little value. Two weeks later, Cohen offered more of his work and this time Dudek spotted "The Sparrows," a five-stanza poem with an elaborate metaphoric scheme. Dudek responded at once: as they walked down a corridor of the arts faculty building discussing the poem, he suddenly stopped and commanded Cohen to kneel. With the manuscript, he knighted him "poet" and bade him rise and join the as-yet-undefined ranks of Canadian poets. Continuity had been established, tradition enacted, and acceptance granted. "The Sparrows" went on to win the 1954 Literary Contest sponsored by the *McGill Daily* which printed the poem on the front page of its December 7 issue.

Cohen's first published works, "An Halloween Poem to Delight my Younger Friends," and "Poem en Prose," appeared in *CIV/n*, a literary magazine started in January 1953 with two hundred and fifty mimeographed copies. Initiated by four recent university graduates, led by Aileen Collins (later to marry Dudek), with Dudek and Layton joining as editorial advisers, it derived its unusual title from Ezra Pound's statement, "CIV/n: not a one-man job," "CIV/n" being Pound's abbreviation for civilization. Its stated goal was to present poetry that would be "a vital representation of what things are, done in strong language (if necessary) or any language, but it [would] rouse the reader to see just what the world around him [was] like." Poets in Canada, Collins added, were "forced to write with maple syrup on birch bark," and this needed to change. The energetic editorial meetings, attended by Layton, Dudek, and Collins, often at Layton's Montreal home, led to the appearance of new and unorthodox writing: it was frank, colloquial, unselfconscious, and experimental. To get the Canadian mind out of storage, *CIV/n* proposed the following new standard:

For Kulchur's sake, at least, let's have a lot of bad *good* poetry in future, instead of more *good* bad poetry—and let the dead-head critics hold their peace until the call of the last moose.

In a letter to Robert Creeley, Layton comically summarized the completion of the inaugural issue: "Last night we celebrated CIV/n with an orgy and to give the issue the proper send-off we all undressed and sat about holding each other's privates (sounds gruesome now)."

Pound was sent copies of the magazine and replied to Dudek that he found it unpolemical and too local. He questioned whether the magazine had any interest in "standing for maximum awareness." The fourth issue of CIV/n, which included Cohen's first effort, was more broadly based. The issue also contained work by both Creeley and Corman; a long article on Pound by Camillo Pellizzi, an Italian author/critic; and an editorial by Dudek on why Pound was being held in a Washington, D.C., mental hospital. It also contained contributions from Phyllis Webb, Raymond Souster, and Irving Layton. Cohen's author's note reveals that "Leonard N. Cohen . . . composes poetry to the guitar; now studying at McGill."

The second poem by Cohen in the issue alludes to his experiences in Cambridge, Massachusetts, during the summer of 1953. That summer Cohen had gone to Harvard, ostensibly to take a poetry course from the experimental French poet Pierre Emmanuel, who was teaching a course on the nature of modern poetry. Cohen convinced his mother that the enterprise would be worth a month or so in Cambridge, though he spent most of his time listening to folk music from the world-famous John Lennox Collection at the Widener Library. In the poem, he describes how the "secret undulations" of the River Charles "swarmed the shadows of ten dozen streetlamps and a moon." The poem appears retitled and revised as "Friends" in Let Us Compare Mythologies. Four other poems by Cohen appeared in CIV/n before publication ceased in 1955.

The literary environment of CIV/n was as important as the publication itself, and through CIV/n Cohen came into contact with older, more experienced writers who sought to challenge the poetic orthodoxy of the country. Aileen Collins later characterized this challenge as the effort, at least in Montreal, to contradict the Canadian Authors Association's notion of poetry as effusive expressions of emotional states, similar in form and taste to a blend of maple syrup; hence her comment about maple syrup on birch bark.

The CIV/n circle included Layton, Betty Sutherland (sister of the McGill poet John Sutherland and Layton's companion from the mid-1940s; they married in 1948), the sculptor Buddy Rozynski, art director of the magazine, his wife Wanda, and later, Doug Jones, Phyllis Webb, Eli Mandel, F.R. Scott, Cid Corman, Raymond Souster, Robert Creeley, and Charles Olson. Aileen Collins and the Rozynskis handled the production and distribution of the magazine, as well as the finances, and also took charge of the correspondence, accounting, art-work, and circulation.

Cohen was soon participating in the group's discussions, debates, and informal readings, often bringing his guitar to accompany his poetry. These gatherings were actually workshops, and Cohen recalls that even an experienced poet like Scott was shaken by some of the candid reactions to his work. There was, Cohen recalls, a "savage integrity" to the Montreal group. Phyllis Webb recollects meeting Cohen in late 1955 when he was preparing to publish his first book with Dudek. Dudek brought him to Layton's house, and she remembers her surprise at learning that this young poet was "voluntarily studying the Bible as an informal on-going project." That evening, as usual, poems "got battered about," but Cohen's was "the most freshly lyrical and genuinely sensuous." Arguments, insults, and praise characterized these meetings, and provided a sounding board for Cohen. The importance of CIV/n, said Dudek, was its role in stimulating a vital Montreal literary environment.

The emergence of the CIV/n group also confirmed the move of new poetry from Toronto to Montreal. Raymond Souster's *Contact*, from which the Contact Press emerged, had ended, and the new CIV/n, in Montreal, had begun. In addition, the magazine solidified the union of Souster, Layton, and Dudek, which had begun with the publication of their co-authored project *Cerberus* (1952). *Canadian Poems, 1850–1952*, an anthology edited by Dudek and Layton, signaled a break from poetry shaped strictly by narrative, exhibiting a modern lyricism. CIV/n was more challenging than the other small magazines in Canada, such as *First Statement, Contact*, or later, *Delta*, and certainly fostered Cohen's early work.

The best-known writer on the faculty at the time was the Governor General's Award winner Hugh MacLennan, whose *Two Solitudes* had startled the country when it appeared in 1945. MacLennan joined McGill in 1951 to teach a course on the modern novel and to run an advanced creative writing seminar. Cohen met MacLennan through Tony Graham, son of the novelist Gwethalyn Graham, who had achieved notoriety with her best-selling novel *Earth and High Heaven* (1944), about the love affair between a young Jewish lawyer and a Gentile from Westmount. While at McGill, MacLennan drafted what would become *The Watch that Ends the Night* (1957), also destined to win a Governor General's Award.

The reading list of MacLennan's novel course, which Cohen attended, included James Joyce's *Portrait of the Artist as a Young Man*. This work had a powerful effect on Cohen, especially the impressionistic "bird girl" section where Stephen Dedalus poetically describes a young woman on the beach. It demonstrated to Cohen how lyrical prose could become within the novel form.

Enrollment in the advanced creative writing course required a submission of material, which Cohen presented and MacLennan approved. Cohen found that he liked MacLennan as a person as well as an instructor. "That's where my life has been mostly," Cohen has said. "I've only gone on these kinds of adventures where there was a personal relationship involved." He remembers MacLennan as a beautiful teacher: "the more restrained he was, the more emotional was the atmosphere in the classroom." For a time afterwards, they continued to exchange letters, and MacLennan expressed interest in Cohen's developing career as a writer. When two of Cohen's poems were published in the February 1954 issue of *Forge*, a student publication at McGill, MacLennan provided an introduction.

F.R. Scott was another influential figure at McGill. An eminent constitutional historian, he was also a noted poet who was able to straddle both the earlier generation of *The McGill Fortnightly Review* and *Preview*, as well as the new efforts of the innovative *CIV/n*. Cohen studied commercial law with him and briefly entered law school, admiring the apparent ease with which Scott could balance poetry and the law. Scott encouraged Cohen's literary efforts and Cohen recalled that visits to the Scotts' were "warm and wonderful [with] a very open, fluid atmosphere; lots of fun; drinking; and talk of politics and poetry."

Several years later, Scott and his wife Marian, a painter, would venture into downtown Montreal to hear Cohen read and sing in the various clubs and coffeehouses. Cohen, in turn, often received invitations to North Hatley, where the Scotts had their summer cottage. He wrote in a lean-to cabin belonging to Scott's brother Elton, which the Scotts made available to Cohen. He began to write *The Spice-Box of Earth* there in 1957 and a year later he returned to work on early versions of *The Favorite Game*. To show his gratitude, he wrote "Summer Haiku for Frank and Marian Scott," which Mort Rosengarten carved on a rock. The Scotts put it to use as a doorstop; the poem also appears in *The Spice-Box*. Scott later wrote a recommendation for Cohen for a Canada Council grant.

Of all Cohen's mentors at McGill, however, Irving Layton was unquestionably the most influential. Layton forced a new vitality into moribund poetic forms and linked the prophetic with the sexual. In Layton's work, Cohen discovered a Judaic voice of opposition, energy, and passion. Who, Layton asked with a flourish, will read the "castratos," the critics? "What race will read what they have said / Who have my poems to read instead?" Northrop Frye, among others, tried to diminish Layton's sexuality: "One can get as tired of buttocks in Mr. Layton as of buttercups in the *Canadian Poetry Magazine*," he remarked in the *University of Toronto Quarterly* in April 1952, when reviewing *The Black Huntsmen*.

In addition to a great and energetic teacher, Cohen found in Layton Judaic prophecy and Hebrew thunder. Layton brought the full force of Jewish identity to bear on his work. He also brought politics to poetry and Cohen absorbed Layton's stance in later works of his own, notably *Flowers for Hitler* and *Parasites of Heaven*. Cohen met Layton briefly in 1949 and again in 1954 when he invited Layton, who had just published *The Long Pea-Shooter*, to read at Cohen's fraternity at McGill. An aggressive figure with two books to his credit, Layton was then juggling a career as a part-time lecturer in literature at Sir George Williams University and as a teaching assistant in political science at McGill.

Layton's ego was relentlessly public. He challenged the entire country to rise to his forthright statements and sexuality. From Layton, Cohen learned to value the excesses of the Dionysian style, to accept the power of prophetic visions, and to extend the poetic to include the Judaic. Layton defiled the sanitary classrooms of poetry in the name of poetry: "with a happy / screech he bounded from monument to monument," wrote Cohen in his poem "For My Old Layton." If Dudek knighted him, Layton took him out on the town. The influence was immense, but over the years, reciprocal: "I taught him how to dress; he taught me how to live forever," Cohen has remarked.

Layton frequently brought Cohen along on reading or promotional tours. On one of their frequent car trips to Toronto, they became so engrossed in talking about poetry that they didn't notice they were running out of gas. Fortunately, they were not far from a farmhouse, where they found help. Several years later they were again driving to Toronto and again ran out of gas. Uncannily, it was in front of the same farmhouse. They sheepishly told their story to the woman in the farmhouse who remembered them from years past. She summed up the entire episode with one word: "Poets!" Cohen and Layton read together at the old Greenwich Gallery on Bay Street, where Don Owen, the filmmaker, remembered that Cohen "always seemed to leave the gallery with the most intesting woman there, the one I'd spent all evening trying to get up enough nerve to say hello to." Cohen was in his pudgy phase at this time, Owen noted, but the extra weight did not deter him from his pursuit of women.

Layton commanded the attention of a public unaccustomed to Whitmanesque gestures and outlandish posturings. With flowing hair, Layton shouted and raved from the heights, addressing crucial subjects. "Poised on a rope stretched tautly between sex and death," the poet, Layton affirmed, can find salvation only in sexual love, a message that strongly appealed to the young Cohen. Layton was responsible for strong-arming Cohen into the wonderful, boisterous, in-your-face world of serious poetry, where dedication to the art was all, and all of you had to be put into the work. The quest for bold experiences was the poet's finest teacher, Layton preached, and in Cohen he had a willing disciple.

No gathering Layton and Cohen attended was more important than the Canadian Writers' Conference held from July 28–31, 1955, at Queen's University in Kingston, Ontario. Organized by F.R. Scott, and supported by the Rockefeller Foundation, the first major gathering of Canadian writers included the established: A.J.M. Smith, Morley Callaghan, Dorothy Livesay, Desmond Pacey, Louis Dudek, Ralph Gustafson, James Reaney, John Sutherland, Earle Birney, Malcolm Ross, and Scott; and the new: Al Purdy, Jay Macpherson, Eli Mandel,

Phyllis Webb, and Miriam Waddington. According to Doug Jones, Layton arrived in staid Kingston "in a car full of women. I guess it was probably Cohen and various friends, but it was like the sultan coming with his harem."

Cohen took his guitar, read in the impromptu poetry sessions and listened to the arguments between the writers, who claimed that the mass media were doing little to promote their work, and the mass media, who claimed that the writers were getting what they deserved, especially the poets whose work was intentionally obscure. Layton argued that poets wrote for the public, not for other poets. The poet was part of the proletariat, not the elite. Layton constantly battled journalists and others at the conference in his conviction that the poet was essential for society and that society had a duty to support its writers through foundations or grants. It resulted in a set of resolutions to formalize the study of Canadian literature, recognizing the need to provide a more prominent place for Canadian writing in schools and libraries.

Attending the Kingston Conference in the summer of 1955 was a heady experience for Cohen. He met the major poets and heard new voices. His career was shaped in response to many of the issues that were discussed and the decisions that were made through the workshops, meetings, and resolutions. A new range of publications soon appeared: *Canadian Literature, Prism,* the McGill Poetry series and the New Canadian Library.

COHEN GRADUATED from McGill in October 1955, one of only five arts students to receive B.A. degrees. He had established himself as a literary figure and campus voice, winning the Chester MacNaughton Prize for Creative Writing for his series "Thoughts of a Landsman," which was made up of four poems, three of which would later appear in his first book. He also won the Peterson Memorial Prize in literature, publicly confirming his talent and renewing his determination to pursue a creative life. The caption under his 1955 McGill Yearbook picture reads "*You have discovered of course only the ship of fools is making the voyage this year . . .*"

"I yearned to live a semi-bohemian lifestyle," Cohen said of his McGill years, "an unstructured life; but a *consecrated* one; some kind of calling." In the fall of 1953, at the beginning of his third year at McGill, Cohen and Mort Rosengarten had taken several rooms on Stanley Street in a rooming house. They had hoped to pursue a modestly bohemian life and to break free of the confines of Westmount. It was a decision that upset Cohen's mother and angered his uncles. His father had lived with his parents until the day of his marriage at age thirty-nine. Cohen's move was seen as a break with tradition and an abandonment of his mother. But its rewards were too seductive. Cohen invited women to his new rooms, serenaded them, and read them poems. As the narrator of *Beauty at Close Quarters* reports, "He knew what minor chords went with what hours of the morning, which poems were too vicious, which too sweet. . . . He wasn't so much trying to accumulate women as he was ideal episodes."

After Cohen graduated, he began law school for a term but his real interest was still in writing. At this time, Layton, Souster, and Dudek created the McGill Poetry Series to provide a new outlet for young poets. Works by Pierre Coupey, David Solway, Daryl Hine, and Cohen appeared. But when Dudek offered the first volume in the series to Cohen, he was, in Dudek's words, "slow and reluctant to present his manuscript for editing." Dudek, in fact, didn't see the completed manuscript of *Let Us Compare Mythologies* until the book was published. Part of the reason for Cohen's reluctance was Dudek's rejection of "the sentimental late-romantic tradition in poetry" to which Cohen was partial. Upholding this tradition was itself a form of rebellion against the modernism of Dudek and others, vividly seen in the work of Pound, William Carlos Williams, and Charles Olson.

Let Us Compare Mythologies contains poems written largely when Cohen was between the ages of fifteen and twenty and went through four drafts before he felt it could be printed. Cohen masterminded the entire publication, assuming responsiblity for the design, typesetting, production, and paper. His friend Freda Guttman prepared illustrations, and he paid the $300 cost to have the work produced in hardcover, rather than paperback, as Dudek had originally planned. Ruth Wisse, then feature editor of the *McGill Daily*, headed the so-called sales team which operated by advance subscription only. She alone sold over two hundred advance copies. Cohen also distributed order forms for the book in campus cafes and bookstores. He sold out the approximately four hundred printed copies.

The book appeared in May with a statement about the series on the back jacket emphasizing its uniqueness and Dudek's role. The inscription on the copy presented to Dudek by Cohen reads:

> To Louis Dudek, teacher and friend, who more than anyone wanted me to bring out this book, and whose encouragement and help is deeply appreciated by every young person writing at McGill —
> Leonard Cohen
> May 1956

Despite increasing differences with Dudek, whose own poetry of ideas and championing of Pound contradicted Cohen's pull toward romanticism, metaphysics, and sensuality, and despite Dudek's later belief that becoming a singer undermined Cohen's talents as a writer, Cohen always valued Dudek's contribution to his work. He knew that Dudek understood him. "Leonard always had an image of himself as a rabbi," Dudek has said. Cohen unexpectedly appeared at Dudek's retirement party in the mid-eighties and was delighted that it was Dudek who presented him to the McGill Chancellor for his honorary doctorate in June 1992. At the ceremony, Dudek summarized Cohen's McGill years with a gentle jibe: "I was fortunate to see him occasionally in my classes in his young days at McGill." He closed with a fatherly question about Cohen's status as a celebrity: "But Leonard, is all this fame really good for you?" After praising Cohen's integrity and search for personal truth, Dudek concluded, "He has won through, so far as anyone can win through, in this difficult struggle of life."

The "personal truth" Dudek cited in 1992 is evident in the forty-four poems of *Let Us Compare Mythologies* (1956). The themes are remarkable for a twenty-two-year-old encountering the power of romantic love and shattered by the reality of loss. "Elegy," a poem marking the death of his father, is the first poem in the text; "Beside the Shepherd," a poem celebrating the resurrection of life, is the last. Patrimony, inheritance, history, and desire emerge as the dominant themes, united by an absorption in myth and integrated with religious sensuality.

A prose statement dated December 27, 1956, written during his year at Columbia, contains Cohen's explanation of the importance of myth in his work. He begins with a declaration:

> I want to continue experimenting with the myth applying it to contemporary life, and isolating it in contemporary experience, thus making new myths and modifying old ones. I want to put mythic time into my poems, so they can be identified with every true fable ever sung, and still be concerned with our own time, and the poems hanging in our own skies.

Cohen cites marriage and adultery as major themes that he will likely explore and then goes on to name poems that illustrate how myth can control poetic image and development. The poems deal exclusively with betrayal or adultery, his third example being the most self-defining, since it narrates the betrayal of the speaker. It reads in part:

> I know all about passion and honour
> but unfortunately this had really nothing to do with either;
> oh there was passion I'm only too sure
> and even a little honour
> but the important thing was to cuckold Leonard Cohen.

Enlarging his sense of myth is his belief that what he does is linked to the folk song. His ballads, Cohen once explained, "strive for folk-song simplicity and the fable's intensity."

Cohen's interest in myth coincided with a shift in literary studies, summarized by the work of the Canadian critic Northrop Frye. In 1957, the year after *Let Us Compare Mythologies*, Frye published his encyclopedic treatment of myth and literature, *Anatomy of Criticism*, initiating a new paradigm for the study of literature via archetypes. Frye reviewed Cohen's first book in the *University of Toronto Quarterly*, providing restrained praise and acknowledgment of a minor talent. During this period, Canadian writers like James Reaney, Eli Mandel, and Jay

Macpherson were also turning to myth as a narrative device. Cohen's book became part of the unconscious but unified development of mythopoetic studies that was evolving in Canada.

Let Us Compare Mythologies contains several other themes that would inform Cohen's later poetry: history, especially related to Jewish persecution, and the Holocaust; sexuality and attraction to women; lyrical sensuality; anger; cultural stereotypes; religion; and frustration with art or history as a means of solving personal crises. It is a young poet's work designed to shock as well as excite ("The moon dangling wet like a half-plucked eye.") One sees his early use of poetry as a form of prayer and the role of the poet as a sacred voice. And it exhibits confidence, demonstrating what Layton said was essential for a young poet: arrogance and inexperience. When asked in 1994 about the quality of his work in those days, Cohen quipped, "It's been downhill ever since. Those early poems are pretty good." Cohen had no strategy for becoming a public figure like Layton. "Mostly what I was trying to do was get a date. That was the most urgent element in my life."

Women were becoming a dominant interest at this time, as an essay from the mid-fifties confirms. The topic was breasts, or as he preferred, "tits," a word he did not use carelessly: "Breasts, in my mind at least, divide, they turn the mind one way and then another." The terminology was significant: "bosom" belonged to the world of feminine hygiene. "Women who have popularity problems talk about their bosoms," he writes. Other terms seem too flippant, "so back to tits which are nothing more than what they are, human and real, the form, the swell, the rosy corrugated nipples all carried plainly in the sound of the word." One particular girl possessed "magic tits" which enraptured him, although he tries to explain that he is not a breast man. The tits of this particular woman deserved a poem, Cohen felt, but who would write it?

Layton would at once attach them to one of his wives or perhaps appropriate the whole body to be mutilated on some fierce landscape. Dudek would spurn them, or if he dared to examine them at all, would compose a travelogue, cataloguing every pore and hair, and having done this thing he'd praise them. Hine does not believe in them. Reaney or Macpherson would turn them to silver, that dear flesh to metal, and etch on them hieroglyphs to prove some current theory of their master who is a Professor of English Literature. Leonard Cohen would embarrass us all by caressing them publically under the guise of praying to a kind of Oriental-eyed suffering Jehova.

The woman with the "magic tits" would not stand out in a crowd, Cohen goes on to say, although while wandering on the "dark southern slope of Mount Royal . . . thinking about all the injustices that had been done me," his heroine suddenly appears and to his astonishment uncovers her "tits."

> And at that moment I knew that upon how I understood and met these tits rested my whole life, that I would climb down to the city from that mountain an empty man or a great one. My heart became a battlefield where compassion struggled with contempt.

It was around this time that Cohen began to experience depression, and also began using drugs. Cohen's depression initially took the form of withdrawl and solitude. He found he had less, not more, in common with his Westmount friends and the feeling of being an outsider began to alter his outlook. It was not so much a conflict as a challenge between alternately attractive ways of living. Nancy Bacal recalls a night in Cohen's fraternity room drinking Armagnac, sitting under an umbrella before a fire with all his typewritten poems spread about, seriously debating whether to burn them. Fortunately, they decided it would be unwise.

Drugs, the panacea of the sixties, began to attract Cohen in the mid-fifties, principally marijuana and LSD. A musician in Montreal provided an introduction to the former; writerly colleagues and hipsters the latter. As he and the times changed, so too did his pharmaceuticals, and he began to favor amphetamines, acid, and hashish. High on LSD or marijuana, Cohen found the freedom to experiment poetically and to attempt new forms for his songwriting. Friends in the artistic community shared in this exploration of hallucinogens. For Cohen, drugs also substituted for religion; the ecstasy and belief that mystical or prophetic religion once held for him was gone. He felt it had been institutionalized and subsequently had lost its magic. But drugs could provide an alternative sacred path. In "Song of Patience," from his first book, Cohen outlines the replacement of religious fervor with the frenzy of art, a theme echoed throughout the text. The visions that came from drugs were both an escape from depression and a release of the imagination.

One night in 1957, Cohen walked to the top of Mount Royal, the hill that juts up in the center of Montreal, and took peyote, the preferred drug of South American Indians. He had always understood drugs to be sacramental and ceremonial, not recreational. Under their influence, he felt he was able to explore psychological and creative states that were otherwise unavailable. In the tradition of Rimbaud, Verlaine, Coleridge, and De Quincey, Cohen sought the expansion of his imagination. He eventually quit drugs because they didn't expand the mind in the way he had hoped, and they were taking a toll on his body.

Initially though, drugs were a sacramental focus in his landscape of religious exploration. There were moments of perception; while writing *Beautiful Losers* on Hydra in 1965 he took acid and wrote on a wall in gold paint, "I am change / I am the same." On an opposite wall he wrote, "Our song led us to the ovens."

Cohen's tendency to depression was exacerbated by the conflict between his desire to be an artist and the obligations of a middle-class life. His two worlds soon became incompatible. A series of destabilizing elements in his personal history contributed to his moods: his father's early death, his mother's depressions, and the suicide of his first guitar teacher among them. "The nightmares do not suddenly / develop happy endings," he wrote in *Parasites of Heaven*, "I merely step out of them." Becoming a writer, stereotypically defined by irregular work, numerous sexual partners, and an uncertain income, created resistance from family and furthered Cohen's inner conflicts.

As he matured, Cohen began to display the characteristics of manic-depressiveness. These symptoms usually first appear around the age of eighteen or nineteen; cyclic and recurrent shifts from manic creativity, sociability, and sexual activity on one hand, and intense lassitude, withdrawal, and anxiety on the other. In addition, victims tend to be obsessive and extremely organized. Cohen was, and is, absorbed by his writing and music, and is unusually tidy and concerned with detail. His homes have all been spotless and almost bare in their furnishings; his notebooks are all ordered by year, and his work habits reflect his concern with discipline and precision. He does not consider a work complete until he is satisified that the lyric, the sound, or the word is absolutely right. He explained this approach in a March 1967 notebook entry: "In principle, everything stands systematized, and it is only in regard to details that success is still to be achieved." Yet he recognizes his own laziness, "which is famous to me, although I have convinced many of my diligence." Nonetheless, his quest for perfection and order characterizes all of his actions: his work, his loves, and his search for spiritual satisfaction.

Cohen would occasionally rent a room in a seedy downtown hotel for three dollars a night, initiating a fascination with hotel rooms. In the 1965 NFB film *Ladies and Gentlemen . . . Mr. Leonard Cohen*, Cohen is seen waking up in a Ste-Catherine Street hotel, staring out the window in his underwear at the bleak, wintry landscape, and lyrically celebrating the release from responsibility that a hotel provides. Two influential hotels for him were the Chelsea and the Royalton, both in New York; each provided creative stimulation and refuge. Epitomizing his identity with the transient hotel world is his 1984 video "I Am A Hotel," in which he dramatizes numerous stories among the hotel's inhabitants. When asked why he found hotels so fascinating, he replied, "My personality cannot go anywhere else. Where else shall a guy like me go?"

Cohen continued to get exposure. In 1956 the CBC recorded *Six Montreal Poets*, which Folkways Records released in the United States in 1957 and which placed Cohen in the company of some of his mentors: Layton, F.R. Scott, A.M. Klein, A.J.M. Smith, and Dudek. Produced by Sam Gesser, an impresario who had brought acts like Pete Seeger and the Weavers to Montreal, the album singled Cohen out as the most important young poet in the city. He appeared on side one, after Smith and before Layton, reading six poems from *Let Us Compare Mythologies*, including "The Sparrows" and "Elegy."

Cohen had now established a local reputation as a poet and was gaining a following from his singing in various coffeehouses. But he was becoming dissatisfied with Montreal and its bourgeois climate. He felt he needed a freer artistic world, one without boundaries or roots. He found it in New York.

3

PASSION

WITHOUT FLESH

EONARD COHEN attended the School of General
Studies at Columbia University in 1956–57. García Lorca had briefly studied English at Columbia
in 1929, and Louis Dudek had received his Ph.D there in 1951. Cohen
followed his mentors. His courses included a survey of seventeenth-
century English literature, a course on the Romantic movement, Literature in Contemporary America, Contemporary Texts, and Introduction
to Literary Research. Graduate school, however, was "passion without
flesh," he thought, "love with no climax." His notebooks from that
time are filled with drawings and caricatures of his professors and
fellow students. In one of them he wrote: "I feel lonely for my uncre-
ated works." He continued the casual study habits he had developed
at McGill.

When Professor William York Tindall allowed Cohen to write a term paper on his own book, *Let Us Compare Mythologies*, Cohen was hard on himself, writing a scathing critique. But he was dismayed by the general absence of rigor in the study of literature. There was no gravity, he felt, evidenced by Tindall's decision to let him review his own work. Cohen finally quit the program and worked briefly as an elevator operator, but was dismissed because he refused to wear a uniform.

Cohen lived at International House, the dormitory for foreign students located on Riverside Drive, close to the Hudson River. But he spent most of his time in the fledgling bohemian scene around the Columbia campus and downtown in the Village. The Beats were emerging and Allen Ginsberg, a graduate of Columbia, had captured national attention with his famous reading of *Howl* in March 1955 at the Six Gallery in San Francisco (memorialized in Kerouac's *Dharma Bums*). Jack Kerouac, who himself had attended Columbia on a sports scholarship, was also part of the Village scene. Cohen recalls hearing him read at the Village Vanguard (with musical accompaniment) and later meeting him at Ginsberg's apartment: "He was lying under a dining room table, pretending to listen to some jazz record while the party swirled on 'round him." Kerouac's novel *On the Road* would appear to great acclaim in September 1957 from Viking, who would go on to publish *The Favorite Game*. Cohen appreciated Kerouac's work, calling him "a certain kind of genius who was able to spin it out that way like some great glistening spider." What Kerouac was "really spinning was the great tale of America." Counterculture writing from Lawrence Ferlinghetti, Gregory Corso, Gary Snyder, and William S. Burroughs shaped a new world of literary recklessness. In New York, Cohen found confirmation of his anti-establishment stance, although he was never accepted by the Beats. "I was always only on the fringe. I liked the places they gathered, but I was never accepted by the bohemians because it was felt that I came from the wrong side of the tracks. I was too middle-class . . . I didn't have the right credentials to be at the center table in those bohemian cafes."

Nevertheless, Cohen drew from this world (and later took back to Montreal) not only a new way of presenting his poetry, reciting it with jazz accompaniment, but also a new realization that spontaneous prose,

"UNINTERRUPTED AND UNREVISED FULL CONFESSIONS ABOUT WHAT ACTUALLY HAPPENED IN REAL LIFE," could both liberate the language and present a genuine account of reality. This would be a key concept nine years later when he wrote *Beautiful Losers*.

Caught up in the mood of literary revolution, Cohen began a short-lived magazine, *The Phoenix*. In his editorial statement, Cohen wrote:

> This magazine intends to publish honest poems, stories and articles of high quality. We intend to make it a vital organ of the community which it represents. We want experiment. We want controversy. We want ideas and song. We invite craftsmen.
>
> Leonard Cohen
> Editor

The issue included poetry by the known and unknown: Louis Dudek, Anne Ruden, Lee Usher, Mimi Hayes, Leigh Van Valen, and Leonard Cohen. Cohen had a series of poems in *The Phoenix*: "Go by brooks, love," "Whatever cliffs are brought down" (to be retitled "You All in White" and published with variant lines in *The Spice-Box of Earth*), "You tell me that silence," "What shadows the pendulum sun," "Perfumed Pillows of night," and most important, "Poem for Marc Chagall," retitled "Out of the Land of Heaven" in *The Spice-Box of Earth*. All six poems reappeared in *The Spice-Box of Earth* four years later. *The Phoenix* only survived one issue, April 1957. But Cohen had again taken control of the means of production, as he had done with his book *Let Us Compare Mythologies*.

Cohen continued to write in New York, occasionally finding New York subjects, like the nearby Riverside Church. An unpublished poem reads:

> Riverside Church frightens tourists
> with a giant carillion
> but is less successful with God
> whose ear grew deaf after
> a century of martyrs

and Bach in bells is dubious
It is a stunned Babel

I told this to a small carved monk
who held a bent stone.

The key event of his year in New York was meeting Anne Sherman, a tall, dark-haired woman whom he first encountered at International House. Cohen was immediately struck by her beauty. She possessed a grace that originated in something "durable, disciplined and athletic." She became the model for the divorcée Shell in *The Favorite Game* and occupied Cohen's erotic and literary imagination. Her beauty devastated him, a beauty that broke down "old rules of light and cannot be interpreted or compared. They [such women] make every room original"; she was, as the novel describes, "formal" and well-educated, and she always presented "the scene the heart demanded." But if she taught Cohen about love and behavior, he taught her "about her body and her beauty."

But the relationship with Sherman didn't last. She was older than Cohen, she wasn't Jewish, and she evidently chose not to continue the affair, although Cohen frequently expressed his love for her after their relationship ended. She had become friends with Cohen's sister and with his friend Yafa Lerner, both of whom were then living in New York. Those close to Cohen at the time believed he wanted to marry Anne but she sought a stability that Cohen could not provide. He wanted her to come to Greece after he settled there in 1960 but she remained in New York, eventually marrying a prominent restaurateur.

Sherman embodied all of the sexual freedom and guiltless love that Cohen had had difficulty finding in other women. For the next five or six years, Cohen continued to write about her in both poetry and prose. A notebook from the summer of 1958 contains a series of references to Sherman as well as the poem "To Anne in the Window Seat," which expresses his grief over having to live without her. In a white notebook from Greece dated September 1961, there is a poem entitled "To Anne":

I'd no sooner forget you
than pretty houses or legends

or success
But sometimes Meadowheart
is lost, Isolde is lost,
the new apartment is lost
and I'm invisible
in the cold machines of universe
that won't stop
or slow to let you kiss.

In the same notebook he adds:

Reader, I am anxious about
your discipline
are you constant as me?
Otherwise, burn this book
Go to the movies
if you aren't doubled up with laughing.

If Freda Guttman was the muse for *Let Us Compare Mythologies*, Anne Sherman was the inspiration for *Beauty at Close Quarters*, the unpublished version of *The Favorite Game*, as well as for *The Spice-Box of Earth*, which has its origin in Jewish tradition and contemporary love. "For Anne," a brief poem in *The Spice-Box of Earth*, records this appreciation and her departure. In a letter of July 1961 to his sister, Cohen writes, "I would appreciate hearing any news about Anne. If you are in contact with her and she is interested please make a book available to her. It is sad, absurd and understandable, that the 'onlie begetter' of these poems should not have a volume in her possession." His sister wrote back in November, saying that Anne was well. "Your report that Anne is happy delighted me. Besides being an extraordinary beauty, she is an extraordinary person and such people often have great difficulty adjusting to the bleak terms that any life presents, no matter how rich and glamourous."

Cohen still expresses affection for Anne Sherman, and as with virtually all of his women, he maintained good relations with her after their association ended. Cohen's lovers have tended to remain his friends, the result of a continued respect, universal graciousness and carefully orchestrated breakups. And with the exception of *Book of Mercy*, which originated in the rediscovery of a spiritual self at fifty, all of Cohen's books are in response to women he has known.

For many years after, Anne Sherman remained in his mind as the image of beauty and love, as a letter to her from the winter of 1961 illustrates. Written from Montreal in a serio-comic style, he asks her to join him:

> Let's run away to Lachine. Let's hide out in Snowdon. Let's go native in Ottawa. Let's meet in Central Station and kiss shamelessly in front of all the trains.
>
> I want to go back to Westmount with you and live on the polished floors of my father's house. I want you beside me when I wear a gold chain and am stoned by the workers. I want your dignity for my scorn.
>
> I will send you flowers when I get some money. You are so beautiful I can be foolish.
>
> I wish you good appetite, peaceful sleep, Happy Easter, easy Lent, hello, sunny weather, new poems, intelligent tv. Be noble, cold, wild.
>
> I urge you to join me in my celebrations.

By the summer of 1957, Cohen was back in Montreal. He had enjoyed the beat culture of New York, but he realized that he would always be an outsider; his roots were in Montreal. As he later explained to an officer of the Canada Council, "Don't worry about me becoming an expatriate. I could never stay away from Montreal. I am a Citizen of Mountain Street." During this time, he worked intermittently at Cuthbert & Co., his uncle's foundry, as a lathe operator, brass die-casting machine operator, and a time-and-motion study assistant. He was faced with a dilemma: would he join his uncles at the Freedman Company, settling down to a life of respectability and responsibility, or would he pursue his creative interests and commit himself to his art? He was plagued with the same ambivalence he had faced at McGill. The poem "Priests 1957" describes his situation and suggests a course of action. The work points to the unhappiness of his uncles and their stunted imaginations, the incompleteness of his father's life as measured by the unread books he owned, and the general unhappiness of his cousins. At the end of the poem he expresses his sense of ironic disappointment: "Must we find all work prosaic / because our grandfather built an early synagogue?"

By the next year, while Cohen was living in Montreal, he worked at the Freedman Company hanging coats, and then as a bundle boy (one who carries bundles of material from one stage of production to another). Layton comically described Cohen's switch from art to manufacturing:

> Now Leonard Cohen has decided to bemuse all our wits by entering the family business, the making of suits for unpoetic characters across the land to buy and wear. Our great lyricist is now a shipping clerk, penning odes to wrapping-paper and string. A handsome way of living brought him to this pass, debt. He puts a good face on the whole affair and mutters something through his strong clenched teeth. If you put your ear close enough you'll make out the words "discipline," "good for my character," and many other sub edifying sounds. May the gods, kind to the erratic ways of poets, be merciful to the three [Dudek, Layton, and Cohen] of us.

Eleven days later, the critic Desmond Pacey responded to Layton's lament: "What will become of Montreal's bohemia now that all of its leaders are becoming tame and respectable?"

Cohen, along with Mort Rosengarten and Lenore Schwartzman, also ran the Four Penny Art Gallery. It was located in a boarding house on Stanley Street, and for effect they painted every picture frame a different color. They exhibited the work of figurative painters, unusual in Montreal at the time, when the abstract expressionism of Riopelle and others was in vogue. They were the first to show the work of Louise Scott, and they also showed the works of Betty Sutherland, Layton's wife, and of Vera Frenkel. A fire, however, destroyed a good many of these works, and because of a technicality there was no insurance coverage. Yet Cohen found the gallery an exhuberant, magical space, as the opening of "Last Dance At the Four Penny" makes clear:

> Layton, when we dance our freilach
> under the ghostly handkerchief,

the miracle rabbis of Prague and Vilna
resume their sawdust thrones,
and angels and men, asleep so long
in the cold palaces of disbelief,
gather in sausage-hung kitchens
to quarrel deliciously and debate
the sounds of the Ineffable Name.

Cohen was also working on various pieces of fiction at this time, including an unusual short story about his now senile grandfather, Rabbi Klein. The impact of the elderly Rabbi's illness led Cohen to write an unpublished short story entitled "A Hundred Suits from Russia." A grandfather, living with his daughter's family, accuses his daughter of stealing his suits. The grandson, unable to face the shouting and madness because he can't write, prepares to leave. "Work," his mother mocks, "fine work. In his room all day listening to records. A poet? A deserter." The grandfather becomes incontinent, and the son tells his mother that the grandfather is not a great Talmudist but senile and must go to a home. One evening the son hears the grandfather sing the most beautiful song. His mother announces that the grandfather has agreed to be quiet so that the son can write and that "one day you would be a great writer and that all the world would know. He [also] said that people would come from miles to hear you speak." The story ends with the grandfather banging his fist on a table for each syllable as he shouts, "One hundred suits from Russia!"

In this early effort, Cohen expresses his frustration with his grandfather's deterioration, a man he adored and recognized as the catalyst for much of his writing. This attachment to the man continued with Cohen's unpublished novel, *A Ballet of Lepers*. The book begins, "My grandfather came to live with me. There was nowhere else for him to go. What had happened to all his children? Death, decay, exile—I hardly know."

The ninety-one-page typescript of *A Ballet of Lepers* tells the story of a thirty-five-year-old sales clerk who takes in his elderly grandfather. They live in a cramped Stanley Street rooming house. The grandfather is given to fits of violence, and the narrator (who remains unnamed) finds an awakening violence within himself. When the narrator discovers a baggage clerk masturbating in a train station washroom, he begins slapping him, reveling in his power: "Defeated he stood before me. I hated him because he would not resist me. I loved him because he was my victim. I slapped him again. He put a freckled chubby hand against his cheek." As the narrator escapes to the street, he concludes that "each of us had his secret art. I embraced the noon-time throngs with a smile." The portrait of the grandfather reflects the difficulties that Cohen faced with his own senile grandfather, although without the degree of violence. Cohen still remembers his grandfather's words to him when he would visit him in the rest home: "Flee from this place, flee from this place!"

A Ballet of Lepers was Cohen's first extended work of fiction, completed in July 1957. He sent the manuscript out to Pocketbooks and to Ace Publications, but both rejected it. In a 1990 interview, Cohen remembers the writing process: "I had a clock on my desk, and I forced myself to write a certain number of hours every day and I watched this clock. It had no glass on it and I always thought I could just move the hand with my finger. I remember writing on the face of the clock the word 'help.'" When an interviewer asked some years later about his productivity, Cohen replied that what an artist really requires is staying power and intransigence and cited Woody Allen's quip that "eighty percent of life is just showing up!"

The theme of the novel anticipates many of Cohen's later works, especially *Beautiful Losers* and *The Energy of Slaves*. There is, for example, the perverse symbiosis that links people, whether lovers or family:

How sad and beautiful we were, we humans, with our suffering and our torturing. I, the torturer, he the tortured, we the sufferers. I, suffering in the clear speared fire of purity, burning, agonized and strangely calm. He, suffering in the dark flames of humiliation, and beginning the journey to purity. I the instrument of his delivery and he the instrument of mine.

Could it be that the reward of the degraded is to degrade others? Could that be the painful chain toward salvation, because I know there is a chain.

In *A Ballet of Lepers*, Cohen also demonstrated a growing sense of Jewish history and tragedy, a theme that would develop in his next three books of poetry: *The Spice-Box of Earth*, *Flowers for Hitler*, and *Parasites of Heaven*. Explaining his violent acts, the narrator says:

It happened, that is all. It happened, just as Buchenwald happened, and Belsen and Auschwitz, and it will happen again, it will be planned, it will happen again and we will discover the atrocities, the outrages, the humiliations and we will say that it is the plan of a madman, the idea of a madman, but the madman is ourselves, the violent plans the cruelties and indignities, they are all our own, and we are not mad, we are crying for purity and love.

A fundamental artistic theme of Cohen's is the necessary cruelty of love. "We are not mad, we are human, we want to love, and someone must forgive us for the paths we take to love, for the paths are many and dark, and we are ardent and cruel in our journey." The predatory nature of love and the need for compassion were explored repeatedly in Cohen's published works, as well as the need to "learn betrayal so that you may not betray." It is also necessary "to learn shame, remember humiliation, be diligent in your recollection of guilt. . . . Understand contamination so you may be pure, violence so you may be peaceful."

COHEN INTENSIFIED his attachment to Layton at this time, acting as best man at the poet's faux wedding in Montreal in the spring of 1958. Incapable of asking his wife, Betty Sutherland Layton, for a divorce, Layton wanted to buy his current love, Aviva Cantor, a wedding ring. Cohen joined Layton and Aviva for lunch and in the afternoon they went to a jewelry shop on Mountain Street, where Aviva looked at gold bands. Layton neglected her, however, and instead bought a chunky silver bracelet for Betty. It was left to Cohen to choose a gold band and he placed it on Aviva's finger, standing in for the ambivalent Layton. Remembering the incident, Cohen said that Layton "probably felt like living with both women. I think he could have handled them both, too. It was the *women* who demanded a resolution." To Layton's mixed pleasure, Aviva Cantor called herself Mrs. Layton from that moment on.

By day, Cohen was still working in the shipping department or office of his uncles' clothing company; at night he would write poems. Sometimes he read the poems in coffeehouses with names like the Pam-Pam or the Tokai. At the Pam-Pam, he and Stephen Vizinczey, a Hungarian writer who would later edit the short-lived magazine *Exchange*, would often spend an evening seated near the door rating the women who entered, issuing invitations to the finalists.

At this time Cohen often projected a mood of despair and angst, especially and perhaps only with women. Vera Frenkel recalled an incident at the Tokai when after a conversation with Cohen about a lost suitcase she telephoned a close friend to express her concern about his state of mind. "Don't worry," her friend remarked, "he often becomes this way with women. He needs to experience this condition in order to work." Such repeated "torment on the bed of love," as Frenkel described it, became a frequent condition for Cohen, which some thought to be theatrics and others a genuine crisis. "Leonard," Frenkel added, "always needed to be saved and lost in the same breath."

Cohen sometimes played host to visiting Canadian writers. Al Purdy recalls a visit with Milton Acorn in the late fifties and the stark contrast between the two poets, Acorn intensely political, "a red fire hydrant in blue denims," Cohen giving "the impression of elegant aristocracy, wearing a fancy dressing gown to putter around the kitchen in . . . perfectly self-aware." Cohen moved "within a slight but perceptible aura of decadence . . . of standing aside in slight weariness, of having been through life before and found it rather boring."

Cohen accompanied Irving Layton to a meeting with another icon of Canadian poetry, E.J. Pratt. Earle Birney had arranged for Layton and Cohen to lunch with Pratt and himself. A photograph commemorating the event shows a businesslike Pratt in suit and hat, Birney casual in jacket and pants, and Layton and Cohen dressed as kibbutzim in slacks and white shirts with their sleeves rolled up. The sartorial clash was mirrored in conversational styles. Layton noted Birney's "sad Duke of

Windsor face" and Pratt's formal anecdotes, explaining to Desmond Pacey that when he and Leonard drove back, "we had lots of impressions to compare and analyze. We haven't stopped talking about it yet."

As Cohen was meeting with his peers and elders, his friends were leaving. He wrote a short story entitled "Goodbye, Old Rosengarten" that describes the last night with his friend Mort Rosengarten before Mort left Montreal to study art in London. The two revisit their favorite locales, including a bistro called The Shrine, their nickname for the Cafe Andre on Victoria Street. Cohen, unnamed in the story, tries to convince Rosengarten of the virtues of Montreal "on the threshold of greatness, like Athens, like New Orleans." At the Shrine, all has changed: the bohemians have abandoned the place, the furniture has been replaced. The story is an apologia for altered lives and an altered city, which both Cohen and Rosengarten must escape to fulfil their promise of greatness. A year later, Cohen also left.

Cohen was adding music to his poetry readings, though not necessarily his own guitar. In February 1958, Layton reported to the critic Desmond Pacey that Cohen was bringing a new Beat style from New York and San Francisco to Montreal: "He's currently reading poetry while a jazz orchestra fills in with strophes of its own." Dudek also tried it one evening but without success, according to Layton, "but Cohen is really laying them in the aisles. A new development in the Montreal School?" Cohen began to appear often at downtown clubs like Birdland, and in March 1958, Layton, Jonathan Williams (an American poet and printer), and Daryl Hine witnessed Cohen's reading accompanied by a jazz ensemble, and then the three joined in.

In April of that year, Cohen gave his first professional poetry recital at Dunn's Progressive Jazz Parlour, a room above Dunn's Famous Steak House on Ste-Catherine Street. Working with pianist and arranger Maury Kay, who usually had a twelve- or fifteen-piece band on stage, Cohen recited his poetry, starting at midnight, often improvising while Kay played piano. Cohen read his poem "The Gift" (which appeared in *The Spice-Box of Earth*), introducing it by saying, "It was written for a girl for whom I had given too many poems and she asked me to refrain. So I wrote her this poem. And it's a serious poem, so don't cackle just because I told you I needed the money."

After Cohen's reading there was a short interview that began with the question, "I wonder how a poet who's meant to be a recluse in his room feels about being a nightclub celebrity?" Cohen responds by saying, "Well, ah, this isn't quite being a nightclub celebrity. What we're really doing is bringing poetry to where it belongs. . ."

"To the people?"
"No, no, no, not to the people. To the hipsters, to the boozers. No really, ah, back to music and back to an informality, away from the classroom."

One night in the spring of 1958, Morley Callaghan visited Dunn's, invited by Cohen. Callaghan had read of "the nightclub poets of San Francisco and Greenwich Village," and was interested in seeing Cohen's work performed. Dunn's, Callaghan writes, "is a kind of triple-decked club, something for the boys on each floor, and naturally the poet is in the attic." Around midnight:

> a waiter placed a high stool near the bandstand and the young poet, Leonard Cohen, black haired and pale, perching himself on the stool, bantered a little with the customers to get everyone and himself cool and relaxed; and at the piano the bandleader too made nice cool sounds. The poet began to read and he read well, just like a pro. In the main he read love poems and the jazz rhythms seemed to give them a little edge and impact. I was watching the faces of the customers. You might say that of all people those in a night club are the least likely to become candidates for listening at a poetry recital. Yet, when you sit around in a night club you are ready for anything, disillusioned, often a little beat. As the boys say, you are down enough to get with it. The poetry mixed with the jazz hits right at the bottom of your spirit. When Cohen sat down with us he said that business had been good or he wouldn't still be there. Even the waiters listened to him he said. What more could any poet ask in a night club. Anyway, we liked it.

Throughout the spring and summer Cohen would appear at Dunn's, performing with a jazz band. He also performed on the McGill campus and in Toronto, honing the musical element that would later eclipse his poetry. It was a fresh genre for Montreal audiences and Cohen established a local reputation as a performer.

In June of 1958, Cohen wrote a short essay that defined his aesthetic, a declaration of poetic intent:

> Whatever I have written about I have tried to remember the violence and destruction and passion of our century. I want my poems to be informed by a sensibility which comprehends the bombing of cities, concentration camps and human infidelity. I do not mean that every poem must have in it a swollen body or a crematoriam[;] most of my poems do not, but a love poem, for instance, must be about a love that encounters and comes to terms with the kind of violence and despair and courage and to which we have been exposed.

THE WORLDLY twenty-four-year-old poet and folk singer spent the summer of 1958 as a counsellor at Pripstein's Camp Mishmar. Pripstein's was started by a Hebrew schoolteacher and educator, Hayim (Chuck) Pripstein, and grew out of a children's camp that was once attached to a Jewish hotel in Filion, Quebec, known for its literary gatherings (Isaac Bashevis Singer, among others, read there). When the river behind the hotel became polluted, the hotel closed and Pripstein transported some of the buildings to a new site in St-Adolphe-de-Howard, north of Montreal. The camp's philosophy was to take children of varying abilities, background, and behavior and integrate them.

When other camps would reject disturbed or difficult childen, Pripstein's took them in. The counsellors attended weekly Saturday afternoon seminars on child psychology, mental health, and Judaism to help them handle the problems. The majority of campers were the children of the middle class and most of the counsellors were McGill students. Instead of a bugle to awaken campers in the morning, the opening bars of Haydn's Trumpet Concerto were played on the public address system. A camp photograph from 1958 shows a robust Leonard Cohen standing in the back row amid a group of healthy campers. Among the graduates were literary critic Ruth Wisse, pianist Robert Silverman, and sociologist Lionel Tiger. Many of the counsellors and campers went on to become psychiatrists, social workers, and child analysts. At Pripstein's Cohen organized folksinging and haiku contests and also took an interest in a young camper named Robert Elkin, an autistic *idiot savant* who had an extraordinary facility with numbers. Elkin appears as the ill-fated Martin Stark in *The Favorite Game*.

The fourth book of *The Favorite Game* carefully recounts Cohen's experiences at Pripstein's, although not his turning up a week late and in shorts for the wedding of Moishe Pripstein (son of the founder) and Florence Sherman. He does describe, however, his emergence from the boathouse in the early morning with a female counsellor, under the watchful eye of Mrs. Pripstein, whose house surveyed the camp from a hilltop perch. Cohen found camp a fertile ground for romance. One close friend was Fran Dropkin, a gorgeous dancer from Brooklyn with thick dark braids who had come to Pripstein's as an art counsellor. Another woman, the camp nurse, became the muse for one of his best early poems, "As the Mist Leaves No Scar." A camper who ran the darkroom at Pripstein's recalls printing a roll of film for Cohen. They turned out to be a series of photos of nude females.

The camp was a cultural mecca and long hours were spent among counsellors and campers in stimulating discussions of poetry, history, and drama. Life in Israel, the status of Jews in Quebec, and the nature of Montreal were also analyzed. It was a time of intense self-expression and Cohen, whose talent was acknowledged, was the leading nonconformist. The counsellor's lounge, underneath the dining hall, became the center for most of these debates.

Part of that year was also devoted to visiting his mother, who was being treated for depression in the Allan Memorial Institute, a psychiatric hospital in Montreal. The depression was triggered by inappropriately prescribed drugs for a skin disease brought on by the stress caused by the return of the now senile Rabbi Klein to the Cohen household. During visits to the hospital, Masha often accused Cohen and his sister of neglecting her and Cohen found the encounters difficult. Once her medication changed, however, she regained her mental balance and was quickly released. But his familial links withered further when he failed to return to the family business at the end of the summer. When asked by his cousin Edgar Cohen why he left the Freedman Company, Cohen replied, "Edgar, I had no choice."

In the December 1958 issue of *Culture* there was a surprising attack on Cohen from his former mentor, Louis Dudek. The newest generation of poets, Dudek stated, is "not even capable of social anger or of pity." Cohen was criticized for his "obscure cosmological imagery . . . a confusion of symbolic images, often a rag-bag of classical mythology." Layton was suitably incensed, calling Dudek's attitude "as stupid as it is false. Cohen is one of the purest lyrical talents this country has ever produced. He hates the mythologizing school of Macpherson, Reaney and Daryl Hine." Cohen overlooked the charges and accompanied Dudek and F.R. Scott to a January 1959 party for Ralph Gustafson at the Montreal Press Club.

In April 1959 Cohen and Layton both received Canada Council grants. Cohen's proposed project was to write a novel drawn from visits to the ancient capitals of Rome, Athens, and Jerusalem. Because he had the support of writers like Layton and Scott, and was gaining attention in reviews from Margaret Avison, Desmond Pacey, Milton Wilson, and Northrop Frye, the Canada Council decided to fund his request. A number of Canadian writers were living overseas at the time: Dorothy Livesay and Mordecai Richler were in London, Mavis Gallant was in Paris, and Margaret Laurence was in Africa. According to Layton, this was to be expected because "the Canadian poet . . . is an exile condemned to live in his own country" without a public or following; hence, one might as well depart to a region where art was at least respected. The arts grant of two thousand dollars made it possible for Cohen to leave Montreal.

That June, Layton introduced Cohen to A.M. Klein who was to become an instrumental figure in Cohen's life. Klein was the seminal Jewish Montreal poet and had been the editor of the *Canadian Jewish Chronicle* from 1938–55. He had won a Governor General's Award for poetry in 1949 and had been the leader of the Jewish literati until his nervous breakdown and withdrawal from writing in the mid-fifties. Cohen grew up reading Klein and Klein had reviewed Cohen's grandfather's book in *The Canadian Jewish Chronicle*. Klein remembered both the book and the rabbi. After their visit, Cohen told Layton that he thought "the fires had been banked" but that Klein was still witty and eager to talk about poetry. Cohen had already written two poems about Klein: "To a Teacher" and "Song for Abraham Klein," later to appear in *The Spice-Box of Earth*.

Cohen interpreted Klein's breakdown as the result of being exiled by his community. In a December 1963 talk by Cohen at the Jewish Public Library of Montreal, Cohen said, "Klein chose to be a priest though it was as a prophet that we needed him, as a prophet he needed us and he needed himself . . ." To avoid such a split himself, Cohen attempts to collapse the divide between prophet and priest and to join them throughout his work—or at least give them equal time. The prophet, Cohen notes, is the visionary; the priest his disciple.

Cohen learned from both Klein and Layton, combining Klein's priestly mien with the prophetic energy of Layton to reformulate the voice of the Jewish poet. Cohen examined Judaism within a broader context, one that allowed the incorporation of Zen Buddhism and traditional Jewish orthodoxy. Cohen's poetic world became a complex mix of tradition and experimentation, conservatism and propheticism. What he called the Montreal tradition was "a certain Hebraic sense connected with Layton and A.M. Klein, and it connected me in a certain way with Scott, whose father was a minister. I'm attracted to a priesthood." But Klein stood out:

> His fate was very important to me, what happened to and what would happen to a Jewish writer in Montreal who was writing in English, who was not *totally* writing from a Jewish position. . . . Klein *came out* of the Jewish community of Montreal, but [he] had a perspective on it and on the country, and on the province. He made a step outside the community. He was no longer protected by it.

Such a move established a paradigm for Cohen, who would himself step outside the Montreal poetry scene. "I always was more interested in the exile," Cohen has commented, "somebody who can't claim the entire landscape as his own."

ON MAY 5, 1959, Cohen wrote an important letter from his Mountain Street apartment:

> Dear Mr. McClelland:
>   I spoke with you on the telephone a few months ago when I was in Toronto and you said that I may send you my manuscript.
>   Here it is. I hope you like it.
>   Sincerely,
>   Leonard Cohen

The manuscript was *The Spice-Box of Earth*, and its arrival marked the beginning of Cohen's long-term relationship with one of Canada's leading publishers. Jack McClelland recalls the young poet self-confidently striding into his office earlier that spring wearing a jacket and tie, carrying a manuscript of poems. McClelland quickly scanned Cohen's poetry, which had been recommended by Irving Layton. In an unprecedented move, McClelland accepted Cohen's manuscript on the spot, without consulting any of his editors. "I think it's the only time I ever—without reading a manuscript or without having it read—made the publishing commitment. . . . I said OK, we're going to publish this guy; I don't give a shit whether the poetry's good, although I did look at a couple of the poems and thought they were pretty good."

In mid-July Cohen received a letter from Claire Pratt, an associate editor at McClelland & Stewart and daughter of E.J. Pratt. It said that the manuscript had been accepted on the condition that certain revisions be made, including reducing its length. She also enclosed a reader's report, which criticized some poems as "too slight to be committed to book form," and suggested lessening the number of erotic poems. But "no other poet can quite match the imagery and expressiveness of these poems" the reader concluded. Pratt anticipated publishing in the spring of 1960.

Cohen was ecstatic with the news, replying,

> I have bought several people several rounds of drinks since your generous and historic letter arrived. One of my uncles smiled, one disturbed relative had an instant of lucidity, the Board of Elders of my family's synagogue has convened to reopen discussion on my occupancy of my father's pew, from which I have been disallowed on account of my last book, which was discovered to be lewd, offensive, and full of christological implications.

Rather than see the book in the McClelland & Stewart "Indian File" series, an expensive hardcover line, as Pratt suggested, Cohen had another idea. He explained that costly, hard-bound poetry books were obsolete. The public wouldn't buy them. He thought that a brightly colored paperback would sell better: "Please understand I want an audience. I am not interested in the Academy. There are places where poems are being bought and embraced." He offered to work with their designer on a format that would appeal to a wide following: "inner-directed adolescents, lovers in all degrees of anguish, disappointed Platonists, pornography-peepers, hair-handed monks and Popists, French-Canadian intellectuals, unpublished writers, curious musicians, etc., all that holy following of my Art." Cohen's preference for a paperback with a potentially large audience contradicts his decision to print his first book in hardcover, the price limiting readership. He concluded his letter with an open and genuine statement: "Thank you for treating me like a professional and making me feel like a Writer."

Pratt and McClelland soon discovered that Cohen operated in an unusual manner, declining to sign contracts for his work after *The Spice-Box of Earth*. As a matter of form, a contract would always be sent, but Cohen would never return it. With the exception of his first book for McClelland & Stewart (and his most recent, *Stranger Music*), this became Cohen's unorthodox procedure. Jack McClelland chose to ignore this aspect of Cohen's behavior, despite his anxiety over certain legal matters, including the right of Cohen, rather than the firm, to control his material.

By September, Cohen had decided to leave the clothing business: "Can't take it anymore. Will try the CBC," which he did briefly, supporting himself by writing reviews and attempting some radio journalism.

He continued to experiment with drugs "to liberate spiritual energy"; at least that was the excuse, he later remarked. "Thanks to drugs," he has sarcastically noted, "for at least fifteen minutes I could consider myself as the Great Evangelist of the New Age!" His role as Evangelist took an unusual form when in early September he joined Layton, Al Purdy, and John Mills at the Ph.D defense of George Roy at the University of Montreal on "Symbolism in Canadian Poetry 1880–1939." Despite the celebrity audience, the candidate passed.

On November 12, 1959, Cohen accompanied Scott and Layton in a poetry reading at the Young Mens' Hebrew Association on 92nd Street in New York, by all accounts a great success. Introduced by Kenneth McRobbie, the trio was in good voice, with Scott possessing "enough Anglo-Saxon dignity to cover the rest of us." A few weeks after the reading at the YMHA, Cohen departed for London. Following his habit of marking a departure or change, Cohen offered a comic farewell:

An All-Season Haiku for my friends
Who are leaving and who have decided
not to leave, who are putting clean
pressed handkerchiefs in their battered
baggage and thinking about trains
chariots and even nobler
wagons only they know about, and
to those who have no clean linen at
all but have to use sleeves or even bare
arms and walk where ever they go
    Goodbye

On October 29, 1959, Cohen was issued his first passport. It is a well-used document, with stamps that record his wanderings over the following decade: Greece, France, Britain, the United States, Morocco, Cuba, and Norway. The accompanying photo shows a serious young man in jacket, tie, and vest, the embodiment of Westmount success.

4

MOLECULES
DANCING IN
THE MOUNTAINS

THE KING OF BOHEMIA and William IV welcomed Leonard Cohen to London on a dreary December day in 1959. The two pubs stood adjacent to 19B Hampstead High Street, a small, three-story boardinghouse which, despite its address, was actually tucked around the corner on Gayton Road. Today the unassuming brown and tan brick building is squeezed between Oxfam and the Cafe Rouge. Across the road and next to a post office is the Cafe Zen. When Cohen arrived, a green grocer, an East Indian restaurant, and a laundromat were the main attractions. Two small windows in the front of the boardinghouse let in a muted light.

Jake and Stella Pullman owned it and their home became a haven of sorts for Cohen. Mort Rosengarten, whose parents knew the Pullmans, had stayed there, and two other close friends, Harold Pascal and Nancy Bacal, were still there, eagerly awaiting his arrival. Cohen was told that the only space left was a cot in the sitting room, where all new guests started out; only after someone left did you graduate to an upper floor. He was welcome to it if (a) he tidied the room every morning and (b) he fulfilled his intention of becoming a writer by meeting his announced goal of three pages a day. "As long as you write your three pages every day you can stay with us," Stella Pullman told him. Cohen agreed to her bargain and got to work, diligently producing at least three pages a day, a practice he followed for years. Stella's strictness, as well as her generosity, paid off: "She is partly responsible for finishing my book in a way," Cohen said, referring to the first draft of The Favorite Game. The Pullmans became a new anchor in his life.

Cohen was excited about being in the capital of English literature and felt he was joining Shakespeare, Milton, and Keats. "London is welcoming another great author!" he declared. A visit to Dublin created similar excitement, and he wrote a short play entitled "Sugar Plum Fairies" (an early version of "The New Step") after visiting the Abbey Theatre and the pubs that Yeats had frequented. But after the initial excitement, Cohen found London dull and its nightlife unpromising. He obtained a "reader's ticket" to the Hampstead Public Libraries and spent a good deal of time at the William (as the local pub, the William IV, was called). He later discovered a West Indian club called the All-Niter, where he found terrific music, marijuana, and dancing. With Nancy Bacal, who was in London to study classical theatre and begin a career in radio journalism with the CBC, he explored late-night London. They played pinball in East End dives, met pimps, explored the drug culture, went to clubs, and encountered some alternative politics. Nancy was then dating a disciple of Malcolm X named Michael X, who later founded the Black Muslim movement in London. He planned to return to Trinidad, take over the government, and make Cohen part of the ruling party, as "permanent advisor to the Minister of Tourism!" Michael X did return, but he was soon arrested. Cohen, with others, attempted to organize support for him but failed.

On the day he arrived in London, Cohen bought a typewriter, a green Olivetti 22, for £40, which would remain with him for years. He also acquired his "famous blue raincoat," a Burberry with epaulets. That, too, remained with him until it was stolen from a New York loft in 1968. In London, these objects acted as amulets, arming him to combat the world. His Olivetti broke only once in twenty-six years, when he threw the machine against the wall of his Montreal apartment after an unsuccessful attempt to type underwater. It was eventually repaired, and he used that Olivetti to type most of his best-known songs and novels.

His raincoat was memorialized in the song "Famous Blue Raincoat," recorded on *Songs of Love and Hate*, his third album. "The last time we saw you, you looked so much older / Your famous blue raincoat was torn at the shoulder" reads two lines of this song that ends enigmatically, "Sincerely, L. Cohen." The song has become a signature of sorts, the raincoat embodying Cohen's early image of mystery, travel, and adventure. The coat itself appears in the 1965 NFB film, *Ladies and Gentlemen . . . Mr. Leonard Cohen*. Jennifer Warnes titled her 1986 album *Famous Blue Raincoat* and used a drawing of the coat on the cover.

Cohen quickly established a new social circle in London. Through Tony Graham, a Montrealer who was studying medicine at Cambridge, he met Elizabeth Kenrick, part of a Cambridge set. She, in turn, introduced him to Jacob Rothschild, later Lord Rothschild. Although Kenrick never became Cohen's girlfriend, he invited her, in jest, to join him when he decided to go to Hydra in March 1960; she declined. Two years later, he was still concerned about her, telling his sister in New York that Kenrick, "very lovely both of flesh and spirit," would soon be visiting and she should help her if necessary.

Cohen's principal activity at 19B Hampstead High Street was writing the first draft of his second novel, *Beauty at Close Quarters*, later published as *The Favorite Game*. At one point he also considered calling it *Stars for Neatness*. He began the book almost immediately upon his arrival, working diligently, despite interruptions from David the cat; he loved to scatter the pages. Cohen read passages to Nancy Bacal, who later said she felt that the lengthy first draft possessed a looseness and honesty that the published work lacked.

The first version of the story, completed in the winter of 1959/1960, opens with the self-conscious narrator, Lawrence Breavman, searching in his papers for a passage summarizing the difficulty of beginnings. He wishes he could be known to the reader in a flash but realizes he must unfold himself through exaggeration and distortion, "until by sheer weight of evidence, you will possess me, knowing when I am false and when I am true." An undisguised autobiographical text follows, with the narrator identifying his birth in Montreal in September 1934, the month and year of Cohen's birth. Cohen's family history follows, essentially a semi-fictional summary of adventures, incidents, and interests of his first twenty-five years.

The actual names of several friends appear, including Freda [Guttman] and [Robert] Hershorn; Mort Rosengarten appears as Krantz; Irving Morton, a socialist folksinger, appears as himself. Other names in the final version change: Freda, presented as a politically motivated student, and Louise, a Montreal artist, merge into a single character, Tamara. Stella, the housemaid from the Maritimes that Cohen hypnotized, becomes Heather. Details about the family home appear, including a careful description of the photograph of Cohen's father hanging in his childhood bedroom. Cohen, through Breavman, narrates his life, including his father's illness, his early girlfriends, and his mother's overbearing love.

After completing the first draft of his novel in March 1960, Cohen then revised the typescript of *The Spice-Box of Earth* and sent it to McClelland & Stewart. Cohen wrote to Claire Pratt, "I'm glad the book is out of my hands. Poetry is so damn self-indulgent. During these past few weeks of intense polishing, I've been making nasty faces at myself in all the mirrors I pass." The work was reduced by the suggested third, while its design became more clarified in the author's mind: "I wouldn't like to see these poems rendered in any sort of delicate print. They should be large and black on the page. They should look as if they are meant to be chanted aloud, which is exactly why I wrote them."

Jack McClelland offered Cohen a choice: he could publish the manuscript in a common edition to appear in the fall of 1960 or do a more expensive and distinctively designed volume for the spring of 1961. In late July, Cohen told McClelland to let Frank Newfeld design the book and publish it the following spring. His choice of the higher-priced, more artistic form for the book contradicted his earlier wish for a mass market paperback. But this format would satisfy his sense of poetry as a formal art that should have an elegant, almost "Westmount" look and feel. The appearance of the volume suited the taste of the author. In his letter to McClelland, he also mentioned that he had almost finished his novel, which he would forward to him. On August 28, 1960, he sent "the only copy in the world," as he admitted to McClelland, to Toronto.

Earlier in March, when he had completed his manuscripts, Cohen was free to consider his position in London, and he found it wanting. After having a wisdom tooth pulled one day, he wandered about the East End of London on yet another rainy afternoon and noticed a Bank of Greece sign on Bank Street. He entered and saw a teller with a deep tan wearing sunglasses, in protest against the dreary landscape. He asked the clerk what the weather was like in Greece. "Springtime" was the reply. Cohen made up his mind on the spot to depart, and within a day or so he was in Athens. "I said to myself that I should go somewhere completely different in order to see how they live," he later explained.

It was actually the island of Hydra that attracted Cohen. English was spoken and an artists' colony was flourishing. He had first heard of Hydra from Jacob Rothschild, whose mother had married Ghikas (Niko Hadjikyriakos), one of modern Greece's most important painters. They lived in his family's forty-room seventeenth-century mansion perched on a hill some distance from the port with a striking view of the sea. Jacob Rothschild encouraged Cohen to visit his mother, promising to write to her to say that Cohen was coming. Layton had predicted Cohen's departure. "I suppose when he's finished his novel," he told Desmond Pacey, "he'll leave London for the Continent, where he'll make love to all the beautiful French and Italian women, and then leave for Greece and Israel!"

COHEN ARRIVED in Athens on April 13, 1960, visited the Acropolis, then spent the night in Piraeus, where he was flattered by a homosexual advance (which he rejected) from a hotel floor sweeper. The next morning he began the five-hour steamer journey to Hydra, which took him first to Aegina, Methana, and Poros, and then to Hydra. (Since the seventies, the Russian-built Flying Dolphins hydrofoils have replaced the once-elegant steamers, reducing the traveling time to one and a half hours.) The trip was an opportunity to relax, drink, and meet women.

At Hydra, the small semicircular port is flanked by white houses rising steeply in an orderly manner, like the seats of an amphitheater. A cobbled esplanade runs along the waterfront, harmonizing the cluster of homes that surround it and reach up the hillside. Only the bell tower of the cathedral attached to the Monastery of the Virgin's Assumption disrupts the horizontal tableau. The structure of the town emulates the classical theater of Epidauros, with the port the equivalent of the orchestra. Access to and from the port follows the theatrical frame of the *parodos* (side entrances and exits) with the houses mimicking the stepped seats of the *theatron*. Towering above the port is the two-thousand-foot Mount Ere, and on a high hill just below it, the Monastery of Profitis Elias (the Prophet Elijah).

In the morning the port is the commercial center where boats are unloaded, where fish and vegetables are sold, and donkeys are hired. At midday and into the evening it becomes the social center, the focus turned toward the restaurants and cafes. During religious or public holidays, it is the site of celebration. When Cohen arrived in 1960, only four coffeehouses and one bar ringed the waterfront.

Tradition, rather than a master plan or building code, determined the urban layout and architecture of Hydra. When a child married, a new house was built within the uncovered space of the family lot, treated as a separate unit, and given direct entry from the public street. The result was odd lot shapes and dead ends (most houses are rectangular or "L" shaped and composed of stone walls, timber or tile roofs, and tile floors.) The doorways are unique in that they face downwards to the port, rather than horizontally to the street. Offsetting the whitewashed walls of the homes are the orange tile roofs and the weathered cobblestone steps. It was the anarchy of the homes that prompted Henry Miller to remark on the "wild and naked perfection of Hydra."

The narrow island was named for water though it actually has little. Rain is rare, the average yearly precipitation being only an inch and a half. When the first home with a swimming pool was built by a Greek

American in the late sixties, the owner had to pay for barges of fresh water to be brought in and pumped up the hilly streets. It is little more than a barren rock, four miles wide and nearly eleven miles long, about four miles off the southeast coast of Argolis.

There are no cars or trucks on Hydra, since the land is too steep and the streets too narrow to permit them. Donkeys, which bray in an agonizing manner throughout the night, and occasionally horses, are the only transportation on the steps and ramps. The widest streets were originally designed so that two basket-carrying donkeys could pass each other; secondary streets provide passage for only one. An important site is *Kala Pigadia*, the Good Wells or Twin Wells. Situated above the port, this is where water was drawn and people gathered to trade news and stories; the two small wells are shaded by several large trees.

When Cohen first arrived on Hydra there was limited electricity, few telephones, and virtually no plumbing. Kerosene or oil lamps lit the homes; cisterns were used to collect water, and no wires obstructed the views. One of the few discos used a battery-operated record player, since the small electrical plant generated power only from sundown to midnight. Except for the kitchen, which was heated by the stove or Turkish copper braziers, rooms were heated with a three-legged tin filled with charcoal embers. Many of the homes were run-down and in desperate need of repair. In 1960, half of the homes were uninhabited, and virtually no new homes had been built for nearly a century.

When Cohen arrived he found temporary accomodation with writers George Johnston and Charmian Clift before renting a house for fourteen dollars a month. After he was settled, Cohen decided to introduce himself to Jacob Rothschild's mother and hired a guide to take him to Ghikas' estate. Jacob Rothschild's sister greeted him but made it clear that no one had heard of him, that her brother hadn't written, and that Cohen's type of Jew was not really welcome. Angered by this reception, Cohen left, casting a curse upon the house. Late one evening in 1961, while wandering back and forth on the terrace of his own house above the port, Cohen was startled to hear an explosion and see a fire high up on the mountain. The Ghikas home had exploded! He felt his curse had taken effect. He later learned that a careless watchman, guarding the empty estate, misplaced some kerosene, which had ignited.

There was already a small community of foreign writers and artists on Hydra. The principal figures were the Australian writers George Johnston and Charmian Clift, the English painter Anthony Kingsmill, and the Norwegian writer Axel Jensen, who headed a small Norwegian contingent. Other writers came and went, including John Knowles, William Lederer (author of *The Ugly American*), Irish poet Paul Desmond, Swedish poet Goron Tunstrom, Israeli journalist Amos Elan, and numerous dancers, artists, and academics. Allen Ginsberg stayed for several nights with Cohen after Cohen hailed him in Syntagma Square in Athens, recognizing him from a photograph. After a lengthy conversation, Ginsberg accepted Cohen's invitation to visit. Don McGill, Canadian broadcaster and director at the Mountain Playhouse, and American sociologist Rienhart Bendix also visited Hydra. Film stars, including Sophia Loren (who filmed *Boy on a Dolphin* there) and Brigitte Bardot, began to appear. Jackie Kennedy would visit, and later Edward Kennedy, as well as Jules Dassin, Melina Mercouri, Tony Perkins, and Peter Finch, who was a good friend of the Johnstons. In several of his letters from 1961, Cohen complains about the influx of movie crews, which upset the peace and quiet of the island.

George Johnston and Charmian Clift were Australian journalists who had moved to Hydra in 1955 to write. *Peel Me a Lotus* is Charmian's engaging account of their survival on an isolated and uncomfortable island with two small children. By 1958, two years after the birth of their third child, their relationship had begun to fall apart. In his 1960 novel *Closer to the Sun*, Johnston recounted the jealousies and liaisons of island life. The couple returned to Australia in 1964 after George contracted tuberculosis, shortly before his novel *My Brother Jack* was published. It was hailed as an outstanding and significant Australian novel. In 1969, Charmian committed suicide, shocking everyone. George died a year later.

Cohen first met George and Charmian at Katsikas' Bar, which consisted of "six deal tables at the back of Antony and Nick Katsikas' grocery store at the end of the cobblestoned waterfront by the Poseidon Hotel." Amid flour sacks, olive jars, and strings of onions, an artist's club of sorts flourished. Evenings were spent arguing, drinking, and entertaining one another. George, the writer-in-residence, held court, often speaking "in a wild spate of words, punctuated with great shouts of laughter and explosions of obscenity." Members of the foreign community appeared, withdrew, and reappeared. The port became a "horseshoe-shaped stage" and the Johnston's circle "the actors of some unbelievable play the intriguing plot of which unrolled in front of the eyes of a totally flabbergasted audience—the locals, who watching it all commented on the side like the chorus of an ancient Greek tragedy."

Cohen soon joined in, absorbed by the discussions, social relations, and sexual maneuverings of his new crowd. He gave his first formal concert at Katsikas' grocery and formed an important and lasting friendship with the Johnstons. They gave him a big work table that he used for writing and eating, as well as a bed and pots and pans for his new house.

Cohen and Johnston made a playful bet occasioned by the spring 1961 upheavals in Iran: in May the Shah had dissolved the representative assembly and senate; by July, he imposed new restrictions on political freedom, while arresting generals and civilans for corruption in preparation for rule by decree. The wager reads:

Bet between LC and George Johnston:
"The Peacock Throne will be
a Shit House Commode by
October 16, 1962."
  – G. H. Johnston

A bet made between George
H. Johnston (a gentile) and Leonard Cohen
(a Jew) on October 16, 1961, and
renewed October 20, 1961, for
10,000 drachmas.
        George Johnston, his Mark,
        [large X] Bassanio [Goron Tunstrom]
P.S. Waiting   Leonard Cohen [written in Hebrew]
for the trial   (Shylock)
yours,
    Portia

Prophetically, what was proposed in the wager nearly came true as land-reform brought major riots causing the Iranian prime minister to resign in April 1962 and allowing the National Front, the religious opposition critical of the government and labeled reactionary, to gain power.

For better or worse, the Johnstons provided both a literary and domestic model for life on the island. The difficulty of the Johnston marriage, with its threats of breakup and numerous affairs, was intensified by George's illness and Charmian's problems in bringing up three children. George shared his ideas, encouraged others, and understood the labor of writing, even if he had difficulty putting it into practice. Charmian was gifted and quite beautiful, but she needed the attention and love of men and her husband was ill and impotent. Cynthia Nolan, wife of the painter Sidney Nolan, remembered there was "a lot of writing talk in the air" around the Johnstons. The island nourished art and destroyed relationships.

Another fixture on the island was the painter, drinker, and gifted conversationalist Anthony Kingsmill, who was to become a close friend of Cohen's. The adopted son of the English writer Hugh Kingsmill, Anthony was plagued by the unknown origin of his biological father, whom he later discovered was not only Jewish but also named Cohen. Kingsmill ended up on Hydra after going to art school in London and spending some time in Paris. Dapper and short, with soulful gray eyes, he would frequently quote long passages from Tennyson, Wordsworth, or Shakespeare. He would also break out into a little softshoe shuffle whenever he was elated or drunk. To the colony of romantically damaged men on the island, he announced that all sex was metaphysical. "Pull up your sex, and get on with it!" His other expression was "Forget the Grace / Enjoy the Lace / Have some fun and carry on."

He survived largely on charm and commissions of never-to-be completed work. When he did finish a painting, he would often resell it to someone else. Cohen commissioned a painting from Kingsmill but when he was away from the island, Kingsmill entered Cohen's house, seized the painting, and resold it. Only years later did he nervously tell Cohen about the ruse. He was expecting the worst from his friend, but Cohen merely laughed. Cohen was constantly commissioning paintings that never materialized, even paying for one painting seven times.

Kingsmill was a difficult and at times exasperating man who drank too much, womanized, and gambled whenever he could. He never had any money but he was always entertaining. By 1964 Kingsmill was having an open affair with Charmian Clift. Island life was intense, and romance was often seasonal: new partnerships would form over the summer, last through the chilly and rainy winter, and then reconfigure themselves in the spring.

But Kingsmill survived his various encounters with women and the bottle. Don Lowe describes Kingsmill as a man with whom you couldn't win:

> He exposed the loser in you. And then took you out, wined and dined you with your own cash, and finally told you that nothing was learned in victories. That it was the losers who proved the most beautiful. So, of course you forgave him. Again and again.

Cohen also forgave Kingsmill again and again, partly because he admired Kingsmill's storytelling skill and talent for life. But Kingsmill also valued Cohen, remarking to Don Lowe that his voice was like a rabbi's, resonant, complex, and full of history. "I don't think he's my father, but he could be. I've tried to tell him that," Kingsmill said. Kingsmill finally married an American woman named Christina in 1973 in Athens. He seemed reasonably settled until his wife left him for someone else and then suddenly died of cancer. He reasoned that he wasn't cut out to be wed; it rhymes too much with "dead," he told everyone. Kingsmill himself died in London in 1993.

George Lialios was another critical figure in Cohen's island life. Several years older than Cohen, he had studied with the concretist musical movement in Cologne and spoke fluent English, German, and Greek. He came from a distinguished family from Patras and was principally interested in philosophy. He first visited Hydra in 1954 where among others he met Lily Mack, a Russian married to Christian Heidsieck of Reims champagne fame, and Patrick Lee-Fermour, a novelist resident in the Ghikas house. Lialios decided to settle there by the fall of 1960, island life being like "living in a past century or in different centuries simultaneously," he commented. Cohen invited Lialios and his Norwegian girl-friend to his home in 1960, and an intense friendship followed. Lialios explained their compatibility: Cohen's "origins are truly and deeply rooted in those ancient cultures which flourished in the eastern part of the Mediterranian basin. This, in part, is why we had such a perfect understanding . . . we could sit together in silence, a virtue which is rare with western people. We never spoke unnecessary words."

Another Hydra friend was Alexis Bolens, a wealthy Swiss *bon vivant* who organized legendary poker games on the island. A friend of Brigitte Bardot, among others, he frequently gave lavish parties at his home in the hills. Kingsmill, Cohen, and Johnston frequently played cards there. Demetri Gassoumis, a Greek American painter; Bryce Marsden and his wife Helen, recognized American painters; Pandias Scaramanga, economist and banker; Bill Cunliff, the Englishman who would later run Bill's Bar, a popular expatriate hangout; Gordon Merrick; and Chuck Hulse rounded out Cohen's immediate social circle throughout the sixties.

At the center of this circle was Marianne Ihlen. Details vary about how Cohen first met her. A poem romantically describes his seeing her reflection in a bookstore window, and in his poem "Island Bulletin" he describes his instant absorption in her. But he also recalls seeing her in the port once or twice and encountering her with her companion Axel Jensen, Norwegian novelist and a student of Jung and the *I Ching*. It may have been at Katsikas', or at the Johnstons'. Cohen's earliest memory of her was seeing her walk arm in arm with Axel and their child and thinking how fortunate they were to have each other.

But they weren't as close as Cohen thought. Jensen soon began an affair with an American painter named Patricia Amlin. They left Hydra in Axel's boat but were soon involved in a car crash in Athens that seriously injured Patricia. She recovered, and they remained together. Cohen took it upon himself to look after Marianne and her child, also named Axel, at first moving into her home:

> I used to sit on the stairs while she slept, they were the most neutral part of the house, and they overlooked her sleeping. I watched her a year, by moonlight or kerosene . . . and nothing that I could not say or form, was lost. What I surrendered there the house has kept, because even torn wordless from me, my own first exclusive

version of my destiny, like a minor poem, is too useless and pure
to die.

Marianne had modeled both in Oslo and on Hydra and had some test
shots taken in Paris. She was beautiful and vivacious and fascinated by
Cohen. His graciousness and generosity touched her. When he bought a
home for himself on Hydra, Marianne and her son moved in with him.
She was quiet, with a domestic bent and Cohen was obsessed with her.
She brought order to Cohen's personal life and encouraged his creativity. On the back cover of Cohen's album *Songs from a Room* there is a
photograph of Marianne seated at Cohen's typewriter in the narrow
writing room on the second floor of his house. She is deeply tanned and
smiles shyly at the camera.

Marianne became both muse and mother for Cohen, fuelling his creative impulse and nurturing his dormant desire for security, home, and
purpose. "It wasn't just that she was the muse, shining in front of the
poet. She understood that it was a good idea to get me to my desk," he
said in 1994. "Marianne is perfect," he wrote to Layton in 1963. "Even
the way she demands masterpieces from me is soft and funny and much
more subtle than she understands." Born in 1935 and raised by her
grandmother, Marianne had the education of an older generation,
Cohen explained. She was "the incarnation of the European woman."
In a BBC interview Cohen said "the way she inhabited a house was very,
very nourishing and every morning she put a gardenia on my work
table." Marianne's son Axel brought out a paternal quality in Cohen.
They lived comfortably as a family.

At the beginning of their relationship, "Marianne and I didn't think
there would be a love story," Cohen has commented. "We thought we
would live together," but it quickly became an intense and enriching
relationship. Her presence sustained his work. He was writing new
poems and by 1964 was beginning his major prose work, *Beautiful Losers*:

There was a woman, she had a child, there were meals on the table,
order in the upkeep of the house and harmony. It was the perfect
moment to start to do some serious work . . . When there is food
on the table, when the candles are lit, when you wash the dishes

together and put the child to bed together. That is order, that is spiritual order, there is no other.

Marianne adored him, although she worried about his drug use. On Hydra, drugs, especially hashish, were easily accessible. It became a common practice for Cohen to smoke either hashish or marijuana, which he believed accelerated his imagination. Cohen got security from Marianne and in return she received Cohen's particular attentions.

"Leonard was unique and amazing," said a longtime female friend. "Leonard *really* loved women, although 'love' is not the right word. He felt that women had a power and a beauty that most did not even know they possessed. To be with Leonard was to begin to know your own power as a woman." Another female friend said he honored them and made them beautiful. Although he was with Marianne, Cohen was not exclusive to anyone. "You could not own Leonard," Nancy Bacal has said.

————————

ON SEPTEMBER 27, 1960, six days after his twenty-sixth birthday, Cohen bought a house in Hydra for $1500, using a bequest from his recently deceased grandmother. This was a "big deal" in the words of one of his friends, a commitment to a place and a world that was mysterious and unusual. Buying the house was a complicated act, needing the assistance of his friend Demetri Gassoumis as translator, adviser, and witness to the deed. Cohen later said that it was the smartest decision he ever made. The three-story, ancient whitewashed building, with its five rooms on several levels, was run-down and had no electricity, plumbing, or running water. Yet it was a private space where he could work, either on the large tiled terrace or in his music room on the third floor. Cohen described his home to his mother:

It has a huge terrace with a view of a dramatic mountain and shining white houses. The rooms are large and cool with deep windows set in thick walls. I suppose it's about 200 years old and many generations of sea-men must have lived here. I will do a little work on it every year and in a few years it will be a mansion . . . I live on a hill and life has been going on here exactly the same for hundreds of years. All through the day you hear the calls of the street vendors and they are really rather musical . . . I get up around 7 generally and work till about noon. Early morning is coolest and therefore best for work, but I love the heat anyhow, especially when the Aegean Sea is 10 minutes from my door.

In a letter to his sister he recounts the nights:

I wander through the rooms with a candle like Rebecca's house-keeper, upstairs, downstairs, the scary basement; my land (presently a garbage heap) is home for a couple of mules and the tinkle of their bells as they pick for food can break your heart as it blends with the music of a taverna two o'clock of a Monday morning. The wind brings you the sound, or three young men, their arms about each other's shoulders, singing magnificent close harmony, nasal[.] Turk-ish minors fill the street with their shared pain of abandoned love, as they reel past your door. . . . There are about sixty countries I've got to visit and buy houses in.

Cohen also adopted the island tradition of keeping cats, although at first he tried to chase them away: "But they came back. I am told that it is the custom of the island to keep cats, and who am I to defy custom?" He relegated them to the basement, since they might have given him hives.

He knew he had been accepted by the community when he began receiving regular visits from the garbage man and his donkey. "It is like receiving the Legion of Honour." Cohen's house gave him a founda-tion. To a friend he explained that "having this house makes cities seem less frightening. I can always come back and get by. But I don't want to lose contact with the metropolitan experience." Buying the house also gave him confidence: "The years are flying past and we all waste so much time wondering if we dare to do this or that. The thing is to leap, to try, to take a chance."

Greece provided Cohen with a base and an observation post on changing social and sexual mores. "The primitive circumstances of my life on this island [are] a condition I hopefully established to attract an interior purity," Cohen wrote, celebrating the discipline instilled by the island. He also liked the natural magic of the island, which could transform a person; in certain seasons, one came out of the sea luminous because of the plankton that adhered to the body. On Hydra, he was freed from the social rituals, obligations, and expectations of his Montreal Judaism. He could take responsibility for his own Judaic identity.

Cohen regularly observed Shabbat, lighting candles and saying the blessings at the Friday evening meal. He stopped his work for a day, dressed more formally, and often walked to the port for Shabbat meetings at noon with Demetri Leousi, an islander who spoke a special, Edwardian English learned at Robert College in Istanbul. Leousi, who had had a love affair with a Jewish woman in New York when he worked there, sustained a deep affection for Jews and congratulated Cohen on being "the first Hebrew to own property on the island. We are honored."

Hydra was also cheap. Cohen could live for as little as a thousand dollars a year, and he quickly worked out a scheme whereby he would return to Canada to earn perhaps two thousand dollars and then race back to Hydra to live for a year or so. And the weather was wonderfully warm. In Hydra, "everything you saw was beautiful: every corner, every lamp, everything you touched, everything you used was in its right place," Cohen wrote. "You knew everything you used . . . It was much more animated, much more cosmopolitan. There were Germans, Scandinavians, Australians, Americans, Dutch who you would run into in very intimate settings like the back of grocery stores." There were no interruptions from work or love. Life was engaging and there was order, but also light:

> There's sun all over my table as I write this, and I'm in love with all the white walls of my house, and anxious to leave them and my stone floored kitchen. I swear I can taste the molecules dancing in the mountains, and I may soon have the privilege of recounting these divine confusions before your fireplace is cold.

The Aegean light had a quality that Cohen felt contributed to his work. "There's something in the light that's honest and philosophical," he told a journalist in 1963, "You can't betray yourself intellectually, it invites your soul to loaf." Not surprisingly, Greece began to play a significant part in the poetry which would appear in *Flowers for Hitler.*

But, just as he felt Montreal both nurtured him and hindered him, Cohen began to feel constrained by Hydra. The attachment to Marianne became both consuming and destroying, a familiar pattern in his later relationships. Island life, with its intense interactions, was becoming difficult. Cohen felt he had to leave for the sake of his art and his peace of mind. The New York poet Kenneth Koch, visiting one summer, reduced the complexities of island life to a single sentence: "Hydra—you can't live anywhere else in the world, including Hydra."

By November 1960, Cohen had returned to Montreal. He needed money, and sought to capitalize on the forthcoming publication of his first book with a major publisher. He applied again to the Canada Council for a writing grant and felt he had to make an impression. He borrowed some money, hired a limousine, and with a friend he sang and smoked marijuana on the two-hour drive from Montreal to Ottawa. At the Canada Council offices, he serenaded the secretaries while chasing them in a wheelchair. Whatever impression he made, Cohen received his grant early in the new year, enough to maintain his life on Hydra. Montreal, meanwhile, ambushed him with "all the old potent guilts."

A month later, the first draft of what would be *The Favorite Game* was rejected by McClelland & Stewart. Cohen tried to find something positive in the rejection. "Since hearing the news, I have been strangely exultant. I feel free again, the way I felt before a line of mine was ever published. . . . I can experiment again, try anything, lose everything. I'm alone with myself and the vast dictionaries of language. It's a joy."

After returning to Hydra, Cohen began to rewrite the novel, which had also been rejected by the New York firm of Abelard-Schuman, although it had had a positive reading. He wrote to Maryann Greene at Abelard-Schuman, "It took me some time to learn to write a poem. It will take me time to learn to write prose. I don't know too much about form right now, but I promise you, I intend to become the best architect in the business." By mid-December 1961, he could tell the Pullmans in London, "I have finished my novel very close to the date at which I began it two years ago in your house."

McClelland & Stewart had objected to his writing prose in the first place and their editorial comments were discouraging; "a protracted love-affair with himself . . . very tedious, not to say disgusting . . . The sex is too damp and morbid." Jack McClelland's first letter about the work told him it was a difficult manuscript to evaluate: it was beautifully written, as one would expect, but was it publishable? And to what degree is the work autobiographical? Cohen replied from Paris in October 1960 that, yes, it was autobiographical: "every event described happened with the exception of the death of Robert at the end of the second section." He "wanted to tell about a certain society and a certain man and reveal insights into the bastard Art of Poetry. I think I know what I'm talking about. Autobiography? Lawrence Breavman isn't me but we did a lot of the same things. But we reacted differently to them and so we became different men."

A later letter from McClelland criticized the novel and asked whether Cohen had other publishing contracts. Cohen responded that in December 1961, Lou Schwartz of Abelard-Schuman had offered him an advance for the revised novel in the presence of Layton, his wife, A.J.M. Smith, and F.R. Scott in a room at the Ritz hotel. He insisted that Cohen take cash right there. Cohen refused and said he would go through regular channels; Schwarz then reneged on his offer. "He managed to offend me and, as you know, I have a saintly nature and am not offended easily," Cohen wrote. McClelland invited Cohen to resubmit the novel, after making editorial changes. "I will always consider you my publisher," Cohen replied, "and I will never forget the wonderful treatment you gave my book of poems and as far as possible I will always come to you first. But I just signed away Commonwealth Rights to Secker & Warburg. Anyway, there'll be other better books." McClelland did remain Cohen's publisher, an important relationship for both of them.

Cohen was ambivalent about the novel himself, describing it as a "miserable" but "important mess." It was "a book without lies," a work with "the atmosphere of a masterpiece; it won't *be* a masterpiece, but people will know that guts were strewn on its behalf." He referred to the revised work as "a book without alibis; not the alibis of the open road or narcotics or engaging crime."

The ambivalence continued, listing between masterpiece and failure. To Seymour Lawrence of the Atlantic Monthly Press, Cohen explained that "perhaps its only value is that it cleared my mind of dogging auto-biographical material," adding that McClelland & Stewart thought the first draft "disgusting, tedious, and dark and that I should stick to poetry. A New York publisher reports that it is one of the most promising first novels they have ever seen. I withdrew the book and began to revise it. That is the whole song." On that same day he also wrote to his sister that "my work limps slowly along to immortality. I am in the phase when I detest the book." A few days later he declared: "It doesn't matter to me whether it's published or not, to tell the truth—I learned so much about writing from that, it's worth it. It makes the next book that much better."

In mid-1961, in the midst of his re-writing, Cohen showed the novel to George Johnston, who thought it had commercial potential as well as artistic appeal. He offered to put Cohen in touch with his literary agents, David Higham Associates in London, and a long correspondence began between Cohen and his soon-to-be agent Sheila Watson. Their letters carefully detailed the drafts, revisions, and rewrites and included a reader's report from January 29, 1962:

> absolutely beautiful writing in most places [but] some of the book is either obscene or near obscene—that is, in the conventionally accepted sense . . . This particular novel is redeemed from being merely erotic by the carefully drawn background and the Jewish phi-losophy of life . . . The title is terrible, vulgar, and out of keeping with the style of the novel.
>
> Very saleable.

Another complaint was that the book was "too long . . . for what it is saying," and that the title, *Beauty at Close Quarters: An Anthology*, was too awkward. Cohen continued his revisions and proposed a series of alter-native titles: *Buried Snows, Wandering Fires, Winged with Vain Desires. The Favorite Game* was not chosen until November 7, 1962. Secker & War-burg finally published the revised novel in September 1963.

DURING A VISIT to Montreal in December 1960, Cohen re-encountered what he called classic Montreal nights: "Three in the morning along Pine Avenue. The black fences and trees from all my old poems canyoned with snow." He was satisfied with his creative life, but had ongoing financial worries. He had a modest yearly annuity of $750, not enough to sustain him. "Except for this tiny desperation about money, I'm happy, productive, and offending all my colleagues with my huge creative joy."

One of Cohen's schemes was to write television dramas with Irving Layton. Every morning Layton came to Cohen's apartment near Mac-Gregor Street, where the two would work on promising ideas which remained unsold. "We did it simply by prodding each other," Cohen said. "He'd get off some line and then I would take the part of a charac-ter and so on and we found ourselves working very beautifully together." Titles like "Lights on the Black Water," "A Man Was Killed," "Up with Nothing," and "Enough of Fallen Leaves" caught no one's imagination. They hoped to write six plays, including "One for the Books," about a Communist bookseller. But the collaboration of poets failed to produce saleable drama.

Cohen was trying his own hand at playwriting at this time and Lay-ton recalls a visit from Cohen one day in which they read his play "The Whipping:" It was a "macabre, compelling thing," similar to an earlier work Cohen had written after his return from Hydra entitled *The Latest Step*. It would later be published as "The New Step (a Ballet-Drama in One Act)" in *Flowers for Hitler*.

Montreal, like every place he stayed, again began to make Cohen rest-less. He sought stimulation elsewhere, and the place he chose was Cuba.

5

H O P E L E S S L Y

H O L L Y W O O D

N 1957 Cohen's sister Esther and her husband Victor had gone to Cuba for their honeymoon and came back with reports of glittering nightclubs, casinos, and risqué floorshows. This had been under the auspices of Batista; in 1959 Fidel Castro had come to power and Cohen wanted to see the socialist revolution firsthand. He took a bus to Miami in late March, and then flew to Havana, which was hot and quietly disintegrating. It was 1961 and Castro was facing off with the Americans. "I am wild for all kinds of violence," Cohen had said before leaving. He later confessed that he went not so much to support Castro as to pursue a fiction: "I had this mythology of this famous civil war in my mind. I thought maybe this was my Spanish civil war, but it was a shabby kind of support. It was really mostly curiosity and a sense of adventure."

Cohen's departure created confusion at McClelland & Stewart: "the day you left for Cuba, the page proofs [of *Spice-Box*] came in, and now I am wondering what we had better do," wrote his editor. On March 30 Cohen was on a Pan American flight from Miami to Havana. Thirty-one years earlier, almost to the day, García Lorca had made a trip to Cuba, and part of Cohen's attraction to the country, as it had been with Columbia University, was that it had excited his literary mentor. Lorca's three-month stay, beginning in April 1930, included lectures, poetry readings, and a crocodile hunt. "The island is a paradise," Lorca exclaimed to his parents. "Cuba! If you can't find me, look for me in Andalusia or in Cuba."

When Cohen arrived, he found a splendid city in decay. The sky-scrapers of Vedado, the business center west of the Old City, were falling into disrepair, the façades cracking, windows broken. The bright pastels of the elegant homes in Cubanacan and El Cerro had faded, the houses now inhabited by peasant families. Walls were crumbling, paint was peeling, and weeds were sprouting. Manicured lawns had turned brown and goats grazed alongside the swimming pools. Elegant cars had been replaced by decrepit taxis. The Havana Country Club was the new National School of Art, and the Prado, once an elite Spanish heritage club, was filled with gym mats for its new use as a gymnastics center.

Havana had once been called "the whorehouse of America," with boatloads of prostitutes greeting tourists as they traveled up the narrow waterway that separates Morro Castle from the city. Under Batista, the government disguised the profitable prostitution rings as dance acade-mies. When Cohen arrived, a program to reform the nearly eleven thousand prostitutes of Havana was underway. The casinos were out-lawed and gambling had been reduced to a back-street operation. But the exotic appeal of the sensual Cuban world could not be erased by socialism, and a violent beauty remained. The rhythm of maracas and marimbas playing the rumba, the *son*, or the cha-cha was heard through-out the city. Sloppy Joe's bar, at one time Cuba's most famous drinking establishment, remained open, although it lacked its former glamor. In Old Havana, the walls of La Bodeguita del Medio, a favorite of Heming-way's, still displayed the signatures of thousands of patrons. Everywhere there was the smell of dust and salt, cigar smoke and cheap perfume.

Despite the new reforms, a certain lasciviousness still hovered about the city, and Cohen rapidly fell into what he referred to as his old bourgeois ways: staying up late to explore the night scene. This teenage habit continued throughout his life and he would often be up writing, drinking, or talking at 3:00 a.m., his favorite morning hour. He soon adopted the fashionable rebel garb: khaki shorts and the fresh stubble of a new beard. But very few citizens were on the streets at that hour and certainly not the East Bloc and Soviet technicians and aides, nor the young female Czech translator he met whose boss would not let her out at night. Only the prostitutes that congregated along the Malecón, the broad boulevard that edged the ocean, or those he met in the Old City kept him company. Of black and Spanish heritage, these chocolate-skinned women with marvelous figures expressed an eroticism that Cohen found irresistible.

Joining the pimps, hookers, gamblers, small-time criminals, and black marketeers who prowled Havana all night, Cohen roamed the urban slums of Jesus del Monte to the swank waterfront suburbs of Miramar. He frequented the back alleys and little bars of Old Havana and the once-renowned Tropicana, which claimed the largest dancehall in the world. Ever since the Shanghai, celebrated for its nude shows, had closed, the Tropicana, with its roulette rooms, cabaret, and open-air dance floor and stage, had flourished. Initially outlawed under Castro, the nightclubs, gambling houses, brothels, casinos, and slot machines soon reappeared. When they were closed, unemployment was too high, compromising the economic goals of the revolution. Cohen imagined himself as "The Only Tourist in Havana," the title of a later poem.

Late one night a Canadian government official knocked on the door of Cohen's Havana hotel, politely telling him that his "presence was urgently requested at the Canadian Embassy." Looking back on the incident, Cohen remembers that he felt apprehensive but excited: "I was Upton Sinclair! I was on an important mission!" Feeling "feisty" and emancipated, Cohen accompanied the dark-suited figure to the embassy. He was immediately ushered into the office of the vice-consul, who took an instant dislike to him, his beard, and his khaki outfit. The official disdainfully conveyed the dramatic news to the pseudo-revolutionary: "Your mother's very worried about you!" It turned out that because three bombers piloted by revolutionaries had staged a minor attack on the Havana airport, exaggerated in the world press as an all-out war on the country, Cohen's mother had contacted Laz Phillips, a Canadian senator who happened to be her cousin and asked him to locate her son to make sure he was alive.

The threat of invasion, however, put everyone on alert and eventually led to Cohen's arrest. Castro had detained nearly one hundred thousand suspected dissidents in the preceding months and Cohen unwittingly joined their ranks. It happened while he was staying at the Hotel Miramar at Playa de Varadero, walking on the famous white sand beach roughly ninety miles east of Havana. Wearing his khakis and carrying a hunting knife, he was suddenly surrounded by twelve soldiers with Czech submachine guns. It was late at night and they thought he was the first of an American landing team. They marched him to the local police station while he repeated the only Spanish he knew, a slogan of Castro's: *Amistad del pueblo*, "Friendship of the people." This made no impression on his captors, but after an hour and a half of interrogation, Cohen convinced them he was not a spy but a fan of the regime who wanted to be there.

Once he had persuaded them that his intentions were innocent, Cohen and his captors embraced, brought out the rum and started a party. The soldiers were *militianos*, and to confirm their good will, they placed a necklace of shells and a string hung with two bullets around Cohen's neck. He spent the next day with his captors and rode back to Havana with them. As they were walking down a Havana Street later that afternoon, a photographer snapped their picture, Cohen wearing his khakis and his new necklace. Afterwards, he stuffed the photograph in his knapsack.

Cohen spent much of his time in the Havana night scene, meeting artists and writers, arguing about artistic freedom and political oppression. He also ran into a number of American Communists. He disagreed with their views and had a violent argument with one of them. The man spat at Cohen and denounced him as bourgeois. The next day Cohen rose to the accusation by shaving his beard and putting on a seersucker suit, confirming their suspicions that he was a "bourgeois individualist."

In Montreal, Irving Layton, as well as Cohen's mother, was now worried. Following the attack on the airport on April 15, Layton wrote to Cohen, advising him to leave as soon as possible. "This is no time for a footloose reckless poet to find himself on the island," Layton told his friend Desmond Pacey. Layton was convinced that within days there would be an invasion and that Cohen was in danger.

Layton was right. The imminent danger was intensified by the January suspension of diplomatic relations between the United States and Cuba. Anti-imperialist rhetoric increased in intensity and daily life became more perilous for foreigners. The Bay of Pigs invasion of April 17, 1961, confirmed the Cubans' fear, although Castro's unexpected success in defeating thirteen hundred U.S.-trained Cuban invaders solidified his power and stature. "Tourists" were arrested daily without explanation, although Cohen found the official attitude of the government "impeccable," even toward someone as "ambiguous and ambivalent as myself."

The day after the invasion, Cohen wrote to Jack McClelland, ostensibly to thank him for his first literary contract, adding, "Just think how well the book would sell if I'm hit in an air-raid. What great publicity! Don't tell me you haven't been considering it." He then gives this report of events the night of the invasion:

> There was a prolonged round of anti-aircraft fire tonight. An unidentified (but we know Yankee) plane. I think the guns were in the room next door. I looked out the window. Half a platoon running down the Prado [Paseo de Martí], then crouching behind an iron lion. Hopelessly Hollywood.

When Cohen decided to leave Cuba, he discovered that most of Havana's middle class was trying to leave as well. Daily visits to the shell-struck Jose Martí airport, sixteen miles southwest of the city, became a fruitless ritual. He was unable to get a seat, although he soon befriended others in the waiting line, including the editor of the socialist magazine *Monthly Review*, who was also eager to escape. Cohen eventually managed to reserve a seat on a flight to Miami. Standing in line on April 26, the day he was to leave, Cohen was surprised to hear an official call the name of the person in front of him and the name of the person behind him, but not his own. Looking at the official's list, he saw that a line had been drawn through his name. Ordered to go to the security desk, Cohen was informed by a Cuban official that he could not leave the country. The reason? A picture of him dressed as a *militiano* and standing with two other soldiers had been found in his knapsack and he was thought to be an escaping Cuban. A copy of Castro's *Declaration of Havana*, condemning American exploitation of Cuba, in his belongings didn't help his claim that he was a foreigner. His Canadian passport was thought to have been a forgery.

Cohen was taken to a security area outside the waiting room, where he was guarded by a fourteen-year-old with a rifle. Arguing with the youth about his detention and his rights as a Canadian citizen had no effect. A commotion on the runway distracted the teenaged guard; several Cubans were being evicted from a plane, and when they resisted, an argument broke out. The guard ran to the scene and Cohen was left unguarded. He quickly repacked his bag and nervously walked to the plane, repeating to himself, "It's going to be OK; they don't really care about me." He climbed on board, telling himself not to look back, took a seat and didn't move. No one asked for tickets. After a few anxious moments, the door shut, the engines started, and the plane began to taxi down the runway. He had escaped.

Eighteen months later during the Cuban missile crisis, Cohen's brother-in-law, Victor Cohen, accused him of being pro-Castro and anti-American. Cohen responded with a lengthy politicized letter, saying that he opposed all forms of censorship, collectivism, and control and that he rejected all hospitality offered by the Cuban government to visiting writers during his stay. He wanted his brother-in-law to understand that he went to Cuba "to see a socialist revolution," not "to wave a flag or prove a point." And although he saw many happy Cubans, he became anxious when he observed the long lines of "scared people outside the secret-police HQ waiting to see relatives, and the sound-trucks blasting the anthem, and the posters everywhere. . . . I left anti-government poems everywhere I went, I talked to painters and writers about their inevitable clash with Authority . . . and they dismissed me as a hopelessly bourgeois anarchist bohemian etc." Although Cohen later suggested that his motives for going to Cuba were personal and slightly shabby, he took a lofty moral stance with his brother-in-law, writing,

> I'm one of the few men of my generation who cared enough about the Cuban reality to go and see it, alone, uninvited, very hungry when my money ran out, and absolutely unwilling to take a sandwich from a government which was shooting political prisoners.

When asked why he went to Cuba several years later, Cohen facetiously replied with bravado: a "deep interest in violence . . . *I* wanted to kill, or be killed."

Cuba was a time for writing as well as revolution, and in addition to poems, Cohen began a novel, of which only five pages survive. At one time called *The Famous Havana Diary*—although in the text the narrator says it might be titled *Havana was no exception*—it opens like a Raymond Chandler mystery: "The city was Havana. That's about all in the way of detail that you're going to get from me." It was a comic, largely autobiographical account of his stay. Cohen the moralist is glimpsed and there is evidence of his preoccupation with sex, his only loyalty, the narrator explains, although voyeurism sometimes suffices: "I enjoyed her from a hundred eyes hung all over the room, telescope eyes, wide-angle eyes, close-up eyes, periscope eyes suspended in fluid."

Cohen's principal literary response to Cuba was poetic: "All There Is to Know about Adolph Eichmann," "The Only Tourist in Havana Turns His Thoughts Homeward," and "Death of a Leader"—all to appear in *Flowers for Hitler*—were written either in Havana or on the bus back from Miami. *The Energy of Slaves* contains "It is a Trust to Me," also written there. Collectively, the poems express disillusionment with Castro as a genuine revolutionary, since his regime had become "oppressive and repugnant." Cohen declared in September 1963, "Power chops up frightened men. I saw it in Cuba."

IN EARLY MAY, Cohen was back in Canada, after stopping in New York to see his friend Yafa Lerner. She remembers him as profoundly changed by the Cuban experience, more aware of his role as a Canadian poet grounded in the international scene. In Montreal, he told Layton that Castro was "a tragic figure." In a later letter, he noted that "Communism is less sinister under palm trees but Cuba is still no place for men bred in the freedom and corruption of North American cities. They are also too concerned with their artists. It makes you uneasy."

On May 4 Cohen appeared on stage at the O'Keefe Centre in Toronto as part of the Canadian Conference of the Arts. He read his poetry (and that of Anne Hébert who was too nervous to read in French) surrounded by luminaries: Northrop Frye, Mordecai Richler, Jay Macpherson, Hugh MacLennan, and George Lamming, although Layton took the spotlight with a reading of his new poem about Jacqueline Kennedy, "Why I Don't Make Love to the First Lady." Layton reported that Cohen read beautifully and looked quite "Dorian Grayish."

By mid-May, Cohen was dealing with the publication and sudden fame of *The Spice-Box of Earth*. Unpacking copies of the book at the McGill bookstore, Marquita de Crevier, at one time romantically linked with Cohen, who gave her a gift of an actual Jewish spice-box, discovered that the books had been mistakenly bound with blank leaves. When Cohen heard of the mix-up, he said that had he been there to witness the event, he would have been unable to continue writing poetry.

Reaction to the finished book was enthusiastic and admiring. To mark its publication, a launch party was held at his mother's house on May 27, 1961, with Layton and McClelland in attendance. The dust-jacket, on what would become Cohen's first Canadian hit, provided a romantic description of the poet:

> Leonard Cohen, 27, McGill graduate, gives his address as Montreal, but as this book was going to press he was enroute to Cuba. He spent last year on the shores of the Aegean Sea, writing as a result of that experience:
>
> *I shouldn't be in Canada at all. Winter is all wrong for me. I belong beside the Mediterranean. My ancestors made a terrible mistake. But I have to keep coming back to Montreal to renew my neurotic affiliations. Greece has the true philosophic climate—you cannot be dishonest in that light. But it's only in Montreal that you can get beat up for wearing a beard. I love Montreal. I hate the speculators who are tearing down my favourite streets and erecting those prisons built in the habit of boredom and gold.*

While he prefers swimming in the Aegean, Leonard Cohen admits a fondness for camping in Northern Quebec. He is currently engaged in writing a novel.

The title, drawn from the spice-box that is blessed and then its contents inhaled after sundown on the Sabbath, marks the boundary between the sacred and the profane. The spice is a fragrant reminder of the link between the religious and the everyday, the holy and the unholy. From the celebration of nature in "A Kite Is a Victim," the opening poem, to the destructive elements of history in the final "Lines from My Grandfather's Journal," the book displayed a joy balanced by tragedy. And the themes that would mark his mature poetry emerged: sexuality, history, Judaism, and love. Whether the subject was fellatio, Jewish mysticism, or death, a vision of promise characterized the work.

Expressing much of the tension found beneath the romanticism of the book is "The Genius." It is a litany of possible Jews the narrator might become, from ghetto dweller to apostate to banker to Broadway performer to doctor. The poem reserves the most disturbing possibility for last:

For you
I will be a Dachau jew
and lie down in lime
with twisted limbs
and bloated pain
no mind can understand

Adulation greeted the book. The critic Robert Weaver found it powerful and declared that Cohen was "probably the best young poet in English Canada right now." Cohen's friends Louis Dudek, Eli Mandel, and Stephen Vizinczey all praised it. Writer Arnold Edinborough suggested that Cohen had taken over from Layton as Canada's major poet, and the critic Milton Wilson in "Letters in Canada 1961" declared *The Spice-Box of Earth* a significant book. The title of the review in *Canadian Literature* summarized the general response: "The Lean and the Luscious." And Desmond Pacey, in the second edition of his respected

Creative Writing in Canada (1961), wrote that Leonard Cohen was "easily the most promising" among a group of younger poets in the country that included Al Purdy and Phyllis Webb.

The Spice-Box of Earth sold out in three months but failed to win the Governor General's Award for Poetry. The winner that year was Robert Finch's *Acis in Oxford*. Irving Layton thought this was an absolute travesty:

> There isn't a single poem in the Finch book that won it. It's dull, academic stuff with not one alive line that can seriously be called poetry. *Exercises*, bloody, or rather, bloodless exercises. Nothing else. What an arsehole of a country this is when this sort of crap can win prizes, but Cohen's genuine lyricism can't and doesn't.

He also relates that Cohen was upset at not winning. "Psychologically, I think he's having a rough time of it," Layton told Desmond Pacey. "It's damn hard to be a young poet!" But if the Governor General's jury wouldn't acknowledge the power of *The Spice-Box of Earth*, the public did. The handsomely designed text continued to sell and won its designer, Frank Newfeld, a major publishing award.

A less publicized event that spring was Cohen's adventure with Alexander Trocchi, a Scottish novelist on the lam from the U.S. for forgery and drug charges. Cohen put him up for a few days and had his first encounter with opium. Trocchi had a wad of it with him and prepared it by cooking it up on Cohen's stove. Trocchi asked Cohen if he would like to lick the pot. Cohen could not resist but found it had little effect. He and Trocchi then headed out to a Chinese restaurant on Ste-Catherine Street but as they crossed the road, Cohen went blind and clutched at Trocchi before he fainted. Trocchi pulled him to the curb, where Cohen gradually recovered. A few days later, Cohen explained to Robert Weaver that he had just left Trocchi on a British ship bound for Scotland: "His passport was two years expired so it was touch and go all the way. He fixed himself every half-hour . . . He's a hell of responsibility. He wants you to feel that. That's why he turns on in public. He's a public junkie. I was glad when we got him on the boat." Cohen's poem "Alexander Trocchi, Public Junkie, Priez Pour

Nous" in *Flowers for Hitler* celebrates Trocchi's bohemian flair. Cohen writes: "Your purity"—of a Baudelairian darkness—"drives me to work. / I must get back to lust and microscopes." A year or so later, Cohen would read *Cain's Book,* Trocchi's once-banned novel of 1960, and it would soon influence *Beautiful Losers.*

In late May Cohen received his Canada Council Arts Scholarship renewal, although only for one thousand dollars. Cohen told the supervisor of scholarships that the council's investment would "yield profits far out of proportion to the original risk. Within the year I promise you a book which will have some importance in our national literature." He then boldly asked for a travel grant, arguing that "distance is essential if I am to get any perspective in this messy semi-autobiography." Before he left, Cohen acknowledged the planting of a tree in his honor by the local Hadassah Chapter of his synagogue, using the occasion to defend his controversial work: "I remind them [Montreal Jews] that it is an old habit of our people to reject our most honest social critics, at least as old as Moses."

———————

BY AUGUST 1961, Cohen was back in Greece, having spent twenty-one days on a Yugoslavian freighter headed for Genoa. Most of the passengers were retirees returning to Yugoslavia to live on welfare, and he tells his sister that "they weep most of the day and eat large meals. Just like home for me." He befriended the thirty-three-year-old captain, spending most nights musing on a destiny "that makes one man the master of a ship, the other an itinerant poet, both exiles." But he knows that he will soon be "rooted on the rock of Hydra, working in that freedom which only an ocean between me and my birthplace can give me."

On Hydra, "his Gothic insincerities were purged" and his "style purified under the influence of empty mountains and a foreign mate who cherished simple English," as he would write two years later. "Thank god for hashish, cognac, and neurotic women who pay their debts with flesh," he wrote McClelland, adding that the products of the island are "sponges, movies, nervous breakdowns, and divorces." He wrote Layton that he had seen corpses in the sea and witnessed "assassins' drugs." Layton was uncharacteristically indifferent: "I gather the Greek wines are too strong for him," he commented to a friend. Meanwhile, Cohen was still seeking extra funds, this time from an advance on royalties of *The Spice-Box of Earth*, encouraging McClelland to "dig deep to keep Cohen out of the Clothing Business."

Cohen was offered six thousand dollars for the house he had paid fifteen hundred for. But the house had given him roots, he later explained, and he was not ready to sell. Hydra freed Cohen from the inhibitions (and intrusions) of Montreal and made his writing less competitive and academic. He realized, however, the price of such isolation:

> I chose a lonely country
> broke from love
> scorned the fraternity of war
> I polished my tongue against the pumice moon.

In Greece, he explained years later, you "just felt good, strong, ready for the task" of writing. This last remark is a key to Cohen's method of composition, whether in verse or in song. He cannot work unless he is "ready for the task," in a state of creative concentration and well-being. Fasting often generated this state, and various friends recall his periods of almost week-long fasts while writing. Fasting also suited the holiness of his dedication to his work, supplemented by his desire for discipline.

Although Cohen experienced long fallow periods of nonproductivity, he retained a rigid daily schedule. Every morning, Cohen worked either on his terrace or in the long, low-ceilinged basement study of his home. Only the midday heat interrupted his work; he would then read, swim, and then return to his writing. In Greece, he wrote to Robert Weaver, "there is my beautiful house, and sun to tan my maggot-coloured mind."

A prose poem entitled "Here Was the Harbour" suggests the purity of life on Hydra that appealed so strongly to Cohen. Describing the harbor and the intense blue of the sky, he proclaims, "Of men the sky demands all manner of stories, entertainments, embroideries, just as it does of its stars and constellations." "The sky," he continues, "wants the whole man lost in his story, abandoned in the mechanics of action, touching his fellows, leaving them, hunting the steps, dancing the old circles." In the silence of Hydra, Cohen found his muse, although Greece plays a surprisingly small part in his writing as a subject or scene. Occasional poems describe his life there, but it has no direct presence in his fiction and appears only sporadically in his songs.

He could not escape politics, however. In October 1961 he provided this analysis of the political situation to his sister:

> everywhere is going Communist and cleaning up corruption and poverty and charm. And the West is too expensive, rigid, and hysterical. What chance has a decent fun-loving literary parasite got in this world? Anyways, your cheque will keep me in hashish yet a little longer.

Drugs on Hydra were becoming increasingly evident and could be obtained without much difficulty—often from a local who regularly made trips to Athens, although marijuana was grown on the island. Cohen soon found himself dependent on the drugs for quickening his imagination and often became desperate when they were not available, as his poem "Indictment of the Blue Hole" makes clear. It reads in part:

> January 28, 1962
> My abandoned narcotics have
> abandoned me
> January 28, 1962
> 7:30 must have dug its
> pikes into your blue wrist

"The Drawer's Condition on November 28, 1961" begins with this question: "Is there anything emptier / than the drawer where / you used to store your opium?"

The most popular drug was hashish, but acid and marijuana were also readily available. Initially, the pharmacist supplied opiates and other drugs, but soon other sources were needed. To a French-Canadian friend he wrote, "I've smoked quite a lot of hash and eaten a fair amount of opium. None of it's any good really, and the O is quite dangerous. Work is better than both—and work is hell." He later relied on a speed-like drug, Maxiton, which could be bought over the counter. He became known to his close friends as Captain Mandrax, Mandrax being an English brand name for quaaludes. By 1964 he found that hashish and amphetamines assisted him greatly in completing *Beautiful Losers*, in a marathon writing session.

A passage from an unpublished essay of 1965 clarifies the nature of drug use on the island. Cohen writes:

> In this part of the planet men have smoked and cooked hashish for many centuries, and as countless American and European homosex-uals can testify, without sacrificing any of the vigourous qualities we would associate with a people so crucial to history, a continuous seminal history including not only the classical and Byzantine peri-ods, but also, and perhaps most important, our own time. We who are here today believe that these lands of the Eastern Mediterranean are still the glistening alembic in which the happiest and purest syn-thesis of the West and Orient must occur. Islanders brew a tea from the wild narcotic poppies which is served to restless children and rebellious mules. . . .
>
> We smoke the occasional common cigarette into which we have introduced a few crumbs of hashish. We cannot rely on this crude device to secure us the visions and insights we hunger for, but it has its use as an agent of relaxation and receptivity. On the recre-ational side I might say that erotic and musical experience is enhanced under its influence. My wife would not listen to Bach without it, nor I to the cicadas at sundown. . . . The lyrics of many bazouki tunes celebrate the aromatic generosity of the leaf as it turns to ash.

In September 1961 a confident Cohen wrote to the editor of the *New York Times* to tell him that he was sending him a new sonnet, written a few days earlier. He believed it to be one of his best poems: "I write a year's verse to keep in training for a poem like this." He titled it "On His Twenty Seventh Birthday." The *Times* did not print it.

He reported to Claire Pratt in Toronto that he was continuing to work on his self-indulgent novel, which nobody, he was sure, would want. He predicted that "the next book will be so orderly that people will mistake it for a geometry theorem." He was also busy with his poetry, saying it was "clearing the mind for some splendid Greek pentalic constructions."

Cohen was living with Marianne again and maintained a six-and-a-half-year relationship with her. Her penetrating blue eyes, high cheekbones, and inquisitive mouth captivated him. Once, when Marianne modeled for a friend's boutique in Hydra, she looked so marvelous in the borrowed clothes and sunglasses that people stopped her in the port for her autograph, assuming she must be a movie star. On one occasion Cohen himself distracted her by asking for her signature on a menu as she crossed the port. For Cohen, Marianne presented an attenuated, lyrical beauty:

It's so simple
to wake up beside your ears
and count the pearls
with my two heads
. . . let's go to bed
right after supper
Let's sleep and wake up
all night

Cohen sought to protect her, as he would seek to protect other women throughout his life, one source of his immense appeal. When Marianne returned to Oslo to visit relatives, Cohen followed. Marianne, he wrote to Layton, "seems to have endured and ruined the women I've known after her and I've got to confront her mystery in the snow. She is so blonde in my heart!" He had to pursue her and while in Oslo wrote a poem: "Lead me . . . into families, cities, congregations: / I want to stroll down the arteries invisible / as the multitudes I cannot see from here."

While Marianne was visiting her mother, Cohen listened to Greek records, smoked cigars, and enjoyed the clean northern beauty of Norway. "Something in the air takes no notice whatsoever of our miniature suffering and invites us, commands us, to join in the insane eternal laughter. Today I'm rolling in the aisles." He enjoyed the contrast of the northern ethic, the cold air and forthright diet. "I've been working on my new book but today I feel like giving up writing. The air is too sweet for all this working of the mind, the herrings are too tasty. When I am not watching blonde girls I am eating herring and sometimes I do both."

Learning that his novel was to be published in Swedish, Cohen told Esther that his book would certainly appeal to the Swedes because "it's so melancholy, and neurotic and dirty." To Stephen Vizicenzy he wrote that he had abandoned himself entirely to oral gratification: "Eating and kissing. Frankly, I hate to get out of bed. I don't think I'm a poet maudit after all. Maybe I'll receive my sense of loss tomorrow." A month later he wrote to Robert Weaver that "Norway is blonde and glorious and I am popular as a negro with my dark nose. I'll travel forever." He danced by himself, listening to Radio Luxembourg. "I can be seen Twisting alone, not even missing London marijuana."

His novel was finished in the spring, and Cohen had a feeling of completion and ennui. He told Yafa Lerner:

> Strange to find myself absolutely lustless. It makes me have to begin everything all over again, find a new structure to hang myself on. Lustless. It's like a kind of amnesia. It leaves me with too much spare time and forces me into metaphysics.
>
> I never thought desire was so frail.
> Write.

He also wrote to a Mr. Dwyer at the Canada Council to report that his manuscript had been accepted by the literary agents David Higham Associates. "This is the same novel I've been working on for two years, the one Jack [McClelland] hates." Quoting the readers' reports, he noted their praise and claimed that if the writing had been any less imaginative, it would have made the "countless passages of remarkable sexual description" inappropriate. He thanked Dwyer for the council's support "and for having created an atmosphere of concern about my work." He added that he was working on a "surrealistic sound poem on the Underground

System for Project '62" of the CBC and is getting "into another novel set in the Eastern Townships." (Only a few pages of this projected work exist.) He closed with a request to inform him about any suitable jobs for him in Canada.

IN MARCH of 1962 Cohen returned to 19B Hampstead High Street in London to work on revisions for his novel. He wrote Jack McClelland to see if he would "be interested in publishing a book of offensive instant poems of mine called *Flowers for Hitler.*" The same day he wrote to Rabbi Cass, in charge of the McGill B'nai Brith Hillel organization, thanking him for a copy of a review of *The Spice-Box of Earth*. He noted that the reviewer had rewritten the first stanza of one of his poems—but "it's the kind of chutzpa I enjoy and indulge in secretly myself, so convey to him my congratulations." The final letter that day was to Robert Weaver of the CBC. He told Weaver that he met the critic Nathan Cohen in Paris and together they had spent an evening praising him. He promised to write a piece on Greece for Weaver but was too busy just then with revisions. "London is horrible," he concluded, "and I long for the honest, brutal massacre of a Canadian winter."

Several days later, Cohen wrote to his Montreal friend Daniel Kraslavsky, complaining about the small amount of money he received for his novel:

Over two years on that book in which I invite the whole world to share my glorious youth and what do I get?

Cashmere? What's cashmere?

I've got to go back to the Greek island. I have reports that my house is crumbling there. I'm meeting a Norwegian girl and her baby there. I shall become a husband and father in one fell swoop. I have no money to live anywhere else. I love it there but it cuts me off from my cultural Roots and the Mainstream. I still have illusions that there are Roots and Mainstreams.

Did I plan it this way?

At the end of the letter he wrote he didn't understand his "blonde woman," adding, "why have I become Scott Fitzgerald but without any loot or social connections?"

In another letter Cohen was darker, complaining that he was working slowly, "twice as slowly as I should be, wasting time in severe depressions, bad dreams, maniacal poems. I am almost paralyzed by indecision." London brought out his vivid dichotomies. After all his praise of Marianne, he admitted to some ambivalence about their relationship. They had seen each other so little that he was "terrified of waking up to find myself broke and stranded on a Greek island with a woman I can't contact and a child to whom I can't even talk in English. I can't help feeling there's some disaster waiting for me if I act in that direction." He wrote that he would probably have to go back to Montreal and "fight for some tiny income . . . otherwise I'll be forced into journalism and all sorts of other excuses for not creating a masterpiece." Loneliness overpowered him:

> I feel I've lost Montreal and not only am I lonely but alone. I am like an eye dangling by a few nerves from a man's socket, and I long for detachment or to be part of the body whole, anything but blind useless pain.
>
> I have not given up by any means so don't let me depress you. There are insights to be gained from the tedious chaos. I could do without such an education but since I have no choice I might as well learn. Laughter is a fist in the face of the gods and I will make those heavenly faces bloody and blue.

A letter to Marianne confirms his romantic vacillation: "There are a million things I want to talk about with you," Cohen wrote, "things I'm frightened about . . . and oceans between us distort things that become very simple when we are together." He reports that he has asked Mort Rosengarten to get him some land on a remote Canadian island, Bonaventure, where they can all live a natural life. He misses everything that he loves, beginning with her:

> I long for you and blind love, brown bodies that speak to one another in a language we don't want to understand, I long for readers

to devour my soul at a feast, I long for health in the sun, woods I know, tables of meat and fruit and bread, children shattering the monarch of the home, I long for cities of preserved elegance and the chaotic quarters of modern cities where the village persists, for loyal restaurants, for parks and battles. I have so much affection for the world and you shall be my interpreter.

I want to get back to Canada and rob a bank.

On the same day that he wrote to Marianne, he wrote to his mother and told her that he always knew that his book would be published, "just as I always knew I wanted to be a writer even when this ambition was discouraged by so-called sensible people and every obstacle of provincialism and caution put in my way." He has also learned that "the things which are given you mean nothing, only what we achieve by struggle and suffering have any value . . . I have no more or less illusions about writing than I had eleven years ago [in 1951] when I began . . . I will continue to fight for the kind of life I want, continue to fight the weakness in myself." He explained that "the secret of my triumph is that I expect nothing, expect to change nothing, expect to leave nothing behind." He said he planned to return to Canada after he completed his revisions in the summer, possibly buy a small house in the country, and return to Greece in the fall.

The dampness and cold of London made him miserable but Secker & Warburg had asked that he stay in London to do revisions. "I want to tear at everything that nourishes me," he wrote to Irving Layton on March 23. "Can I help it if she [Marianne] is a priestess whose nature it is to make everything difficult and prosaic?" He also told Layton that "I've been working on my novel with a scalpel. I won't be able to save it, but it's one of the most interesting corpses I've ever seen."

Another letter to his sister noted his disappointment at not winning the Governor General's Award for *The Spice-Box of Earth*: "Too bad because *Spice-Box* was the last book anyone will understand. I am now running three and a half years ahead of enlightened poetic taste and the time-lag is increasing daily." And Secker, he explained, took his manuscript because they wanted his next book and that his manuscript is a "beautiful book that will be misunderstood as a self-indulgent childish autobiography, disordered and overlong. . . . In actuality," he tells her, "it's an extremely subtly balanced description of a sensibility, the best of its kind since James Joyce's *Portrait of the Artist as a Young Man*. I am perfectly prepared to be ignored or slaughtered by stupid men of letters." He ends with an indictment:

> What a joyless farce we make out of our lives, especially the cautious, especially them because what they hoard is leaking away day-by-day. Give me a war, give me complicated divorces and disgrace, give me broken lives and alcoholic fantasy, give me anything but pettiness and safety.

A final passage in the letter records his enjoyment of the Twist, danced at a West Indian club called the All-Niter, where the marijuana smoke was so thick, he reported, that you could get high without taking a puff. "It's the first time I've really enjoyed dancing. I sometimes even forget I belong to an inferior race. Their stuff compares very favorably with Greek hashish. The Twist is the greatest ritual since circumcision—and there you can choose between the genius of two cultures. Myself, I prefer the Twist."

6

COCKTAILS IN THE SHAVING KIT

ACK ON HYDRA, two distractions interrupted Cohen from the strenuous effort of rewriting *The Favorite Game*: the first was the arrival of his mother; the second, the arrival of many so-called friends. Since he had bought his house, Cohen's mother had remained unconvinced that his life was secure, that he was eating well, and that he knew what he was doing. Through letters at first to his sister and then to his mother, Cohen stressed the regularity of his life: he had a cleaning lady, caring friends, and a well-looked-after home. He sent his mother recipes, described social events and chronicled his literary progress. But nothing would substitute for a visit, and in the summer of 1962, in the midst of work on his novel, Cohen had to prepare for his mother's arrival.

First he had to placate his mother's fears. Masha was worried about rain, about dampness, and cold. "In the last six thousand years it hasn't rained once on the island during the summer, so I doubt if it will begin in 1962," he assured her, telling her to bring light clothes because it was hot. "You would suffocate under a mink jacket, and if you didn't suffocate you'd be eaten by several thousand cats who have never seen a mink jacket and would suppose you to be some new kind of animal."

It was unthinkable that she stay at a hotel. Why be uncomfortable and hot in their rooms when she could be uncomfortable and hot in his, he asked. Cohen wrote, "My house is big and you won't interfere with my work or my several wives, mistresses, and children." The house, he explained, was being whitewashed, some rotten wood replaced, stones repaired, and despite the absence of running water and electricity, she would find it clean and private. "Buying this house was the wisest move of my life. I think you and Esther will probably settle here."

Masha Cohen's visit precipitated some drastic changes, the most important being Marianne's removal from the house. According to Jewish law, a Cohen (member of a priestly caste) cannot marry a divorced woman, and living with a divorced woman and her child would have been even more upsetting to his mother. So Marianne had to disappear from Cohen's daily life. This upset Cohen as much as it did Marianne, who found temporary lodging elsewhere. The visit, meanwhile, was a disaster. The heat bothered his mother, she felt unwell, and Cohen didn't do any writing for a month. "She's a little overwhelmed," he wrote his sister, "and I'm expecting disaster from moment to moment. My own routine has been completely wrecked, of course." His mother brought with her "all the old chaos. . . . She exists on my energy. I have nothing left for anything, books or humans," he told a friend, adding:

A nomadic animal should sleep in hidden places. Once he digs a permanent home and the hunter learns where it is, he invites destruction. It's my own fault for not moving light. It's strange to be trapped in the house I built for freedom.

Cohen had an obligation to revise his novel. He had assured his editor Roland Gant at Secker & Warburg that the new version would be much, much better. Half of the original first section had been eliminated, and the book would be a third shorter. He proposed several titles: *The Mist Leaves No Scar* or *Mist Leaves No Scar, Only Give a Sound, Only Strangers Travel*, or *No Flesh So Perfect*, though felt "nothing sounds any good . . . THE MOVING TOYSHOP isn't bad, but this isn't just a book about youth, it's an allegory for a lost perfect dim impossible body, the one that escapes us when we kiss, the one that hovers over the best dancer and ruins her dance or makes it sad." Other possibilities he listed were *Fields of Hair, The Perfect Jukebox, The Moonlight Sponge*, and *The Original Air-Blue Gown* (from Hardy's poem "The Visit").

Visitors from Montreal became another nuisance and disruption. They relied on him to make hotel arrangements, find restaurants, and act as interpreter. To Esther he announced:

> I don't intend to open my gates to Everybody whose only excuse for bothering me is that they can afford the fare and know my name . . . My commitment here is serious and they are on holiday. They want their kicks out of every moment while I am here for work and order. This is a workshop.

In the same letter he complained about Tony Perkins, Melina Mercouri, and Jules Dessin, who were shooting a movie on "the very spot where I happen to swim." He received surprise visits from people like his witty cousin Alan Golden, "whom I had never spoken to except over my shoulder at shul . . . In fact, had he not come, all the Goldens would be to me is a row of blurred faces arranged above a Freedman Company shoulder pad."

He and Marianne began to avoid people and the port: "I've greeted people so fiercely that nobody dares to drop in. I've got a notice DO NOT DISTURB nailed on the front door," he told his sister. Occasionally an encounter proved interesting, as when he met a troupe of Russian dancers from the Bolshoi Ballet and compared notes with them on the status of artists in Russia and Canada. But soon he and Marianne prepared to visit Kiparissi on the Peloponnesus because Hydra had become "intolerably touristic which is fine for one's real estate but bad for Canadian Literature." He also admitted, "It is hard to be a poet *maudit* when you have a good tan."

But a poet with a good tan is an attractive commodity, and women sought Cohen out. There was Astrid, a tall, stunning redhead from Germany; a willowy blonde from Australia who typed the manuscript of his novel; Phyllis, an American who was in love with his songs; and another Australian, who climbed over his daunting wall to get to him. Some of these women were welcomed, some were passed on to other willing hosts, such as Don Lowe or Anthony Kingsmill.

With his mother gone and the tourists and the women deflected, Cohen could get back to writing. By August he told Roland Gant that he had "eliminated a kind of self-conscious melancholy that is fine for a 'first-novel'—but I want to put a polished and precise weapon on the market. The new book is tough. The author isn't sticking his personal pain at you in every chapter; that's why the new version hurts more. Mostly it's a question of cutting away the blubber and letting the architecture of bone show through." He finished the work in October, cutting the book virtually in half, confessing to a friend that "I think I have rewritten myself, and like the book, I'm not sure I admire the product. We all have several images of ourselves. It is a surprise to see which one we assume."

His self-assessment was unsparing:

> One day I found that I was a man leading a sunny uncluttered life with a very beautiful woman. The man was poor, all his clothes were worn and faded, he had no Sunday suit, he was happy much of the time, happier than I ever thought he could be, but tougher, crueller, and lonelier than I had ever planned.

To Layton he wrote that he was not entirely satisfied with this rewritten version, but "anyone with an ear will know I've torn apart orchestras to arrive at my straight, melodic line . . . In a way that means more to me than the achievement itself. I walk lighter and carry a big scalpel. Everything I've read in the past week is too long . . . I don't know anything about people—that's why I have this terrible and irresistible temptation to be a novelist."

November gave Cohen an unexpected opportunity to travel. The CBC invited him to Paris to participate in a panel with Malcolm Muggeridge, Mary McCarthy, and Romain Gary. To Robert Weaver he exclaimed, "Has the world gone completely mad? Also fee and expenses!" The hour-long radio program, which he would moderate for a fee of six hundred dollars, would address the question "Is there a Crisis in Western Culture?" It was to be recorded in the Hotel Napoleon. Cohen arrived two days early for the taping, and settled into a "coffin-colored room in the Hotel Cluny Square" on the left bank, to read the work of the other participants. A short story, "Luggage Fire Sale," published in *Partisan Review* (1969) narrates his adventure, including picking up a female medical student at 2:00 a.m. in a Boulevard St Michel cafe and writing on his hotel wall *"change is the only aphrodisiac."* The story also hints at his pleasure at being away from Hydra and from "a couple of women who knew me too well." He arrived in Paris with a small piece of Lebanese hashish "and a complete suntan which recorded my major life success, the discovery of hot beaches where I could live naked with someone worth watching." He added that "the sweetest aspect" of this unnamed woman of Hydra "was the way she let me know that I could neither hurt nor miss her."

Before the taping, the participants shared an expensive dinner at the Hotel Napoleon where the principal topic was marijuana. During the taping, Muggeridge stressed culture as embellishing the human condition, and McCarthy allowed that culture was integral to society. Cohen, wondering why he was getting paid, threw in Russia as a topic. They agreed on the existence of a new world culture that encompassed both China and Russia, but could not agree on the issue of greatness in contemporary culture. Cohen reported that the discussion had been neither witty nor profound. The reason, Cohen felt, was that they had been too well fed: "Cultural crises, especially permanent ones, have little effect on bodies so recently nourished on expensive French food and liquor. We should have been starved three or four days."

By February of 1963 he was back in North America, partly to replenish his bank account, but partly to celebrate the forthcoming publication of *The Favorite Game* by Viking in New York. "It's a perfect little machine," Cohen said of the book, "not spectacular, but new and nothing sticks out, and it even sprays a shower of sparks from time to time."

Cohen began a long and satisfying association with Cork Smith, his new editor at Viking, who had accepted *The Favorite Game*. In May, when Viking received the corrected galleys of the book (it had been published in London in October), Cohen told Smith that the possibility of an epigraph by Yeats was unthinkable.

[Yeats] has had too much already and what have I had? Do you see my poems in the front of every book? . . . No, no, I refuse, I resist, must we be forever blackmailed by the Irish merely because a few hundred thousand perished of starvation? . . . No Yeats, no Wilde, Behan, Thomas. And don't try and tell me he wasn't an R.C. Oh no. And I suppose Roosevelt wasn't Jewish? I'm on to you. The book will be bare.

A perceptive editor, Smith would play a critical role in the development of *Beautiful Losers*, guiding the publication of that difficult novel. Cohen sent the final revisions of *The Favorite Game* to Smith, and included a poem:

Tell all your gold friends
that Cohen has been struck down by their melting beauty
that he no longer contends with desire
but lies stricken under Law.

Cohen of Mountain Street
Cohen of Juke Boxes
Cohen The Moonlight Sponge
Cohen The Jewish Keats

has tied it with a string.
Could this austere historian be he who once succumbed
like a public epileptic
to pretty faces in every window

Yes
Cohen has been struck down
He lies on a couch of snow
Therefore blonde dancers
do not expect him to rise for an introduction.

In July, after he had returned the galleys, Cohen received a copy of the book jacket and quickly wrote to Cork Smith to express his dismay at the author photo:

The photograph is of a first novelist I never wanted to be: over-shaven, pale, collector of fellowships, self-indulgent, not mad enough for an insane asylum, not tough enough for alcoholism, the face that haunts Hadassah meetings. But I swear to you I am cruel-eyed, hard, brown. In the mountains they call me Leonardos the Skull.

Cohen was restless in New York where he stayed with his sister. He wrote to Sheila Watson:

I haven't been to sleep for a long time. I wear sunglasses along Park Avenue at four in the morning. . . . I have spent my advance on escargots. I have a plastic Edgar Allen Poe doll. Finland cares nothing for me. The gypsies on Eighth Avenue are breaking up that old gang of mine. There is a cocktail party in my shaving kit and it threatens me with Arizonian wastes. I didn't mean the old guy any harm when I spoke with the tongues of angels.

Jack McClelland had not been keen to publish *The Favorite Game*, saying that Cohen did not have to write such a "first novel" work, both autobiographical and egotistical. Cohen responded by declaring it "a third novel disguised as a first novel. . . . I use the first novel form the way a good technician uses the first person." (He actually had written two others: *A Ballet of Lepers* and *Beauty at Close Quarters*, both never published.)

For his next novel, Cohen predicted, "I will write a book about pure experience which will make THE FAVORITE GAME look like a grotesque gimmick. You will have to come to my cell to pick up the manuscript." McClelland thought *The Favorite Game* was "a beautiful book," but it was still "a first novel" and not what he should have done. McClelland forecasted that the book would be a critical but not a commercial success, adding that "one of the great dangers of staying in this business is that you begin to think you know something about books. My greatest virtue as a publisher for years was that I knew nothing about books." In response to McClelland's criticism, Cohen explained that:

> I've never written easily: most of the time I detest the process. So try and understand that I've never enjoyed the luxury of being able to choose between the kinds of books I wanted to write, or poems, or women I wanted to love, or lives to lead.

FOLLOWING THE REVISION of his novel, Cohen returned to writing poems. They became the core of *Flowers for Hitler*, which Cohen had originally titled *Opium and Hitler*. The book drew together a series of new and immediate themes: Hydra, history, and politics. He considered the poems radical and challenging, and anticipated the negative reception they would receive from McClelland & Stewart. The poems, he told Jack McClelland, "will speak to nobody because nobody enjoys my grotesque kind of health. I would have rather read these poems than have written them. Enjoy your authoritarian life." He closed the letter with, "Goodbye forever / Leonard Cohen / The Jewish Keats."

Unlike the lyrical *Spice-Box of Earth*, *Flowers for Hitler*, with its tough, unpleasant topics, would offend people, but he accepted responsibility, telling Cork Smith that "I accept the hemlock for the evils it will work against established order, for I will turn son against father, beloved against lover, apostle against guru, pedestrian against traffic light, eater against waitress, waitress against maitre d', and they will all lie down, unconnected and free and loving as mating flowers." He celebrated the importance of the poems as "a fairly original study of Authority," writing to his sister that the collection would be complete in a couple of weeks and that the last ten days had been one of his "best creative periods ever: I've really

Above left: Nathan B. Cohen: the photo-portrait that hangs in Leonard Cohen's childhood bedroom in Montreal. *Above right:* Lyon Cohen, father of Nathan B. Cohen and a founding figure in the Montreal Jewish community. Leonard Cohen's paternal grandfather.

Above left: Rabbi Kleinitsky Klein, Leonard Cohen's maternal grandfather, standing with Leonard Cohen in Brooklyn, New York, in 1953. *Above right:* Masha Cohen, Leonard Cohen's mother, in Montreal.

Leonard Cohen performing at Dunn's Jazz Parlour in the summer of 1958.
On the left is Morley Callaghan. Photo by Sam Tata.

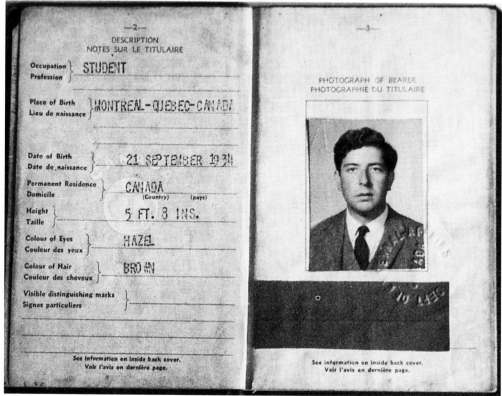

Cohen's first passport, issued on October 29, 1959, initiating decades of international travel.

On the plank in Hydra. Cohen with his back to the harbor in sixties regalia in a photo used to publicize the NFB film "Ladies and Gentlemen . . . Mr. Leonard Cohen."

Above left: Leonard Cohen, center, standing between two militianos in Havana shortly after the Bay of Pigs. This photo, found in his knapsack at the airport on the day of his departure, forced his detention. *Above right:* Marianne Ihlen in Hydra. Photo by L. Cohen.

Above left: Leonard Cohen on the terrace at Hydra working on *Beautiful Losers.* Note the Olivetti and the record player. *Above right:* Cohen and his sister Esther in a formal photo taken in the late sixties.

put the book into wild, evil, and revolutionary working order. I imagine it is the best study of the authoritarian psychology ever written."

In June Cohen submitted a selection of the poems to a CBC poetry contest for poets under thirty. In the covering letter he wrote that *Opium and Hitler* was a collection of "prose poems which studies the totalitarian spirit of our century." Several months later he said to his U.S. agent Marian McNamara, "I gave my mental health to that book and hereafter I am released from the bondage of logic and sanity. It feels good." Yet the real challenge came from finding a means to express his revised values. He admitted to Cork Smith, "So many of my values have been challenged and strengthened or destroyed. I want to say something but every form I use seems to cramp, or limps under a kind of self-indulgence which I have to clean out of my system."

Jack McClelland's response, though negative, surprised Cohen. He thought that the uneven quality of the poems would harm Cohen's reputation. But then he added: "Because you are Leonard Cohen, we will publish the book as is without concern or apology." Cohen took offense, telling McClelland that he did not want the book published, "feeling as you do, so cautiously honoring my place in Canadian letters." He added that he had ten more poems to include, as well as a verse play. And yes, he was willing to make changes, although his confidence in the work was unchanged:

> I know this book is a masterpiece, a hundred times better than Spice-Box. I also know that there is no one in the country that can evaluate these poems. My sounds are too new . . . Jack, there has never been a book like this, prose or poetry written in Canada . . . Believe me, I could produce another Spice-Box and everyone would be happy. I know the formula. But I'm moving into new territory.

Cohen emphasized the language of his new work, telling McClelland that various young writers had read it:

> they've been staggered . . . This book moves me from the world of the golden-boy poet into the dung-pile of the front-line writer. I didn't plan it this way. I loved the tender notices Spice-Box got but

they embarrassed me a little. HITLER won't get the same hospitality from the papers.

Publication was delayed by last-minute revisions. The title and the so-called "gas-chamber" poems, works dealing with the Nazis and the Holocaust, received the most severe criticism. One reader's report begins, "This is a manuscript which I find on the whole to be disappointing. After a while it has the same effect as a dentist's drill, and I have to stop reading." Cohen's "natural, sensuous gifts as a poet don't shine through." Another reader begins with "This poetry is full of bitterness and hate . . . How marketable is hate?" The same reader declares that Cohen is being "immature," but "*if* he intends to go on endlessly and tiresomely parading the same old theme, then by all means make the most of him while he's still saleable."

The original manuscript had a scornful dedication, which was also offensive to readers. Cohen agreed to remove it, although it revealed his current state of mind:

With scorn, love, nausea, and above all,
a paralysing sense of community,
this book is dedicated
to the teachers, doctors, leaders of my parents' time:
THE DACHAU GENERATION

Asked to revise the manuscript, Cohen worked on it during his winter 1963–64 visit to Canada and added new work. "I was ambushed by fifty new poems which I had to integrate into the book," he wrote, following a triumphant reading tour of Western Canada in March. In May, he was still arguing about the title with McClelland, wishing to keep *Opium and Hitler.* "The title is damn intriguing and the diseased adolescents who compose my public will love it." What disturbed Cohen most was the proposed cover, again by designer Frank Newfeld, which was a drawing of a female body "with my face for tits . . . It doesn't matter what the title is now because the picture is simply offensive . . . It hasn't the sincerity of a stag movie or the imagination of a filthy postcard or the energy of real surrealist humor."

Cohen ended up designing six covers of his own. The final jacket cover amalgamated these images into nine separate boxes, containing drawings of a dog, a parachutist, a house, two roses, and a baby-faced Hitler. A heart is the principal motif, evoking the romance implicit in the reference to flowers in the title. The cover is printed in red with a white background, suggesting a Valentine's Day card of sorts. "The whole point of the title is that the word HITLER has to be set against a domestic background, and that's the point of the book too. Nothing scary, arty, or fearsome. Just let people see the word without all the tympani and squeaky doors and the effect is powerful," Cohen explained. On the half-title page of the printed book the reader encounters this enigmatic "Note on the Title": "A while ago this book would have been called SUNSHINE FOR NAPOLEON, and earlier still it would have been called WALLS FOR GENGHIS KHAN."

Cohen actually suggested canceling the project, since McClelland & Stewart was not incorporating his changes into the galleys, including a new dedication, replacing the Dachau reference with "FOR MARI-ANNE." He added an epigraph, a sentence taken from Italian writer Primo Levi's memoir *Survival in Auschwitz*, which reminded readers to resist the destruction of one's conscience and the creation of evil.

It turned out that the book had already been printed by the time McClelland had received Cohen's letter, but the sheets were unbound. They agreed to scrap that printing, make his changes, and reprint. McClelland had not actually read the full manuscript, only a few of the poems: "I don't profess to be a lover of poetry . . . I'm flattered to think that you think that I have read your goddam poetry. Heh! When we have the Beatles we sure as hell don't need poets."

Cohen eventually agreed to change the title to *Flowers for Hitler*. But the jacket copy, which Cohen had asked to be suppressed, "has made me and the book a hell of a lot of enemies. It was very important that a Jew's book about Hitler be free from arrogant personal promotion." The blurb, taken from a September letter to McClelland, stressed his move from romantic lyricism to history in all of its horror. Cohen also objected to the austerity of the book's production, especially in the paperback edition; he thought that the book looked cheap and that the poems were mutilated by their awkward placement on the page.

Earlier, in the summer of 1963, Cohen had tried to place portions of his *The Favorite Game* in various magazines. *Playboy* said no, but *Cavalier* said yes. Encouraged, Cohen wrote to his New York agent that the novel could easily become a movie and that she should pitch it to Hollywood. Unfortunately, a series of studios turned it down.

———————

PUBLICLY, their lives appeared rich: Cohen was preparing for the publication of his novel, Marianne was modeling for a chic island boutique run by Magda-Slovak. Privately, their lives were falling apart. A short vacation in late July 1963 attempted to patch things up but a letter to Irving Layton in August suggests that the difficulties remained. "The Mediterranean doesn't help," Cohen wrote. "Everything breaking up here. . . . Gurdjieff was right when he shouted from his deathbed to all his teary followers: 'Abandon the System!'" Cohen's idyllic relationship with Marianne was unraveling.

Travel and contact with others stimulated his creativity but dimmed his love. His song "So Long, Marianne," expresses these sentiments:

> Well, you know that I love to live with you
> But you make me forget so very much
> I forget to pray for the angel
> And then the angels forget to pray for us.
>
> For now I need your hidden love
> I'm cold as a new razor blade
> You left when I told you I was curious
> I never said that I was brave.

To renew the "holiness" of his work, he had to pursue his artistic quest, as he would summarize in *Death of A Lady's Man* several years later: "I had the woman I loved. I wanted to end it, but it would not end: my life in art."

A letter of September 1963 to a New York editor stressed "a violent disintegration that lets me catch fewer and fewer bright sparks . . . I can go for a week without feeling anything." The time is "filled not so much with violence as with lies . . . I feel deprived, and I want even ugly women, I want nakedness, I don't want to talk to anyone who isn't naked." A note of self-criticism creeps in: "What I want from people, mostly women, is outrageous, and I begin to see how hilarious and just it is that no one gives it to me." To Cork Smith Cohen wrote, "The further a writer gets from his malice, his bitterness, his selfish problems, the more full of wounding pain his writing becomes."

Cohen's personal life was in turmoil but visitors continued to appear on the island: John Knowles, novelist and author of *A Separate Peace*; Howard Bacal, Nancy Bacal's brother, who was training to become a psychiatrist; Marcelle Maltais, a French-Canadian painter; Sharona Aaron, an Israeli folksinger; and others: "A tall blonde girl who wears Oriental robes and carries a book called *The Mystery of Life* came here with my name."

He continued to monitor the sexual scene on Hydra, writing to his sister in late August:

Lots of French lesbians here this week. . . . Perverts of both sexes tell me that this was not a good sexual season, nothing compared to last year. Police beat up an elderly homosexual for sport and two masochists left the island in indignation at having been overlooked!

He also added that "from a sexual point of view," he was completely

obsolete . . . and I've just got to face the facts. Mother doesn't realize what a freak I am, a real live artist living with an actual woman, Christian or not.

That summer one of his close friends was arrested for drug possession, taken off the island, and beaten in a prison in Piraeus. The event became the catalyst for his poem, "I Threw Open the Shutters."

In September his novel appeared in New York and by October, Cohen returned to Canada to accept a five-hundred-dollar first prize in the CBC competition for new Canadian poets. Prompted by the attention his novel was receiving, *Holiday* magazine suggested that he write a story about pianist Glenn Gould. The idea was to interview Gould and record his impressions about a series of cities. The editor was concerned that Gould and Cohen would be recognized and suggested that they wear false beards as they walked around Montreal, the first proposed site. Cohen actually met Gould in the basement of the Hotel Bonaventure in Ottawa to begin the piece but became so enthralled by Gould's conversation that he forgot to pursue the line of questioning he had prepared. For months afterward he avoided answering the phone, convinced that the caller was the disgruntled editor waiting for his story.

In mid-October, Cohen participated in the Foster Conference, an informal gathering of poets and critics, held in the Eastern Townships of Quebec. The major speakers were John Glassco, A.J.M. Smith, Irving Layton, F.R. Scott, Milton Wilson, Louis Dudek, and George Whalley. Delegates included Ralph Gustafson, Eli Mandel, Seymour Mayne, Henry Moscovitch, Ronald Sutherland, and Leonard Angel. Cohen's presence signaled his involvement with the emerging Canadian literary scene.

Following Layton's address, entitled "The Creative Process," Cohen announced that "there were thousands of poems and thousands of poets in the world and that most of the poems don't get written down. The poets are specifically anal characters who like to collect it all." Layton took a different view, describing poetry as "a self-authenticated speaking, a reaching down into the roots of one's being . . . doubts, perplexities, inner conflicts, joy, desire, chagrin—the terror and ecstasy of living daily beyond one's psychic means. The major poets have large-sized, terrifying demons inside their psyches."

In response to Louis Dudek's presentation "The Little Magazine," Cohen excited discussion by stating that little magazines had fulfilled their purpose and had no real role. "The mass magazines will print the most sensationally daring of material, so that good writers do not need to resort to the little magazines." *Esquire*, he argued, was certainly open to the kind of writing that in the past could only be found in little magazines. His position here may have been influenced by having just placed part of *The Favorite Game* with *Cavalier* (actually a men's magazine noted for its pinups). He criticized his friend Layton for becoming a cardboard rebel, his antics recorded for the middle class by CBC television. Cohen's participation in the three-day conference sustained his place in the public

imagination, while renewing friendships with those from the days of
CIV/n. At the conference he read his poem "Alexander Trocchi, Public
Junky, Priez Pour Nous."

While in Montreal, Cohen met Suzanne Verdal, a dancer who was
one of the inspirations for two poems that would appear in *Parasites of
Heaven* in 1966. He first saw her dancing flamboyantly with her husband,
sculptor Armand Vaillancourt, at a *boîte* in Montreal called Le Vieux
Moulin. The first poem, beginning "Suzanne wears a leather coat," celebrates her dangerous beauty. The second, better-known poem is a version of his well-known song "Suzanne," from his first album, *Songs of
Leonard Cohen* (1968). He wrote the poem in the summer of 1965,
although it lacked focus until Suzanne took Cohen to her loft near the
St. Lawrence river. She remembered that they would spend hours talking by candlelight. Cohen maintained that they "were never lovers, but
she gave me Constant Comment tea in a small moment of magic."

Images in the song were drawn from a visit to the seventeenth-
century La Chapelle de Bonsecours, the mariner's church in old Montreal with the figure of the golden virgin at the top with her body turned
away from the city to bless the departing mariners. Inside the sanctuary,
hanging from the ceiling of the triple-steepled church, are votive lights
suspended in model ships. Yafa Lerner can remember walking with
Cohen in September 1965 and his excitement about the poem.

In a 1986 interview on the life of John Hammond, the Columbia
Records executive who gave Cohen his first record contract, Cohen
explained that the opening verse of his song was more or less *reportage*:
"Suzannne takes you down / to her place near the river / you can hear
the boats go by / you can spend the night beside her." Verse two represented the religious symbols of Montreal, a city filled with religious
iconography. "And Jesus was a sailor / when he walked upon the water /
and he spent a long time watching / from his lonely wooden tower . . .
forsaken, almost human / he sank beneath your wisdom like a stone."
Cohen summed up verse three as the "compassionate attention that a
man looks to receive from woman":

Now Suzanne takes your hand
and she leads you to the river

she is wearing rags and feathers
from Salvation Army counters
And the sun pours down like honey
on our lady of the harbour
And she shows you where to look
among the garbage and the flowers

And you want to travel with her
you want to travel blind
and you know that you can trust her
for she's touched your perfect body
with her mind

Cohen recalled that he had the chord progression before the lyric and outlined his process of composition: "Most of my songs began with the phrase of music and a phrase of the lyric." The tunes were usually completed before the lyric. Then Cohen would begin the long process of "uncovering the lyric and fitting it to the melody."

In Canada, Cohen had been saddled with that unfortunate sobriquet, "The voice of his generation." "TV stations pay me one hundred dollars a half hour for any blasphemous nonsense I can dream up," he wrote in a 1963 letter. He had become a literary personality, his persona better known than his work. "I was mailing a letter yesterday and a man came up to me and said, 'I bet there's not a decent poem in that envelope!'"

In the same 1963 letter, Cohen announced, "this Sunday I address the Jewish Public Library and I shall have become a Rabbi at last." This was a controversial event described in the *Canadian Jewish Chronicle* under the headline "Poet-Novelist Says Judaism Betrayed." Speaking at a December 29 symposium entitled "The Future of Judaism in Canada," Cohen gave an address he called "Loneliness and History." He startled the audience with an indictment of the community's neglect and indifference to its artists. The emphasis on the corporate survival of Jewish institutions, he said, was wrong; Jews must survive in their loneliness as witnesses, for if they forego that role, they abondon their purpose. Jews are the witnesses to monotheism, and that is what they must continue to declare. Jews had become afraid to be lonely. The prophet had vanished; only the priest remained. And the last great poet who tried to be both prophet and priest, A.M. Klein, had fallen into silence; rabbis and businessmen had taken over. Replacing the loss of Jewish values was the wealth of Jewish businessmen. Klein saw this change and decided to become a priest rather than prophet. Young Jewish writers would not make this mistake; they would remain alone and seek to honor their prophetic roles, Cohen declared.

This indictment of the Montreal Jewish community confirmed their worst suspicions: Cohen had turned against them, first in print in *The Favorite Game* and now in person. The reaction at the meeting was strong, but because of the late hour the chair, Dr. Joseph Kage, curtailed discussion and suggested that the symposium be continued the following Sunday. At this second meeting, a packed hall was disappointed to learn that Cohen would not be there. The community took his absence as an insult, but in a later interview Cohen said no one had confirmed to him the date of the second meeting. In his absence, several speakers lashed out at him, launching personal attacks. They quoted from his novel and identified Cohen with anything that was critical or vulgar in the book. A few of the younger members of the audience attempted to defend Cohen, although with little success.

Cohen frequently found his Jewish identity tested. The structure of his Judaism, like his quest in music, became a plea for union with a higher being and confirmation of his priestly function. "Draw me with a valuable sign, raise me to your height. You and I, dear Foreign God, we both are demons who must disappear in the perpetual crawling light, the fumbling sparks printing the shape of each tired form."

The controversy initiated by his December 1963 talk did not abate when early in the new year Cohen traveled to Western Canada. He stopped in Winnipeg for a reading/performance with the Lenny Breau Trio at the Manitoba Theatre Center and a reading at the University of Manitoba, then moved on to Vancouver, where he spoke at the University of British Columbia, the Jewish Community Center, and the Vancouver Public Library, all the while promoting the image of the poet as alienated spiritual iconoclast—cool rather than beat, mysterious rather than angry. His readings were uniformly successful and sensational.

In Vancouver he spent time with Earle Birney, who had promoted his work. In a letter thanking him for his hospitality, Cohen playfully chided

him: "Please quit soon. Layton and I will take over. Then we will quit."
At the Jewish Community Center on February 12, he again spoke on "the
distinction between the Prophet and the Priest, probably sparking a religious revival." The library talk generated the most displeasure, however:

> there's something about the West that invites you either to disarm or
> consider yourself in a state of permanent seige. I chose the latter.
> Went slightly insane before crowd at Library giving them "new
> insights into my irrelevant Eastern complexities."

Many found his behavior offensive, especially his use of frank language
and his invitations to the women in the audience to join him in his hotel
room after his talk. Despite the furor, he wrote to a Canada Council official who sponsored the tour that "Vancouver is a beautiful Polynesian
city and I will stay there forever."

By March, he told his U.S. agent, Marian McNamara, that his trip
had been "fairly triumphant. . . . As far as the prose goes," he complained, "much work, many breakdowns," adding that he would "tap
Easter and Passover and all festivals of renewal."

Cohen felt a new purpose and desire: "Most of all what I want is to
be able to seize some discipline and consecrate myself to ten years of real
labor." This consecration occurred with *Beautiful Losers*, which was
written in two intense eight-month periods, the first in 1964, the second
in 1965. His goal was to prepare a "liturgy, a big confessional oration,
very crazy, but using all the techniques of the modern novel . . . pornographic suspense, humor and conventional plotting," as he told Eli Mandel and Phyllis Gotlieb. In February 1964 he said that he wanted to
isolate himself "in the country and work on the new lunatic novel."
Seven months later, he wrote Jack McClelland that his "new novel,
PLASTIC BIRCHBARK, is deep into its asylum."

When he started, he worked only long enough to write three pages a
day, sometimes one hour, sometimes eight, typing away on the terrace of
his house in Hydra with a portable record player beside him. After the
book began to take shape, he would work for longer periods of time, up
to twelve or fifteen hours a day, aided by amphetamines and a Ray
Charles record, *The Genius Sings the Blues*. His favorite song, played over

and over, contains the line "Sometimes I sit here in this chair and I wonder." Speed, he thought, would strengthen his mind, but at a certain point "the whole system collapsed. It isn't a very good drug for depressed people because coming down is very bad. It took me ten years to fully recover."

Work on the novel was interrupted by his October visit to Canada to receive the four-thousand-dollar Prix litteraire du Québec for *The Favorite Game*. He also participated in a reading tour organized by Jack McClelland. Four poets traveled in two cars; an exuberant Irving Layton, a white-bearded Earle Birney, a nervous Phyllis Gotlieb, and the leather-jacketed Cohen. Beginning with a October 25, 1964, reading at the North York Public Library, they visited six eastern Canadian universities in five days: Waterloo, Western, Toronto, Queen's, Carleton, and McGill, reading to audiences of up to three hundred students. Receptions, book signings, and publicity accompanied them, as well as TV and radio broadcasts. The poets, however, did not mix well with each other. According to McClelland, Birney drank and was shy; Gotlieb was withdrawn; Layton was a showman; and Cohen went along but didn't enjoy himself. At Western, *Time* reported that "Leonard Cohen in a black leather jacket, Caesar haircut and expertly mismatched shirt and tie looked around and asked, 'Is this a church?'" The report unfavorably described Cohen's book as "more shackled by despairs exclusively his own" than by history. When an undergraduate demanded to know 'What makes a poem?' Cohen replied, "God. It's the same kind of operation as the creation of world."

Although the poets made no money—five months later, after all expenses, they had only one hundred and fifty dollars to divide four ways—the venture did result in an added benefit, especially for Cohen. Donald Owen filmed the tour for the National Film Board of Canada. He dutifully traveled with the group, filming their various readings. Birney's and Gotlieb's were remarkably dull. This resulted in a re-edited and partially re-shot film by Donald Brittain about Cohen rather than the group. *Ladies and Gentlemen . . . Mr. Leonard Cohen*, released in 1965, was the first of several films about Cohen.

The tour did generate publicity, but Cohen complained to Jack McClelland in March 1965 that:

the reading-tour made me an enemy of the whole country and ruined my Canadian life. This was not due solely to my obnoxious personality. It also resulted in the minimum attention for the book it proposed to promote. And worst of all it doesn't look like we're going to get any money out of it. Yankel, Yankel, why did you lie to us?

DURING HIS VISIT political events in Canada intruded into Cohen's artistic world. To Marian McNamara in New York he explained he had been:

> torn on the conflicts arising from the so-called quiet revolution here in Quebec. The separatist feeling is very powerful and many of us are engaged in an agonizing reappraisal of the *idea* of Canada, the *value* of Confederation, and what the risks of independence would be . . . It is not easy to talk or resist the dreams of people who feel they have been humiliated and who are ready, today, now, to throw bombs.

On his return to Hydra, he got down to work and began to rewrite *Beautiful Losers*, often listening to a radio tuned to the Armed Forces network broadcast from Athens, which played mostly country and western music. Cohen incorporated Canada's political turmoil into his work. The Quiet Revolution was changing the landscape of Montreal, turning it into a secular, francophone city, quietly assaulting the ruling anglophone business class. In 1963, the Front de Libération du Québec began its campaign of violence; in May, the explosion of a time bomb in a Westmount mailbox seriously injured an explosives expert. In a October 26, 1963, interview, Cohen remarked that the exploding mailboxes were an invitation to Canada to re-enter history and that the survival of the nation depended on the response to this event. On July 12, 1963, a bomb destroyed the statue of Queen Victoria on Sherbrooke Street. The brass head of the lifesize statue hurtled fifty feet away and the statue toppled. Chalked on the monument were the words "You're coming to your goal," and on the street, near the severed head, was scrawled "Here is the answer."

Cohen refers to the bombing in *Beautiful Losers* as a proposal by F., who tells the narrator that he will commit suicide as he lays sticks of dynamite in the lap of the statue. "Queen Victoria and Me," a poem in *Flowers for Hitler*, emphasizes the symbolic power of the figure. Cohen included the poem, with minimal musical accompaniment, on his *Live Songs* album of 1973. Cohen includes the October 1964 visit of the Queen and Prince Philip to Montreal in his novel, contrasting the new revolutionary fervor of Quebec with its decaying ties to the monarchy. The erotic mood of a separatist rally in the text is testimony to the link between politics, history, and sex.

Cohen's own response to the movement was complex, although in a February 1964 letter from Montreal he wrote that "in ten years Quebec may not be part of Canada and I will stay in Quebec. Our government has recently established a Ministry of Culture, the first in North America." He told George Johnston on Hydra, "I have made a commitment: to Art and my Destiny. All the other commitments are not commitments at all, but contracts, and I don't like the legal world of compulsion."

IN *Beautiful Losers* F., a young Montreal poet, asserts that "the texts had got to me." This was true of Cohen himself, who based his novel on several core readings: P. Edouard Lecompte's *Une vierge iroquoise: Catherine Tekakwitha, le lis de bords de la Mohawk et du St. Laurent (1656–1680)* (1927); *Kateri of the Mohawks* by Marie Cecilia Buehrle; a volume entitled *Jesuits in North America*; an American comic book from 1943, *Blue Beetle*; a farmer's almanac; a passage from Nietzsche's *Twilight of the Idols*; and Longfellow's *Song of Hiawatha*.

Cohen had become very interested in the life and history of Catherine Tekakwitha, the Mohawk who may become the first Native Canadian saint. He found her fascinating because she "embodied in her own life, in her own choices, many of the complex things that face us always. She spoke to me. She still speaks to me," he said in 1990. He most likely learned of her through her picture in the apartment of his friend Alanis Obam-sawin, an Abenaquis Native, though Kahntineta Horne, a First Nations woman who later became a politician, may have told him about her. A statue of the saint sits on the stove of his Montreal house, and prints of her hang in his Los Angeles home and office. When he was in New York he would put flowers on her bronze statue in front of St. Patrick's Cathedral.

He also drew from Swedenborg: *Arcana Caelestia* or *Heavenly Arcana*, volumes 1 and 2, the *Divine Providence*, and *Divine Love and Wisdom*. He studied these volumes in January–February 1966 and each is heavily annotated and marked. He refers to the *I Ching* in his work, echoing his poem, "How We Used to Approach the Book of Changes: 1966," published in *The Energy of Slaves*.

At this time, Steve Sanfield, Axel Jensen, George Lialios, and Cohen regularly met on Hydra to discuss such texts as the Book of Revelation, the *I Ching*, or *Book of Changes*, *The Secret of the Golden Flower*, and *The Tibetan Book of the Dead*. Jensen provided the key texts, which also included *Tibetan Yoga and the Secret Doctrine* and the translations of Evan-Wentz. Cohen introduced Hasidic thought into this mix, notably the work of Martin Buber and Gershom Scholem, as well as the Jewish prayer book.

In an unpublished essay from 1965, Cohen summarizes the importance of his education on Hydra in "esoteric enterprise":

We have among us adepts of telepathy, telekinesis, levitation, *apporte*, teleplasty, dematerialization, telesthesy, psychometry, kryptoscopy, and other minor ocular skills which at best assume the importance of parlour games in relation to our ultimate goals, and which at worst may be viewed as a dangerous distraction from those high purposes. I, for one, am rather disposed to the more pessimistic interpretation of these phenomena, but the charity we all practice in regard to another's discipline forbids me to treat the subject with any further aggression. We also have among us students of tantric sexual systems, and I regret to say, misplaced as my regret may be, that these students have often found themselves in adulterous predicaments.

In March 1965 Cohen told Jack McClelland that *Beautiful Losers* would be finished in a month "and if it gets by censors it could make money. I need cash—so would you decide how much you'd like to pay me." Three weeks later Cohen reported that he had "written the Bhagavad Gita of 1965" and that "what happens to this book doesn't matter because I have discovered a way to write a novel in three weeks and will turn out four in 1965. That is serious." He then proposed new titles:

> *SHOW IT HAPPENING* or *SHOW IT HAPPENING EVERY DAY* is the novel's new title, or maybe *THE HISTORY OF THEM ALL*, or maybe *THE BEAUTIFUL LOSERS*, or just *BEAUTIFUL LOSERS*. Just these titles are worth a fortune to Ideal Hollywood. So you'll get the mss. in April.
>
> One of us is cracking up.

Two separate draft title pages of the novel read "*BEAUTIFUL LOSERS* / A Pop Novel" and, correspondingly, *PLASTIC BIRCHBARK* / A Treatment of the World." Note sheets contain other variant titles: *IT WAS A LOVELY DAY IN CANADA, INDIAN ROCKETS, INDIANS*. One experimental section has the prose set to guitar chords.

The narrative of *Beautiful Losers* encompasses history, politics, and sex. As F. outlines it to the narrator, "You have been baptized with fire, shit, history, love, and loss." The novel uses a multiplicity of narrative forms and languages, incorporating journals, letters, grammar books, historical narratives, advertisements, catalogues, footnotes, poetry, and drama. Encyclopedic, all-encompassing, and energetic, the text almost bursts its form, and at times the narrator must interject to remind the reader that "a man is writing this . . . A man like you." Writing *Beautiful Losers* taught Cohen "how to treat big themes with a fast, personal technique," although his work still went through many transformations.

Cohen assessed the novel in a letter to Cork Smith:

> As far as the prologue goes, I can't think of anything to put in a prologue, and I think it would interfere somehow with the way the whole book is launched, its continual *forward* motion. A prologue would seem to say to the reader: you see, it was all really make-believe, and here am I, your faithful author, standing with a pipe in my library, just another book in my career. But I swear it wasn't like

that at all. I have written some things, even parts of *The Favorite Game*, that came out of my sense of a career, but every word of the new book is antagonistic to the very idea of career. Your colleague hit on something very true, I think, in his concern for the reader mistaking the book for non-fiction. It *is* non-fiction, although it would serve none of us to let this get around, in fact the notion must be rigorously suppressed. I believe this will be a problem of the presentation of the book on the market. It is non-fiction in the sense that there is more of the unscreened author on every page than usually appears in a work of the imagination, and this is because the book is really a long confessional prayer attempting to establish itself on the theme of the life of a saint, meditation on a tight rope, slipping off to circus screams, catching it again in the crotch, and all the men in the audience blink—they know what it feels like. To get pretentious, more than anything the book resembles the Spiritual Exercises of St. Ignatius, in the way that he requires the student to Visualize the stages of the life of Jesus, to actually see Nazareth, the real landscape, never to leap into glory, but to move from the *fact* into mystery, mystery is always grounded in the ordinary fact, mystery has a narrow entrance. It is fiction because I use a fictional construction, characters, scene setting, parodies of pornographic suspense—because all of the apparata of religious perception have withered, in me and in you, and we are offended by any accounts of Mystery which are not presented in fictional or anthropological terms. Because I could not write or believe in a book called Cohen's Meditations, I had to make a story out of prayer. I believe I had enough craft to be able to pull it off, and a lot of the joy in the book comes directly from pride in craft, ordinary fictional craft. Again and again, I had to reassure myself and the reader that it was only fiction, and when we believed it and relaxed, then I could really dive into the prayer which itself (I think) is composed, at the bottom, of real facts, buttons, doubts, garbage, pie-throwing, and you have to move through all the shit before you can use the pure vocative. Anyhow, this is all postmortem. If the book is one of those rare books that is still read three years after it is published, or maybe even five years, it will have become less and less fictional.

During the writing of *Beautiful Losers*, Cohen had continued his practice of fasting. He felt that it helped focus the mind on creation and also produced a physical manifestation of the holiness of his calling. The absence of food, the denial of pleasure, revivified the importance of his task, following the Judaic tradition of sanctifying the self through exerting control over the appetites. The sanctity was somewhat compromised by the aid of amphetamines, however, which kept him awake and killed his appetite. "My fast has been following me and I have been following my fast," Cohen writes. His spiritual sustenance diminishes his physical hunger, he explains, and he rejoices in the emptiness of his body.

After he completed the novel, he broke down. With the text finally finished, he decided to take a break and go to another island. He hadn't prepared himself, however, for the hot afternoon sun when he returned by boat. He nearly passed out when he got home and had to drag himself to bed. He didn't eat for more than ten days. He hallucinated and lost weight, going down to 116 pounds. Too many amphetamines coupled with sunstroke had caused his breakdown. But the day the storks came to Hydra was the day he recovered. Every year the storks stop over on their way to Africa and nest for one night on the highest buildings, usually churches, and then leave the next morning. When the storks left, Cohen had regained his strength.

The unorthodox nature of the novel made for some difficulties. Viking required eight readings of *Beautiful Losers* before deciding finally to publish it. Even then, they were not sure of what they had approved. One reader referred to the book as "Canada with the Maple Leaf snatched off—it is a serious put-on, rich and raunchy, terrifying and funny. It is a truly experimental novel, in which, I admit, I don't always know where he's going, but I like the way he travels." Brendan Gill of *The New Yorker*, Norman Holmes Pearson of Yale, and Leslie Fiedler of Buffalo all offered praise, Fiedler writing that it was an "honest-to-God pop art novel, with an R.C. Pocahontas and all." McClelland also went to outside readers to confirm his judgment that it was a brilliant book. "It astounds and baffles me and I don't really know what to say about it. It's wild and incredible and marvellously well written, and at the same time, appalling, shocking, revolting, disgusting, sick, and just maybe it's a great novel. I'm damned if I know."

Cohen's response to McClelland's letter of acceptance was a six-page statement beginning with a parodic dialogue between offended Canadian critics and a defensive Cohen. It opens with Cohen telling these critics that he was the author only "for a brief period. Soon it will be the book that *you* have written, and you will treasure it." The letter continues in the tradition of the trial scene of Leopold Bloom in the "Circe" episode of *Ulysses*:

— Fiend of the Kaballa! Explain yourself! We happen to know that even Milton Wilson hates your book.

— The authorship of the book is already among you. I have already lost it. I am the one man who has not written it.

— The associates of Jack McClelland are easily certain that you are a sick phony and they have conveyed this opinion to their associate, Jack McClelland, who resists it with that true and baffled courage with which a man who longs to be a pagan resists the voice of his conscience.

— Sirs, do not apply for pity.

— Eeeek! Jew Cohen, you've condescended too far this time. You have written a disgusting book and we intend to punish you with the G[overnor] G[eneral's] award, so that you will be hidden forever from the Americans.

The dialogue continues with charges of the novel's filth, fetishism, and fantasy. Cohen responded by declaring "the book I hold is absolutely empty, it contains not a trace of anyone, especially me." He also outlined his terms for publication to McClelland, including control over the cover and jacket copy. He was still smarting at the poor job with *Flowers for Hitler*: the "exhibitionism I argued off the front cover turned up on the back. We've got to avoid all hints of this sort of thing with Beautiful Losers." He also didn't want quotes from critics on the back cover. Of "Canadian critical opinion, I say this in all truthfulness, there is not a single mind in the whole dreary heap that I can take seriously, whether they turn their attentions to me in attitudes of censure or praise." As always there was the matter of money: "if you can get that $500 [the advance] to me quickly you would be contributing to my mental health. So let's say, to put it in writing, that I accept your publishing offer in general, and that we will work out details in our usual unofficial gentlemanly way."

McClelland agreed to Cohen's supplying biographical copy and approving jacket copy for the novel. Part of Cohen's own description of the book was adopted for the jacket, which reads:

Driven by loneliness and despair, a contemporary Montrealer tries to heal himself by invoking the name and life of Catherine Tekakwitha, an Iroquois girl whom the Jesuits converted in the 17th Century, and the first Indian maiden to take an Oath of Virginity. Obsessed by the memory of his wife Edith, who committed suicide in an elevator shaft, his mind tyrannized by the presence of F., a powerful and mysterious personage who boasted of occult skills and who was Edith's lover, he embarks on a wild and alarming journey through the landscape of the soul. It is a journey which is impossible to describe and impossible to forget . . . *Beautiful Losers* is a love story, a psalm, a Black Mass, a monument, a satire, a prayer, a shriek, a road map through the wilderness, a joke, a tasteless affront, an hallucination, a bore, an irrelevant display of diseased virtuosity, a Jesuitical tract, an Orange sneer, a scatological Lutheran extravagance, in short a disagreeable religious epic of incomparable beauty.

The categories are there, Cohen is saying; take your pick.

But even the manuscript, it seemed, would not cooperate: after the book had been accepted, Cohen wrote, "I lost my only carbon of the original when a sudden wind sent pages scattering to the sea during an outdoor reading in Hydra. Only because my NY agent could get another copy could I proceed with revisions." But advance sales were promising; pre-publication orders reached a surprising 3100 copies. It was also being read by a number of movie producers: Otto Preminger, the MCA group, Ulu Grosbard, and Alexander Cohen, for a possible movie option.

Release of the novel in Canada created a problem for Jack McClelland: censorship. He expected the book would be banned, hence, the small advance. The marketing strategy proceeded with advance copies and notices to the trade that the book was a strong, rewarding work. Promotion, McClelland explained, would avoid the sensationalist approach.

Replies from advance readers were too cautious or negative to use. But McClelland went forward with a gala launch party at the Inn on the Park in Toronto, held on March 29, 1966, nearly a month before the official publication date. The launch was attended by journalists, academics, politicians, broadcasters, and publishers, as well as writers, filmmakers, and general readers. The original invitation list included over four hundred names and read like the Who's Who of Canada: Robertson Davies, F.R. Scott, Earle Birney, Hugh MacLennan, Northrop Frye, Douglas LePan, Milton Wilson, Phyllis Gotlieb, Nathan Cohen, Morton Shulman, Irving Layton, Peter Desbarats, Peter Gzowski, Robert Fulford, William French, Pierre Berton, Mavor Moore, Patrick Watson, Harold Town, Timothy Findley, Adrienne Clarkson, Morley Callaghan, Marshall McLuhan, Ramsay Cook, and George Grant.

Posters showed a photograph of Cohen dressed in a turtleneck and jacket, staring intensely at a manuscript with pen in hand. It was a meditative posture designed to offset the potentially scandalous novel. Also on display was the cover art by Harold Town. Nearly three hundred people turned up at the lavish party, where the following telegram was received and read out: "Live Forever Leonard Cohen / Assorted Shy Bacchantes."

The University of Toronto, which had begun acquiring Cohen's papers in 1964, bought the manuscript of *Beautiful Losers* a month before the book was to be published, paying Cohen almost six thousand dollars, a substantial sum for him. The purchase underscored his stature in Canada at only thirty-one and showed confidence in his new work, since it had yet to be released.

Reviews of the novel began to appear in April and reaction was intense. Journalist and critic Robert Fulford both praised and damned the book, dismissing it as "a fantasy wrapped in a fable," adding:

> this is, among other things, the most revolting book ever written in Canada. Far from encouraging sexual drives, it will if anything mute them. The book is an important failure. At the same time it is probably the most interesting Canadian book of the year.

A few days later, Fulford reported that a Toronto bookstore had failed to sell any of its twenty-five copies of the novel in the first eight days of publication. Cohen's appearance on the current affairs show *This Hour Has Seven Days* on CBC television helped sales despite unfavorable reviews across the country. Austin Clarke in the *Toronto Telegraph* objected to the paper-thin characters, stilted dialogue, and exhibitionist pedantry. Miriam Waddington could say no more than "the story concerns three sexually versatile people." The Deer Park Public Library in Toronto circulated its three copies of the novel with Fulford's review attached as a warning. Poet bill bissett responded more positively; in the magazine *Alphabet* he wrote, "i give the book of Cohens a good review, a great review, easily million stars." Few critics shared his enthusiasm, although Cohen maintained, "It's the best thing I've ever done. It's a technical masterpiece."

Cohen was unhappy with distribution of the book, however. Jack McClelland pointed out that such stores as Simpson's and W.H. Smith had decided that they didn't want to take the risk of handling such a controversial work. McClelland had strenuously defended the book as a work of great energy to George Renison of W.H. Smith, explaining that "most of the people interested in pornography would not begin to understand either Cohen's purpose or his accomplishment," but to no avail.

On the matter of the $6.50 price, which Cohen thought too high, McClelland cited his production costs; he had imported printed sheets from the United States and bound them in Canada; the duty on the sheets was ten percent and there was an eight percent exchange on the U.S. dollar. An expensive jacket and a good binding had been used. More than three hundred copies of the four-thousand-copy run had been distributed as review copies. Then there was the cost of the posters, promotional materials, press releases, and the expensive launch party (which McClelland thought had been of little value "because you [Cohen] didn't think it suited your image or were unwilling to put yourself out"). McClelland implored Cohen to do more radio and TV interviews but to avoid "calling it a pornographic book yourself . . . People have been hanged for less."

By the summer of 1966, Cohen's popularity had reached a new height when it was reported that he had accepted a position as a TV commentator for the CBC in Montreal. Robert Fulford began a column by saying, "It is pleasant to think that Canada may soon have a poet who is also a TV star, or a TV star who is also a poet." Interviewed about this unusual development, Cohen replied, "I thought it was time to get into mass communications." With a female co-star, he was to do short interviews and films. "I'd like to make something beautiful. I'd like to get close to the viewers, get them to participate in the show, even send in home movies. And I'd like to help re-establish English Montreal as a community," he explained. But the television show never came off; nor did the proposal in November that he become part of a new CBC network show produced by Daryl Duke and titled *Sunday*. Though his heart lay in novels and poetry, Cohen had begun to realize the power of the electronic media.

Poetry expressed his longing and it nurtured him artistically, but it didn't pay the bills, and poetry, Cohen wrote, "is no substitute for survival." *Parasites of Heaven*, a collection of poems, was published in 1966, containing poems that dated back to 1957. An enigmatic four-line poem begins the slight book: "So you're the kind of vegetarian / that only eats roses / Is that what you mean / with your Beautiful Losers." The chief value of the collection is that it registers a shift in Cohen's outlook from satisfaction to discontent with the isolation of Hydra. He felt the need to join, in some fashion, the experiences of his audience and redefine his past. "How can I use the gull's perfect orbit / round and round the hidden fish, / is there something to do as the sun / seizes and hardens the ridge of rocks?" he asks. The collection received mixed reviews and modest sales and Cohen contemplated another career.

7

B L A C K

P H O T O G R A P H

C OHEN BEGAN a serious singing career in 1966,
when he realized that he couldn't earn a decent,
or even an indecent, living as a writer. In January
of that year he had become interested in the work of Bob Dylan. At an all-
day poetry party organized by F.R. Scott, and attended by Layton, Dudek,
Purdy, A.J.M. Smith, and Ralph Gustafson, Cohen played his guitar, sang,
and raved about Dylan. No one had heard of him, but Scott rushed out to
buy *Bringing It All Back Home* and *Highway 61 Revisited*. He returned and to
the chagrin of everyone, put them on. After a few minutes, Purdy
"bounded out of the room as though booted from behind," shouting,
"'It's an awful bore. I can't listen to any more of this.'" Only Cohen listened intently, solemnly announcing that *he* would become the Canadian
Dylan, a statement all dismissed. The remainder of the afternoon was

spent watching two new NFB films: *A.M. Klein: The Poet as Landscape* and *Ladies and Gentlemen . . . Mr. Leonard Cohen*, which Cohen did not view. At 10:00 p.m. Scott replayed one of the Dylan records, and this time the result was dancing, not criticism.

At Dylan's concert at the Place des Arts in Montreal the following month, Layton announced Cohen's decision to start a singing career to a group of students. At the intermission he said, "Do you know that Leonard is going to start singing?" The students replied, "He can't sing!"

Cohen had little choice but to try another career: *Beautiful Losers* had had good reviews but marginal sales, selling only one thousand copies in Canada and three thousand in the U.S. *The Favorite Game* had sold approximately two hundred copies in Canada and one thousand in the United States. Cohen realized that unless he chose the unattractive path of a university post, he could not survive as a writer, despite the critical praise. So he thought of music as his financial salvation. "In hindsight, it seems like a very foolish strategy, but I [said] to myself, I *am* a country musician, and I *will* go down to Nashville. . . . I have songs, and this is the way I'm going to address the economic crisis. It seems mad." On his way to Nashville, Cohen stopped in New York and ended up staying, off and on, for two years. The mood of the city echoed Cohen's own and he reveled in its energy and bleakness.

His friend Robert Hershorn provided Cohen with some funds and an introduction to Mary Martin, a Canadian living in New York and an assistant to Albert Grossman, who managed Dylan, as well as Peter, Paul, and Mary. Martin had previously arranged for The Hawks, with Robbie Robertson and Levon Helm, to be hired as Dylan's backup group. They were renamed The Band in 1968 and toured with Dylan before going on to become seminal rock figures themselves. For a short while, Martin also managed Van Morrison.

Cohen arrived in New York in the fall of 1966 with no sense of the folk renaissance that had occurred during his years in Greece. He had no idea of the sudden fame of Judy Collins, Joan Baez, or Phil Ochs. But he found a sensibility with which he was compatible: "I felt very much at home," he remarked years later. In New York Cohen first stayed at the Penn Terminal Hotel on 34th, then at the Henry Hudson Hotel near Eighth Avenue, and finally, at the Chelsea on West 23rd. At the Henry

Hudson Hotel, where he stayed just before taking up residence at the Chelsea, he was surrounded by drugs, down-and-outers, and dope addicts. Life in a hotel was losing its glamour. But it was there that he met an intriguing Swedish woman who was part hooker and part teacher. In an elevator a few days later, she told him that he was dead but that she could restore him to life. She undertook a therapy that involved yoga and an odd psychology. He became fascinated by her teaching and gave her nearly six hundred dollars. He decided to record her, with the idea of perhaps writing a book about her. But when the machine was on, she stopped talking. Their relationship continued for some time, Cohen frequently singing songs to her before he recorded them for his first album.

"Once I hit the Chelsea Hotel, there was no turning back," he said. The place was "rich in character and opportunities," and it was possible for him to establish "the rudiments of a social life." In between forays to New York, Cohen would return to Montreal, living either at his mother's or in downtown hotels such as the Hotel de France on Ste-Catherine Street.

In 1966 the Chelsea was notorious as *the* residence for the emerging underground music and writing scene, with its thick walls, high ceilings, and a management that had an "iron regard for privacy." Its marble halls and elegant wrought-iron central staircase contrasted with the slow, rickety elevators. It had a faded elegance, a romantic decay. In the sixties, the Chelsea also had a flourishing drug culture; Cohen has commented that one went "on a lot of involuntary trips [there] just accepting the hospitality of others."

The Chelsea had a diverse bohemian history that included Mark Twain, Eugene O'Neill, Dylan Thomas, William S. Burroughs, Arthur C. Clarke, Arthur Miller, Virgil Thomson, and Thomas Wolfe. While Cohen was at the Chelsea, Joan Baez, Bob Dylan, Jimi Hendrix, Allen Ginsberg, Kris Kristofferson, and Janis Joplin all stayed for varying periods. Harry Smith was one of the figures in residence at that time, a filmmaker, anthropologist, ornithologist, and mentor to Allen Ginsberg, an intriguing man, Cohen recalled. Stanley Bard, the appropriately named manager/owner, encouraged the experimental and the offbeat. Cohen once witnessed the arrival of a virtual zoo on the upper floors, as a dress rehearsal of Katherine Dunham's production of *Aïda*, with lions, tigers, and other animals took place; acrobats limbered up in the hallways and singers practiced in the elevators. Cohen's small, cupboard-sized room on the fifth floor held two single beds and his guitar. From the lobby the guests walked directly into a Spanish restaurant that was open all night; a few doors to the east was a synagogue. His affection for the hotel remained, and even during his time in Nashville, he would frequently return to the Chelsea.

Cohen recounts his most famous meeting in the hotel in "Chelsea Hotel #2" from *New Skin for the Old Ceremony* (1974). In his well-known concert introduction to the song, he outlines his first encounter with Janis Joplin:

> Once upon a time, there was a hotel in New York City. There was an elevator in that hotel. One evening, about three in the morning, I met a young woman in that hotel. I didn't know who she was. Turned out she was a very great singer. It was a very *dismal* evening in New York City. I'd been to the Bronco Burger; I had a cheeseburger; it didn't help at all. Went to the White Horse Tavern, looking for Dylan Thomas, but Dylan Thomas was dead. Dylan Thomas was dead. I got back in the elevator, and there she was. She wasn't looking for me either. She was looking for Kris Kristofferson [laughter]. "Lay your head upon the pillow." I wasn't looking for her, I was looking for Lily Marlene. Forgive me for these circumlocutions. I later found out she was Janis Joplin and we fell into each other's arms through some divine process of elimination which makes a compassion out of indifference, and after she died, I wrote this song for her. It's called the Chelsea Hotel.

During a more recent performance in Norway, Cohen revised the story of the original meeting between Joplin and himself: in the elevator Cohen asks, "Are you looking for someone?" "Yes," she replies, "I'm looking for Kris Kristofferson." "Little Lady—you're in luck. I'm Kris Kristofferson." He was significantly shorter than Kristofferson, but as he says, those were generous times. Yafa Lerner recalls that at the Chelsea it was common for women to offer themselves to Cohen as he rode the elevator. Cohen began writing "Chelsea Hotel #2" in a Polynesian bar in Miami in 1971 and finished it at the Imperial Hotel in Asmara, Ethiopia, in 1973.

There was also a "Chelsea Hotel #1," which had different lyrics and a much slower beat. Cohen performed "Chelsea Hotel #1" on his 1972 tour, often on Mandrax, which tranquilized both him and the song. It had a deadening beat; he realized that it had to be rewritten, and his guitarist, Ron Cornelius, provided him with a chord change that made the new version possible. But the song embarrassed him, and he later felt that it was indiscreet of him to reveal that Janis Joplin was the subject.

Cohen encountered Joan Baez at the Chelsea one night and she and Cohen got into an argument about Gandhi. Cohen had read a biography of the Indian leader and discovered that he regularly chewed rauwolfia, an Indian weed that is the active ingredient of Valium and other tranquilizers. Cohen had a vision of the nonviolent movement as an army of people stoned on Valium. Baez, who has called herself the only straight one at the party of the 1960s, took offense at Cohen's suggestion that drugs were an integral part of the movement. "She had this deep investment in being the straight girl," Cohen remarked. Baez also had an antipathy to mysticism and the occult and couldn't accept the last line of "Suzanne": "And you know that you can trust her / For she's touched your perfect body with her mind." Whenever she sang the song, she altered the last line because she found the action unreal. Only when she and Dylan came to Montreal in 1975 with the Rolling Thunder Review and sang at the Montreal Forum did she sing the correct line. Backstage she told Cohen, "I finally got it right."

Since his arrival in New York, Cohen had been on the edge of what he called the New York Renaissance of folk music. Clubs like the Bitter End were showcasing new and important talent. But until Mary Martin took him on, visits to several agents led only to the criticism that at thirty-two Cohen was a little old for this gig. Cohen was distressed, thin, and disappointed. He recalls sitting over a cup of coffee in a Greenwich Village cafe, feeling lonely and unwelcome, writing in frustration on a placemat, "KILL COOL!" He then held it up for the patrons to see.

Cohen's problematic professional life was mirrored by his equally complicated personal life. Marianne and her son Axel had come to New York at Cohen's request. He was living in the glorious chaos of the Chelsea Hotel, an inappropriate setting for a family, even one as loosely structured as theirs. He rented a loft space for Marianne and Axel on the lower east side, near Clinton Street. But he remained at the Chelsea, although his romantic energies were directed elsewhere. He and Marianne's life made sense on Hydra, within that simple, ancient context. In New York they didn't have a foundation, they didn't have a pattern that worked.

At times they still operated as a family, going to Montreal to attend the wedding of Carol Moskowitz, a friend of Cohen's. Cohen was dressed in a beautiful gray suit that he had had made and spent his time leaning in a doorway looking "professionally tortured," as someone noted. As well as the difficult romantic tribulations, Cohen also had to deal with the fact that several of his friends had recently been charged with drug dealing.

Cohen kept a sporadic journal in which he recorded hexagrams of the *I Ching*, which he was throwing, and the occasional poem that expressed self-criticism or desire, two favorite subjects. A poem from March 1967 offered this assessment:

> I am so impatient, I cannot
> even read slowly.
> I never really loved to learn.
> I want to live alone
> in fellowship with men.
> I'm telling you this because
> secret agreements bring
> misfortune.

The romance and sunsets of Greece evaporated into the realities and exhaust of New York. The order he had established with Marianne in Hydra had disappeared, replaced by darkness and chaos. He was taking more drugs, finding temporary refuge from a singing career that was not taking off. His behavior was skittish. Staying for a few days with a friend, he would unexpectedly disappear for a day or two if someone he didn't like arrived, even for a short visit. He would often leave a party moments after arriving. He was depressed but he still worked and wrote and sang. "Everything serves his work," his friend Yafa Lerner remarked, "which is arrived at only by tearing at the skin."

In 1966, Cohen walked into the silver foil-lined La Dom, Andy Warhol's club on 8th Street in the East Village, in search of "the scene." He saw, and instantly fell for, a statuesque blonde with a misty, wavery voice and a German accent who was singing in a monotone. She was Nico, "the perfect Aryan ice queen." Amid the looped projections of parachutists on the walls, "I saw this girl singing behind the bar. She was a sight to behold. I suppose the most beautiful woman I'd ever seen up to that moment. I just walked up and stood in front of her until people pushed me aside." The art critic David Antrim described Nico as possessing a "macabre face—so beautifully resembling a *memento mori*, the marvellous death-like voice coming from the lovely blonde head." Cohen visited La Dom every night she sang and finally introduced himself. Accompanying her on guitar was a handsome young man, Jackson Browne, then just eighteen years old.

Nico had lived in New York since 1959, modeling and then taking acting lessons with Lee Strasberg; Marilyn Monroe had been one of her classmates for a short time. Dylan, who was a lasting influence on Nico, had introduced her to Warhol, suggesting that he make movies with her. Warhol decided to let her sing instead and foisted her on his rock band, the Velvet Underground, which included John Cale and Lou Reed. Paul Morrissey saw that the group needed something beautiful to counteract "the screeching ugliness they were trying to sell." The critic Richard Goldstein described it as a "secret marriage between Bob Dylan and the Marquis de Sade." Nico was soon singing with the group, and in 1967 their first album was released. Its signature image was an erotic banana drawn by Warhol.

Nico made it clear that nothing would happen between her and Cohen; she preferred younger men. But she introduced Cohen to Lou Reed, who surprised him with his knowledge of his work. Reed had a copy of *Flowers for Hitler*, which he asked Cohen to sign, and was an early reader of *Beautiful Losers*. Cohen confided, "in those days I guess he [Reed] wasn't getting very many compliments for his work and I certainly wasn't. So we told each other how good we were." One night at Max's Kansas City, someone insulted Cohen, but Reed told him not to pay any attention to it since he was the man who had written *Beautiful Losers*.

The infatuated Cohen followed Nico around the city, but she was clearly not interested in him. He was madly in love with her though, and persisted: "I was lighting candles and praying and performing incantations and wearing amulets, *anything* to have her fall in love with me, but she never did." A journal entry from the Chelsea Hotel dated March 15, 1967, highlights Cohen's fascination with Nico, his entanglement with depression and his art: "Terrible day, hopeless thoughts of Nico. The guitar dead, voice dead, tunes old and fake . . . Nico in terrible mood. Tried to reach her, tried to make her stay beside me for a second, impossible." The journal that day also records a visit by Phil Ochs, Henry Moscovitch, a young Montreal poet, and the advice of a friend to see a psychiatrist, prompting this notation: "poet maudit ca. 1890. Cut the call short. Visited Judy Collins, taught her 'Sisters of Mercy.'"

Overwhelmed by Nico's beauty—she had modeled in Paris and had had a bit part in Fellini's *La Dolce Vita*—Cohen wrote "Take This Longing" for her. She sang it to him several times but never recorded it. He also wrote a confessional prose piece about his longing for her. After defending his writing as the result of "too much acid," too much loneliness, or an education beyond his intelligence, the narrator offers the following self-defense:

> It's a pity if someone . . . has to console himself for the wreck of his days with the notion that somehow his voice, his work embodies the deepest, most obscure, freshest, rawest oyster of reality in the unfathomable refrigerator of the heart's ocean, but I am such a one, and there you have it. . . .it is really amazing how famous I am to those few who truly comprehend what I'm about. I am the Voice of Suffering and I cannot be consoled.

The speaker then identifies himself as "the creator of the Black Photograph," the photographer who after the setup puts his hand over the lens and takes the picture. Only Nico, he writes, could understand his black pictures. "My work among other things, is a monument to Nico's eyes." He continues:

> That there was a pair in my own time, and that I met them, forehead to forehead, that the Black Photograph sang to other irises, and yes, corneas, retinas and optic nerves, all the way down the foul leather bag to Nico's restless heart, another human heart, that this actually happened constitutes the sole assault on my loneliness that the external has ever made and it was her.

Only after many weeks of being with Nico did Cohen finally understand her mysterious manner of speaking and singing: she was partially deaf. He was "perplexed by her conversation and paralyzed by her beauty" and thought that she was a terrific singer. "Completely disregarded . . . but she's one of the really original talents in the whole racket." Years later they re-met accidentally at the Chelsea, by then a dangerous place: the previous week a murder had occurred, and hustlers and drug dealers were everywhere, as were the police. Whether it was the drink or old times remembered, Nico suggested that the two of them go up to his room to talk because the bar was closing. They sat close to each other on his bed, and "I put my hand on—I think it was her wrist—and she hauled off and hit me so hard it lifted me clean off the bed, and she screamed and screamed. And suddenly the door came down and about twenty policemen came in, thinking I was the killer they were looking for. . . ." Several lines from "Memories" on *Death of a Ladies' Man* refer to her:

> I pinned an Iron Cross to my lapel
> I walked up to the tallest
> and the blondest girl
> I said, Look, you don't know me now
> but very soon you will
> So won't you let me see
> Won't you let me see
> Won't you let me see
> Your naked body.

"Once in my room," Cohen said, Nico whispered "I can't bear anything that isn't artificial." Nico's sad decline into drug addiction later troubled Cohen; she died in Ibiza in 1988.

COHEN PLAYED some of his songs for Mary Martin. Martin, who would become his first manager, introduced him to Judy Collins. In the fall of 1966, Cohen visited Collins and sang several of his songs for her. "She said she loved the stuff, [but] there wasn't anything there [for her], but if I ever did anything else, would I keep in touch with her," Cohen recalled. Several months later, Cohen sang "Suzanne" to her over the telephone from his mother's house. Collins liked it immediately and recorded it for *In My Life*, which was released in November 1966. He knew he was on to something, telling Sam Gesser, a Montreal producer, "I'm really in the middle of writing a wonderful song and I never said that before or since to anybody. I just knew. It sounded like Montreal. It sounded like the waterfront. It sounded like the harbor." Gesser replied, "There are a lot of songs like that around, Leonard."

On December 2, 1966, Cohen received a copy of Collins' album at his small Alymer Street apartment in Montreal. He couldn't stop playing "Suzanne" over and over, as three McGill students reported when they arrived that afternoon to interview him. Cohen talked about Dylan and how pop music would be the future of poetry. He noted that the local community had dropped the word "pseudo" from his poetry only when he gained a sizable reputation. Cohen remarked on the spiritual division between the old and young, and supported any belief system that would work: "Roman Catholicism, Buddhism, LSD." The students asked about his singing and Cohen explained that even if you don't have a voice or play well, "just speak from the center, tell people where you are and you'll reach them."

Collins' next album, *Wildflowers* (1967), included three of Cohen's songs—"Sisters of Mercy," "Priests," and "Hey, That's No Way to Say Goodbye"—as well as her own hit, "Both Sides Now." Collins acknowledged that it was Cohen's example that encouraged her to try her own songwriting. Until she met him, she had not written any of her own songs. In turn, Collins encouraged Cohen's first major singing performance, on April 30, 1967, at a Town Hall rally in New York for SANE, the National Committee for a Sane Nuclear Policy. Cohen walked out and played a few bars of "Suzanne," but then froze and walked off stage, a combination of stage fright and the fact that his Spanish guitar had gone out of tune because of the temperature change between the overheated backstage and the frigid stage out front. However, the audience shouted for him to come back and, with Collins encouraging him, he returned to finish the song.

After Cohen's success with Judy Collins, Mary Martin called John Hammond, Columbia Records' leading artist and repertory executive. Hammond had discovered and signed Billie Holiday, Count Basie, Aretha Franklin, Bob Dylan, and, later, Bruce Springsteen. On the advice of Martin, Hammond viewed the 1965 NFB film about Cohen and then invited Cohen to lunch. They ate at White's on 23rd Street, and later went back to Cohen's room at the Chelsea, where Hammond asked to hear a few songs. Cohen played "Master Song," "The Stranger Song," "Suzanne," "That's No Way to Say Goodbye," and a still-unrecorded song about rivers. At the end of six or seven numbers, Hammond simply said, "You got it, Leonard." Cohen didn't know if he meant he had talent or a contract. Hammond thought that Cohen had a "hypnotic effect"; he was "enchanting" and unlike anyone he ever heard before: "Leonard set his own rules and was an original."

Columbia Records, however, was not so keen, and Bill Gallagher, acting head of the record division, opposed the deal on the grounds that a thirty-two-year-old poet was not a good bet to become a singing sensation. Over the years the relationship between Cohen and Columbia reflected this ambivalence. In 1984 Walter Yetnikoff, then president of CBS Records, said to Cohen, "Leonard, we know you're great, but we don't know if you're any good." Columbia had sensed the problem eighteen years earlier: Cohen had talent but would he sell? They decided to take a chance. Within a week of Hammond's meeting him, Cohen was in Columbia's Studio E on 52nd Street.

Recording the album was no simple task. Cohen had never been in a studio to record before and he could not read music. Hammond had arranged for first-rate studio musicians to accompany him, but Cohen found that he paid more attention to their musicianship than his lyrics. Cohen hadn't sung with professional musicians, and he didn't know how to work with them. The relaxed Hammond read a newspaper behind the console, displaying what Cohen called "a compassionate lapse of attention." He knew Cohen had to find his own way. He thought Cohen should then lay down a simple track, just guitar and bass. He brought in Willie Ruff, a bass player who taught at Yale. Ruff was also a linguist and understood Cohen's songs and their meanings implic- itly. He was able to anticipate Cohen's musical moves. With Ruff's sup- port, Cohen recorded the vocal tracks of "Suzanne," "The Master Song," "Hey, That's No Way to Say Goodbye," and "Sisters of Mercy." "Leonard always needed reassurance of some kind," Hammond remem- bered, and Ruff provided it. To establish the mood for the songs, Cohen had the studio lights turned off, lit candles, and burned incense; but he needed one more object to feel at home: a mirror.

In Montreal, Cohen had always sung in front of a full-length mirror, partly because he needed to see himself perform and partly to imagine what an audience might see. He asked Hammond if a mirror could be placed in the studio. At the next session, Cohen sang while staring at a reflection of himself. But the sessions were still not coming together. Cohen visited a hypnotist to see if he could recreate his moods when he was writing the songs but it didn't work. Cohen did not believe that his voice was com- mercial enough, and he was insecure about his guitar playing.

Hammond became ill and had to remove himself from the project. A new producer, John Simon, was brought in and he added strings, horns, and "pillows of sound for Cohen's voice to rest on." Cohen disagreed with Simon's enhancement and felt he was losing touch with his own songs. Simon added a piano and drums to "Suzanne," arguing that it required syncopation. Cohen removed both, thinking that the song should be "linear, should be smooth." With "So Long, Marianne," Simon introduced a stop or blank moment, and then restarted the music. Cohen objected and changed the stop in the mix. The arrange- ments on Cohen's first album remained Simon's, but the mix is Cohen's. He felt the "sweetening"—adding the strings and horns— was wrong, but it couldn't be removed from the four-track master tape.

On the lyric sheets accompanying the album, the following note by Cohen appears:

> The songs and the arrangements were introduced. They felt some affection for one another but because of a blood feud, they were forbidden to marry. Nevertheless, the arrangements wished to throw a party. The songs preferred to retreat behind a veil of satire.

Songs of Leonard Cohen was unofficially released on December 26, 1967, although the year is always listed as 1968. For the most part, the arrangements on the album work against the songs. "Sisters of Mercy" uses a calliope and bells as background; "So Long, Marianne" contains a female rock and roll chorus; "Suzanne," also has a chorus to deepen the sound. "Master Song" does benefit from unusual electronic sounds, as does "Winter Lady." The most unnerving element is the scream or wail at the end of "One of Us Cannot Be Wrong."

In advance of the album, the folk music magazine *Sing Out* published two articles on Cohen, the first a casual biographical piece by Ellen Sander, the second an analysis of his music by the Saskatchewan-born Cree singer Buffy Sainte-Marie. She criticized his lack of musical knowledge but celebrated his sometimes outrageous modulations, shifting keys within a song. His melodies, she wrote, were largely "unguessable," while his musical figures repeated themselves so gradually that a casual listener could miss the patterns. Yet he lifted one off "familiar musical ground." "It's like losing track of time," Sainte-Marie wrote, "or getting off at Times Square and walking into the Bronx Zoo; you don't know how it happened or who is wrong, but there you are." His songs seemed to lack "roots or directions" because of his unusual chord patterns, but once absorbed they became enchanting.

Cohen had already mistakenly signed away the publishing rights to three of his most important songs: "Suzanne," "Master Song," and "Dress Rehearsal Rag," unaware of the consequences. Mary Martin knew an arranger, Jeff Chase, who also promoted himself as a music publisher and who she thought would enhance these songs. He worked with Cohen to put together a demo tape for promotion, but Cohen soon realized that he and Chase had conflicting ideas. But he convinced

Cohen that it would be useful for him to sign certain documents that "temporarily" gave Chase rights to the three songs and allowed him to represent Cohen. When things didn't work out musically, Chase told Cohen he was contractually bound. If he pulled out, Chase would retain the publishing rights to those songs as compensation for damages. Cohen was inexperienced and unsure and sought Mary Martin's advice. She suggested Cohen let it go. Cohen had lost the rights to Chase on a bluff of sorts, since Chase never did more than prepare the lead sheets.

In 1970, after his first tour, Cohen realized what a mistake he had made. He also realized that Stranger Music, a music publishing company he formed in 1967, was partly owned by Mary Martin, with whom by then he had become disenchanted. He went to Columbia producer Bob Johnston's lawyer, Marty Machat, for advice, and Machat, who soon became Cohen's lawyer, worked a deal whereby Mary Martin was bought out of Stranger Music. But that still left the matter of the song rights, which Cohen later described as having been "lost in New York City but it is probably appropriate that I don't own this song ["Suzanne"]. Just the other day I heard some people singing it on a ship in the Caspian Sea." In 1983–84, Chase contacted Barry Wexler, a friend of Cohen's, to tell him that Cohen should have the rights to these songs and that he was open to offers. A meeting subsequently took place at the Royalton Hotel in New York between a nervous Chase and an angry Cohen. Asked by Cohen how much he wanted, Chase replied, "What do you think?" Cohen thought for a second and said, "One dollar, you motherfucker!" Chase ran out of the room. But Cohen still wanted the rights to the songs and in 1987 successfully negotiated a sum that was more than his first offer but less than what Chase wanted.

Songs of Leonard Cohen introduced Cohen to the arcane financial machinations of the music world, a dark contrast to the book publishing industry which had relatively little corruption simply because it had relatively little money. But the album remains a coherent artistic statement, and it raised issues that would be addressed in later songs. Cohen has said on occasion that an artist has only one or two songs or poems that he constantly reinvents and that his earliest work contains all his later themes and variations. This is true of *Songs of Leonard Cohen*.

The back cover of the album shows a portrait of a Joan of Arc figure engulfed by flames. Her blue eyes and enchained hands are raised upward, while the flames reach her breasts. The unattributed image was actually a widely available Mexican postcard of a saint Cohen found in a Mexican magic store. It shows the *anima sola*, the lonely soul, seeking release from the chains of materiality. "I sort of felt I was this woman," he remarked years later. The reappearance of the image on the reverse of the 1995 tribute album *Tower of Song* was "closing the circle," he explained.

"Stories of the Street" documents Cohen's despair and dislocation during his early days in New York. As he says at the beginning of the song, "the stories of the streets are mine," elaborating his experiences in narrative: "I lean from my window sill / In this old hotel I chose / One hand on my suicide / One hand on the rose."

"Sisters of Mercy" had been written in Edmonton after he ducked into a doorway during a blizzard, and encountered two young women with backpacks taking refuge. Since they had no place to stay, Cohen invited them to his hotel room. They had hitchhiked across the country the previous week and quickly fell asleep on his double bed. He sat in the armchair near the window, and as the storm abated and the sky cleared, he studied the moonlight on the North Saskatchewan River. A melody had been rattling in his head (he recalled playing it for his mother in her Montreal kitchen), and wrote the stanzas as they slept: "It was the only time a song has ever been given to me without my having to sweat over every word. And when they awakened in the morning, I sang them the song exactly as it is, perfect, completely formed, and they were . . . happy about it. Barbara and Lorraine were their names."

"The Stranger Song," which addresses loss, departure, and the constant need to move on is essentially a confessional. Love is necessary yet also destructive; the warmth and comfort that love provides also weakens one's will. All of Cohen's later themes were contained here; *Songs of Leonard Cohen* became a template for the songs to come.

IT WAS IN NEW YORK that Cohen met Bob Dylan in the fall of 1969. Cohen remembers being in the dressing room of the Bitter End, a

Greenwich Village folk club, where he had gone to see Phil Ochs or Tim Buckley perform. Dylan had returned to live in the Village after spending several years secluded in Woodstock, N.Y., following his near-fatal motorcycle accident in 1966. Dylan heard Cohen was at the club and sent Paul Colby, his assistant and friend, to summon Cohen, who then met Dylan at the Kettle of Fish, Dylan's hangout on MacDougal Street.

Cohen's talent had some of the same elements as Dylan's: both wrote sophisticated lyrics, surprisingly elegant melodies, and neither had much of a voice. Dylan drew heavily from two of the same sources that Cohen did; the bible and Hank Williams.

Cohen has stated his appreciation of Dylan's work many times, calling him, at one point, "our most sophisticated singer in a generation . . . nobody is identifying our popular singers like a Matisse or Picasso. Dylan's a Picasso—that exuberance, range and assimilation of the whole history of music." And Dylan has said that one of the people he would not mind being for a minute is Leonard Cohen (two others were Roy Acuff and Walter Matthau).

WHILE LIVING in New York, Cohen began to make appearances on Canadian television. He was the perfect Canadian cultural commodity; articulate, sexy, and living outside the country. His first show was CBC's *Take 30*, hosted by Adrienne Clarkson. He appeared with the Toronto folk group The Stormy Clovers, who had been singing his songs in Montreal and Toronto clubs. On *Take 30*, Cohen sang "Traveller" (an early version of "The Stranger Song"), "Suzanne," and "So Long, Marianne." Afterwards, Clarkson asked if he now wanted to sing rather than write poetry. Cohen replied, "Well, I think the time is over when poets should sit on marble stairs with black capes."

In 1967, Cohen began a romantic relationship with Joni Mitchell, whom he first met at the Newport Folk Festival. He would visit her at the Earl Hotel on Waverly Place in the Village and since Mitchell frequently played in Montreal, she would spend time with Cohen there, writing the song "Rainy Night House" about their visit to his mother's home. When Cohen went to Los Angeles in the fall of 1968, he spent nearly a month with her at her new Laurel Canyon home. Cohen, Mitchell acknowledges, inspired her, giving her another standard in songwriting, although sometimes his presence surprised her—as when she found his name inscribed on the back of a heavy pendulum that fell off an antique clock she owned. He and Dylan, she has remarked, were her "pace runners," the ones that kept her heading to new and higher musical ground. Cohen characterizes their relationship as "the extension of our friendship," a friendship that has endured.

Based on the belief that he was the voice of the new counterculture, Cohen was flown out to Hollywood in 1967 by a producer to score a film that was to be directed by John Borman. It was his first time there, and what he remembers most distinctly were the matchboxes with his name on them in his hotel room. The producer thought Cohen would be a kind of authority on the new movement in music and the culture. It didn't work. "They showed me the film but I couldn't relate to it." He went out again a year later to score a movie tentatively called "Suzanne," an art film based loosely on his song. The filmmakers were unaware that Cohen had lost the rights to the song and the project didn't work out. But Cohen took the opportunity to spend time with Joni Mitchell, who was becoming an important part of the west coast music scene, and then rented a car and drove up to northern California to visit his friend Steve Sanfield, whom he knew from Hydra.

Back in New York, Cohen began to perform more. On April 6, 1967, he was introduced to a standing-room only crowd at the State University in Buffalo, New York, with these words: "James Joyce is not dead; he lives in Montreal under the name of Cohen." He read from *Beautiful Losers* and sang "Suzanne," "The Stranger Song," "The Master Song," "Love Calls You by Your Name," and "The Jewels In Your Shoulder" and did three encores. On April 30 he had his Town Hall debut for SANE and, shortly after, performed at EXPO '67 in Montreal in a small pavillion with a club-like setting. Walking out with his guitar and a handful of candles, Cohen engaged the audience by announcing that "I cannot sing unless you all agree to take a candle and put it in the middle of your table and light it." The audience thought this was pretty tacky but humored the singer. A guest that night recalled that Cohen's "guitar

157

playing was terrible and his voice was not much better. But he got to you and the women were quickly taken in; the men were less sure of him, but the mood was fabulous."

Cohen also performed at the Rhinegold Music Festival in Central Park and the Newport Folk Festival on July 16, where he joined Joni Mitchell, Mike Settle, and Janis Ian at the first singer-songwriter afternoon, which had been arranged by Judy Collins. In the car to Newport, Cohen confided to his lawyer Marty Machat that he had little confidence in his singing. "None of you guys know how to sing," Machat replied, "When I want to hear singers, I go to the Metropolitan Opera."

In September, Cohen appeared on CBS-TV's Sunday morning cultural affairs program *Camera Three*, eliciting the largest audience response in the fourteen-year history of the show. In November, Judy Collins released *Wildflowers*, which included three of Cohen's songs. The album became her biggest hit, reaching #5 on the charts. All of this set the stage for the release of *Songs of Leonard Cohen*.

A January 28, 1968, article in the *New York Times* captured Cohen's state of mind. The interview took place in his hotel room in the dilapidated Henry Hudson Hotel, where Cohen was enjoying the trappings that go with being "strictly an underground celebrity." With his album now released, he seemed "on the verge of becoming a major spokesman for the aging pilgrims of his generation, the so-called Silent Generation." Cohen offered his views on sex, women, revolutionary movements, the Greek colonels who came to power in 1967, and suffering, an area where people increasingly looked to him for advice. He offered diet tips; three years earlier he had been a vegetarian, now he only ate meat, and even proposed a new language: "When I see a woman transformed by the orgasm we have together, then I know we've met. Anything else is fiction. That's the vocabulary we speak in today. It's the only language left . . . Everybody I meet wipes me out. It knocks me out, and all I can do is get down on my knees. I don't even think of myself as a writer, singer, or whatever. The occupation of being a man is so much more." He praised women as mankind's salvation: "I wish the women would hurry up and take over. It's going to happen so let's get it over with . . . then we can finally recognize that women really are the minds and the force that holds everything together; and men really are gossips and artists. Then we could get about our childish work and they could keep the world going. I really am for the matriarchy."

Commenting on his work, Cohen says his novels "have a pathological tone. What I find out from my mail is that the best products of our time are in agony. The finest sensibilities of the age are convulsed with pain. That means a change is at hand." Mankind, he summarizes, must "rediscover the crucifixion. The crucifixion will again be understood as a universal symbol, not just an experiment in sadism or masochism or arrogance. It will have to be rediscovered because that's where man is at. On the cross." The headline of the interview, taken from a statement he offers, was "I've Been On the Outlaw Scene Since 15."

The next day, an unsympathetic review of the album appeared in the *Times*. The second sentence reads: "On the alienation scale, [Cohen] rates somewhere between Schopenhauer and Bob Dylan, two other prominent poets of pessimism." Yet the critic believed that the album would be fairly successful, although "*weltschmerz* and soft rock" are not always big sellers. "Suzanne," the critic said, "has its moments of fairly digestible surrealism." A comparison with Dylan emphasized their differences: "whereas Mr. Dylan is alienated from society and mad about it, Mr. Cohen is alienated and merely sad about it." However, the review concludes positively: "popular music is long overdue for a spell of neo-Keatsy world-weariness and Mr. Cohen may well be its spokesman this season."

By the spring, *Songs of Leonard Cohen* was a modest hit, reaching #162 in the United States, sandwiched between the *Young Rascals' Collection* and Petula Clark's *These Are Songs*. In Britain that summer, he hit #13, forecasting his popularity in Europe. Columbia also released "Suzanne" as a single, but it did not reach the charts. Cohen did not support the album with a tour, largely because of his insecurity as a performer. In Canada, the national news magazine *Maclean's* disliked the album, beginning its review with "Pity." An article in the *Village Voice* entitled "Beautiful Creep" criticized the folk poetry movement and identified Cohen as its leading proponent. "Cohen suffers gloriously in every couplet," the article said. Cohen's work was characterized as depressing, dark, and despairing. Eight months later, the *New York Times* linked Cohen with Dylan, Paul Simon, Rod McKuen, and Laura Nyro as the new voices of folk rock poetry.

Cohen went to London to appear on BBC-TV, performing twelve songs on two of his own shows, both entitled "Leonard Cohen Sings Leonard Cohen." The shows included "You Know Who I Am," "One of Us Cannot Be Wrong," and "Dress Rehearsal Rag." The introduction to the last song indicated Cohen's gloomy state. He talked about a Czechoslovakian singer who used to perform a song so depressing that afterwards people would leap out of windows. Cohen then reported that the singer himself had recently leapt to his death. "Dress Rehearsal Rag" was Cohen's equivalent song, and he performed it only when "the environment was buoyant enough to support its despair."

Although he was labeled a sixties poet and singer, Cohen remained aloof from the larger movements. "I never married the spirit of my generation because it wasn't that attractive to me. . . . Mostly I'm on the front line of my own tiny life. I remember that I was inflamed in the 60s, as so many of us were. My appetites were inflamed: to love, to create, my greed, one really wanted the whole thing." In particular, Cohen felt that the folk movement had been rapidly usurped by commerce. "The thing died very, very quickly; the merchants took over. Nobody resisted. My purity is based on the fact that nobody *offered* me much money. I suppose that had I moved into more popular realms, I might have surrendered some of the characteristics of my nature that are now described as virtues."

Cohen's dislocated situation in New York led to his exploring different sexual, spiritual, and pharmaceutical pathways, and one was Scientology. In 1968, as he was driving down Sunset Boulevard in Hollywood with Joni Mitchell, she spotted a building with a number of women wearing saris and handing out material. Above the door a large sign which read "Scientology." "What is Scientology?" she asked Cohen. "Oh, some crackpot religion," he replied. A few weeks later, he called from New York to say that he'd joined them and that they were going to rule the world. But a few months later, Cohen told Mitchell he was disenchanted and that he'd had some difficulty extricating himself from it. Initially, Scientology offered the goal of a "clear path" ("Did you ever go clear?" he asks in "Famous Blue Raincoat"). Cohen had also heard it was a good place to meet women. On June 17, 1968, Cohen received a Scientology certificate awarding him "Grade IV—Release."

By this time Cohen's relationship with Marianne was ending. He was seeing other women, defending his behavior as acts of generosity; he was restless in New York. He saw Marianne and Axel often, but he also knew that their future was bleak, as a number of his songs record. "So Long, Marianne" is the musical denouement to their arrangement. They finally separated in 1968. Although Marianne was still mad about him, she understood that she could never completely possess him. "My new laws encourage / not satori but perfection," Cohen wrote. In subsequent relationships, he sought to enact this principle, building on his earlier experiences. He required a serious, monogamous relationship, but one that allowed for his need for the freedom which sustained his creativity. Marianne was both the inspiration for, and casualty of, this need.

8

A I N ' T   N O   C U R E

F O R   L O V E

L EONARD COHEN met nineteen-year-old Suzanne
Elrod in an elevator at the Plaza Hotel in New
York. Cohen was there to attend a Scientology
session, one of the potholes on his road to enlightenment, and Elrod was
living at the Plaza, supported by a businessman. Elrod stepped out of the
elevator as Cohen was going in. He looked at her, spun around and
quickly introduced himself. Their relationship began almost immediately. She soon left the Plaza and moved into Cohen's downscale apartment at the Chelsea.

Suzanne was radically different from Marianne; whereas Marianne
was domestic and protective, Suzanne was direct and domineering.
With her dark, sultry beauty and aggressive sexuality, she sustained
Cohen's interest for nearly a decade, and he never learned to refuse her

various demands, whether they were for clothes or homes. A longtime friend from Greece commented that both women "had catlike characters": Marianne was "a puma," whereas Suzanne was "a Persian in a lady's parlor" who could jump with claws at any instant. Marianne seemed difficult to get to know, as if she had a wall of glass around her. She was loving, compliant, and understanding. With Suzanne, Cohen felt he had found an equal, someone who could meet him at the same level of intensity. He found her beauty inescapable and her sensuality irresistible. She hung erotic woodcuts beside religious icons on the white-washed walls of his house on Hydra. She was Jewish, from Miami, a beautiful, difficult woman. "God, whenever I see her ass, I forget every pain that's gone between us," he once remarked. When he discovered that she had small handwriting much like his own, he said, "I fear we are to be together for a long time."

Their difference in age never affected their relationship, although once when Cohen was doing an interview and gave his real age, thirty-four, she interrupted to say, "Leonard, don't say how old you are." He laughed and quoted John, 8:32: "The truth shall set you free." In their first year together, Cohen and Suzanne were itinerant, living on Hydra, at the Chelsea in New York, and briefly in Montreal where, after a short stay with Robert Hershorn, they rented a small house in the Greek section near Mount Royal. He wrote and composed, while she dashed off a pornographic novel, written "to make us laugh." He gave Suzanne a filigreed Jewish wedding ring, although they never actually married. They eventually settled in Nashville.

Cohen decided to go to Nashville to record his second album, *Songs from a Room*, after meeting Bob Johnston, Columbia's leading producer of folk rock, in Los Angeles in 1968. Johnston, who had produced Dylan, had heard Cohen's debut album and was interested in producing his next.

Nashville was the bible publishing capital of America, referred to as the "buckle of the Bible belt" and seen by many as a Christian, largely Republican theme park. The juxtaposition of a lugubrious, urban Jew and the rural, country backdrop of Nashville seemed odd. Musically, Nashville leaned toward bad puns and cloying musical arrangements. The television show *Hee Haw* debuted in 1969 and Merle Haggard's anti-protest song "Okie From Muskogee" was a number one hit. But its aw-shucks, hillbilly veneer belied the level of musicianship and innovation that thrived in Nashville. Chet Atkins and producer Owen Bradley were pioneering new sounds. Johnny Cash was doing interesting work. Kris Kristofferson was writing songs and working as a night janitor at Columbia Records. Elvis was recording at the RCA studios. Bob Dylan had recorded two albums there (*John Wesley Harding* and *Nashville Skyline*) and Buffy Sainte-Marie was developing one. Ever since his first band, the Buckskin Boys, Cohen had had an odd fondness for country music, and saw himself, incongruously, as a country singer.

When he arrived in Nashville, a pop/country crossover trend was beginning, blurring the distinction between the two. Bobbie Gentry's "Ode to Billie Joe" had been a number one hit on both the country and pop charts. Glen Campbell had recorded "Witchita Lineman" and Ray Charles, a longtime favorite of Cohen's, issued Volume 2 of "Modern Sounds in Country and Western Music." More experimentally, a series of twelve duets between Bob Dylan and Johnny Cash was recorded in March 1969. The crossover philosophy would be revived in cycles through the ensuing years, with varying degrees of success. In Nashville, Cohen found enthusiastic, professional musicians who were ready to accept him as a slightly older poet and budding folk-rock singer.

When Cohen decided to go down to Nashville in 1968, he was initially opposed to Suzanne coming with him. She spent the night before his departure carousing with several men, an unsubtle message. Cohen was upset but slightly overpowered. He was in thrall and it was decided that she would go with him. They stayed briefly in the Noel Hotel but decided to move to a small cabin in Franklin, Tenneessee, a rural town twenty-five miles southwest of Nashville. It was their home for the next two years. Producer Bob Johnston rented the place from Boudleaux Bryant, songwriter of "Bye, Bye Love" and other hits for the Everly Brothers, but let Cohen have it for seventy-five dollars a month. It came with twelve hundred acres of virgin forest filled with hickory, chestnut, oak, beech, and black ash trees. It also had a stream. Wild peacocks roamed the area and Cohen would amuse his occasional guests by imitating their cry.

He and Suzanne led a quiet rural life, driving in to Nashville only to record or to meet friends. Suzanne made long dresses, worked at her loom and dabbled with pottery. Guests to the farm found it isolated and Cohen's life there simple. At the time he was continuing with his mac-robiotic diet (between 1965 and 1968 he was a vegetarian). Cohen often had nothing to offer guests but soy tea.

In Tennessee, Cohen was able to fulfill his fantasy about being a cow-boy. One of his favorite places in Nashville was the Woodbine Army Sur-plus store. A journal from that period contains photographs of various gun counters; he became the poet with a gun. On one occasion, friends came over for an afternoon of shooting, bringing a carload of weapons. Leonard joined them with the largest weapon he had at the time, a Walther PPK pistol. He noted the comic imbalance in firepower, commenting that he was impressed with the way the South protected its women.

Cohen decided he needed a horse, and he bought one from Kid Mar-ley, a sometime cowboy and full-time drinker. A legend in the area, Marley could sing and play the harmonica and did so often with Cohen. The horse was lame and consistently uncooperative, spending most of its time in the pasture avoiding the Montreal cowboy, although Cohen did eventually learn to ride him.

One of Cohen's neighbors was Willie York, a notorious figure who had an illegal still and had once shot a revenue officer. He became the subject of a hit song called "Willie York, Big East Fork, Franklin, Ten-nesssee" by country singer Johnny Paycheck. York looked after Cohen's cabin and land while he lived there, but he also made off with a variety of goods, including Cohen's rifle. An erratic neighbor, he would pound on Cohen's door in the middle of a raging storm, demanding twenty dollars, and Cohen would give it to him. Yet his individualism appealed to Cohen and he enjoyed his company.

For the most part, Suzanne felt comfortable in Tennessee, although she made regular trips back to New York or Florida. "Diamonds in the Mine," from Cohen's third album, refers to her failure to write to him and his disappointment at not finding any letters from her in his mailbox on the farm. But in composing, recording, and living far from the pres-sures of Montreal or the intensity of Hydra, he was content: "I moved there. I had a house, a jeep, a carbine, a pair of cowboy boots, a girlfriend ... A typewriter, a guitar. Everything I needed." Suzanne's view of their life there, however, was touched with cynicism: "As long as someone like him [Cohen] was in the universe, it was okay for me to be here. I was walking on tiptoe—anything for the poet. Our relationship was like a spider web. Very complicated."

In rural Tennessee, Cohen had successfully transposed what he had in Hydra—the romantic isolation that allowed him to work. Yet he never quite escaped his melancholy, as a poem from the "Nashville Notebook of 1969," entitled "The Pro," makes clear. It is a serio-comic poem of departing:

> I leave to several jealous men a second-rate legend of my life.
> To those few high school girls
> who preferred my work to Dylan's
> I leave my stone ear
> and my disposable Franciscan ambitions.

The recording of *Songs from a Room* went well. Bob Johnston understood the fragility of Cohen's songs and their blend of poetry with music and, like John Hammond, helped him to overcome his nervousness in working with other musicians. They worked in Columbia's large, new 16th Avenue studio, which Johnston had had refitted. Johnston chose the sidemen, including Charlie Daniels, an imposing Texan and a fiddle player who had worked with Dylan and would go on to his own successful career. The first session though, was unfocused. Cohen came in and asked, "What do you want to do?" Johnson said, "Let's get some hamburgers and beer." When they returned, Cohen again asked, "What do you want me to do?" Johnston replied, "Sing." After the first taping, Cohen came into the control room and asked, "Is that what I'm supposed to sound like?" "Yeah," said Johnston.

Charlie Daniels recalled the way Cohen appreciated the musicianship of the players but also brought his own unique talents to bear. In the studio, Daniels and the other sidemen were told to listen to Cohen in order to get into the songs. It was like mixing colors; you had to be one of the colors for it to work. Johnston later referred to the album as a painting, not a record, and described his role as "a musical bodyguard," protecting Cohen and his music from artificial intrusions and falsification of sound. There was a fragile, gentle feel to the album. Johnston attempted "to make his voice sound like a mountain" without sacrificing the purity of his sound. When Cohen sang "The Partisan," one of the few songs he has recorded that he didn't write, Johnston felt that French voices would enhance it. So he and Cohen went to France and overdubbed three female French singers.

The music on *Songs from a Room* was produced in such a way as to enhance the language; no drums were used, and an electric guitar only sparingly. The sessions were quite loose, with plenty of time allowed for each take. Johnston had recently done *Blonde on Blonde* for Dylan, as well as *Folsom Prison* for Johnny Cash, so he was prepared for the new sound that Cohen brought.

Johnston has said that Cohen swept one's psychic energy away. "Leonard has always had his finger on the future, Dylan his eye on tomorrow," Johnston explained in an interview. He described Cohen's guitar playing, with its beautifully constructed chords, as a black widow spider. Johnston recognized the offbeat power of Cohen's voice, its ability to mesmerize.

Cohen himself maintained doubts about his voice. Of one song, "Lady Midnight," he wrote, "The voice is uncertain. In those days it took me fifteen minutes to decide whether or not I should wear my cap when I went outside and a half hour whether or not I should take it off when I came back."

Yet in the studio, Cohen was sure of what he wanted. Johnston "created an atmosphere in the studio that really invited you to do your best, stretch out, do another take, an atmosphere that was free from judgement, free from criticism, full of invitation, full of affirmation." It was the way he moved while you were singing; "he'd dance for you" and "sponsor a tremendous generosity in the studio." The recording process was becoming easier for Cohen and he was relaxed. In his journal he wrote, "read [the] Zohar, exercised, slowly came alive."

The album was released in March 1969. Grim, hard, and emotionally powerful, it did nothing to dispel his reputation as the crown prince of pessimism. In "You Know Who I Am," he sings:

Sometimes I need you naked
Sometimes I need you wild

I need you to carry my children in
And I need you to kill a child.

"Bird on the Wire" became an anthem and Cohen used it to open his concerts, explaining that it "seems to return me to my duties." Kris Kristofferson, who had begun selling his own songs, told Cohen at a Nashville party that Cohen had stolen part of the melody from Lefty Frizell's "Mom & Dad's Waltz." But Kristofferson admired the song and said that the first three lines—"Like a bird on the wire, / Like a drunk in a midnight choir / I have tried in my way to be free"—would be his epitaph.

"Bird on the Wire" began in Greece: when Cohen first arrived in Hydra, there were no wires on the island, no telephones, and no regular electricity. But soon telephone poles appeared, and then the wires: "I would stare out the window at these telephone wires and think how civilization had caught up with me and I wasn't going to be able to escape after all. I wasn't going to be able to live this eleventh-century life that I thought I had found for myself. So that was the beginning." Then he noticed that the birds came to the wires. The next line referred to the many evenings Cohen and friends climbed the endless stairs up from the port of Hydra, drunk and singing. Often you'd see "three guys with their arms around each other, stumbling up the stairs and singing these impeccable thirds." He finished the song in a Hollywood motel on Sunset Boulevard in 1969.

A single, "The Old Revolution," hit #63 on the U.S. charts and a surprising #2 in England. In France the popularity of the album led to Cohen being named *le folksinger de l'année* by *Le Nouvel Observateur*. Cohen entered the cultural grammar; it was remarked that if a Frenchwoman owned but one record, it was likely to be by Leonard Cohen. It was later reported that the president, Georges Pompidou, often took Cohen's records with him on vacation.

While still living in Nashville, Cohen made a trip to Italy. In June of 1969 he joined Franco Zefferelli and Leonard Bernstein at a villa outside Rome to score a movie on St. Francis of Assisi, titled *Brother Sun, Sister Moon*. Music was to play a leading part, with Bernstein composing the music and Cohen writing the lyrics. With Zefferelli, Cohen visited the tomb of St. Francis, taking away some small metal birds blessed by the abbot. There were long meetings and luxurious Italian meals served by attractive young men but little real work. Cohen was unhappy with the scene and left for Rome, where he unexpectedly ran into Nico. He was seized with his old obsession but nothing came of it. Zefferelli eventually made his film but Cohen was not a part of it. He was replaced by Donovan.

After several false starts, Cohen did get involved in scoring films, providing songs for Robert Altman's *McCabe and Mrs. Miller*. Cohen was in Nashville recording some tracks for his third album, *Songs of Love and Hate*, and ducked into a theater to see Altman's film *Brewster McCloud*. That night he was back in the studio again when, by coincidence, Robert Altman called him, telling him that he had built a film around Cohen's songs from his first album. He said he had been writing the script while listening to Cohen's record. Cohen said, "Who are you?" Altman replied, "Well, I did *M*A*S*H*, that's my film." "I don't know it," Cohen replied, asking if there was anything else he had done. "Well, I did a picture that's been completely buried, that you wouldn't know about; it was called *Brewster McCloud*." To that replied Cohen, "Listen, I just came out of the theater. I saw it twice; you can have anything of mine you want!"

For *McCabe and Mrs. Miller*, Cohen did some additional instrumental music, although eventually the only piece used was guitar background for a soliloquy by Warren Beatty. The soundtrack for the movie, released in 1971, included "The Stranger Song" (the opening piece), "Sisters of Mercy," and "Winter Lady," with various instrumentals added. When he saw the finished picture—without the music—Cohen candidly told Altman he didn't like the film. Several months later, however, when he saw the completed film with the soundtrack in Montreal, he managed to reach Altman in London. "Forget everything I said; it's really beautiful!" he shouted into the phone.

Reaction to the film itself was mixed. Vincent Canby in the *New York Times* thought that its intentions were "not only serious, they are meddlesomely imposed on the film by tired symbolism, [and] by a folk-song commentary on the soundtrack that recalls not the old Pacific Northwest but San Francisco's Hungry i." Several months later, John

Simon complained in the same paper that the dialogue was "delivered sotto voce out of the corners of people's mouths in a remote corner of the screen or entirely off it." He continued, "There is not much to see in the film and even less to hear—often no more than a pretentious ballad by Leonard Cohen, the Rod McKuen of the coach trade, which has nothing to do with the matter at hand." *Time* said that Cohen's craggy voice sounded "like Villon with frostbite." The movie did poorly at the box office, and Altman has called it "the biggest failure of all my films."

WHILE LIVING IN NASHVILLE, Cohen went to Los Angeles for the wedding of his friend Steve Sanfield. It was Sanfield who introduced Cohen to his Zen master. An American from Massachusetts, Sanfield had been involved with LSD, Tibetan Buddhism, and mysticism. On Hydra he had peddled antique comic books and hashish. Planning to work at a Tibetan refugee camp, Sanfield left Hydra and went first to California where he learned of a Japanese Zen Buddhist missionary, Joshu Sasaki Roshi, who had come to the United States in 1962 to establish a militaristic brand of Zen known as Rinzai. Unlike Soto Buddhism, which emphasizes gradual enlightenment, Rinzai stresses sudden, explosive enlightenment earned through austere regimes of *zazen* (meditation), *sanzen* (meetings with the master where a *koan*, or a question, is posed), and daily rituals of work and rest.

Sanfield met Roshi when the Zen master was fifty-seven. He had spent forty-one years as a monk in Japan, fifteen of them as a Zen master, and was now leading a small but committed Zen group in Gardena, a Los Angeles suburb. He had transformed his garage into a *zendo*, or meditation hall, and the bedroom into the *sanzen*, or spiritual examination room, and was sleeping on a mattress in the living room. After an excruciating session of *zazen* the evening of his first visit, Sanfield was unexpectedly admitted to *sanzen* and presented with his first *koan*: "Show me the voice of God." Unable to answer, he was immediately shown out. He returned the next day and stayed for three years, soon moving into the attached garage/*zendo* to sleep.

In order to raise funds for Roshi's growing roster of students and the expanding *zendo*, Sanfield went to New York in the fall of 1967 and there, at the Penn Terminal Hotel, re-met Cohen, then recording his first album. Cohen suddenly became very interested in learning about Sanfield's teacher. Judaism was still important for both men, and one Sunday, Sanfield, Cohen, and Mort Levitt traveled downtown to visit a group of young Hasids. As they crossed Washington Square Park, they saw a large circle with Swami Bhaktivedanta seated in the center leading a mantra. This was his first visit to America, and the Hare Krishna movement was just beginning. Allen Ginsberg soon joined the growing circle of dancing, chanting figures. Cohen stayed while Sanfield and Levitt continued to their meeting. When they returned, the circle was just breaking up and Cohen offered his only comment: "Nice song."

After his return from New York, Sanfield fell in love with the wife of a fellow student and was ordered by Roshi to leave the *sangha*, or community, for six months. He and his lover moved to the Santa Ynez mountains south of Santa Barbara. Several weeks later Roshi sent word that he wanted to see him; he expressed hesitant approval of the match. Thirteen months later, in 1969, the two were married in a ceremony presided over by Roshi at the Cimarron Zen Center in south central Los Angeles. A former home built within a compound, the Cimarron center quickly became the new focus of the Rinzai movement and is still the home temple of Rinzai-ji in America. Sanfield asked Cohen to be his best man.

Cohen, who was now in Nashville, never replied to his request. He did, however, send Sanfield an unusual photo of himself apparently hunting; hanging from his belt were the guts of some animal. But when Sanfield walked into the Cimarron center on the day of the wedding, Cohen was there. In the kitchen before the ceremony, Cohen was helping with the dishes when a small Japanese monk came in, took some food from the refrigerator, propped up his feet and ate. He then left and in hushed tones Cohen was told that that was the Roshi. At the ceremony there was much celebration of the Ten Precepts of Zen—a decalogue that includes no killing, no misuse of sex, no lying, and no indulgence in anger—but after the fifth precept, which states no dealing in intoxication, they broke out the saki and enjoyed themselves. Cohen's twenty-eight-year relationship with Zen was baptized on this ambiguous note, one that would define his continued involvement.

IN APRIL 1969, Cohen received the Governor General's Award for Poetry for his *Selected Poems, 1956–1968*. Over two hundred thousand copies were sold in the United States. It was his first book of poetry to be published in the U.S., but his second album had just appeared and he was becoming well known as a singer. A full-page ad for the album reads in part, "What makes Leonard Cohen a very different poet is that he turns his poetry into songs . . . now there's actually a demand up front for Leonard Cohen."

Selected Poems also sold well in Canada, although the numbers did not equal those in the United States. Including selections from his first four books and twenty new poems, the collection presented a timely overview of Cohen's work. It was published in England in 1969 and in the following four years in Germany, Israel, Sweden, France, and Spain. When Cohen learned that he had received the award, he sent a telegram from Europe: "May I respectfully request that my name be withdrawn from the list of recipients of the Governor General's Award for 1968. I do sincerely thank all those concerned for their generous intention. Much in me strives for this honor but the poems themselves forbid it absolutely." No one in English Canada had ever before turned down Canada's most prestigious literary award (and the accompanying twenty-five-hundred-dollar prize money), although the previous month Quebecois writer Hubert Aquin had rejected the award because accepting it "would not conform to [his] political beliefs." As a separatist and member of the *Rassemblement pour l'independance nationale*, Aquin felt he had to reject it. After the embarrassment caused by two recipients declining the award, winners in subsequent years have been asked whether or not they would accept the award before the public is informed.

Unexpectedly, Cohen turned up with Quebec novelist Diane Giguere at the party Jack McClelland gave for the Governor General winners at the Chateau Laurier the night of the Ottawa ceremony. Upon seeing him, an angry Mordecai Richler motioned him into the bathroom

173

with the words "C'mere. I want to talk to you," closed the door, and then pointedly asked him why he had turned down the award. "I don't know" was Cohen's halting protest. "Any other answer and I would have punched you in the nose," Richler heatedly replied. Cohen believed that it wasn't necessary to "get behind Canada then." In 1969 the country did not seem, as it does today, an entity that needed such support, he later explained. And he felt that receiving an award from the federal government at a time when the separatists were crying for recognition was, for someone from Quebec, not quite timely. He had friends in the separatist movement, and he couldn't divorce himself from it so easily. "I have no idea why he came to the party," McClelland remarked.

Most of the material in *Selected Poems* was first chosen by Marianne. The collection reflected the changing focus of Cohen's writing, from his early concentration on religion and identity to a lyrical celebration of love and then the pain of history and loss. One of the best known of the new poems in the collection was a comic plea entitled "Marita." It reads:

MARITA
PLEASE FIND ME
I AM ALMOST 30

Cohen had scrawled it on a wall behind one of the outdoor tables of a famous Montreal cafe/bar on Mountain Street, Le Bistro chez Lou Lou les Bacchantes, located under the old Crêpe Bretonne. The bistro was open from 1962 to 1982, and was a gathering place for journalists, writers, artists, politicians, and riff-raff. Pierre Trudeau, Rene Levesque, Jack Kerouac, Genevieve Bujold, and Harry Belafonte were likely to turn up around the famous zinc bar or at the marble-topped tables set outside. The Marita in the poem is Marita La Fleche, a petite, attractive brunette from Manitoba who managed three Montreal women's dress shops. After leaving her shop on Mountain Street, she would go to "Le Bar Zinc," as it came to be called. Cohen was a regular himself and tried unsuccessfully to pick Marita up one evening. She patted the young poet on the head, and said, "Go on your way, young man and come back when you're thirty." Cohen's poem was his response, although he recently admitted to no recollection of Marita in the flesh.

Critical praise for the book was strong in both Canada and the United States, although the love poetry rather than the spiritual searchings received the greatest attention. An ad for the book in the *New York Times* included "a modern housewife's lament," plucked from the *New York* magazine: "It's so difficult, you know, wearing miniskirts and keeping up with Leonard Cohen, and not going insane when the diaper service doesn't come!" In an interview in the *Times* from April 13, 1969, Cohen explained that there was no difference between his poems and songs. "Some were songs first and some were poems first and some were situations. All of my writing has guitars behind it, even the novels." He was fond of citing Ezra Pound's dictum: "When poetry strays too far from music, it atrophies. When music strays too far from the dance, it atrophies."

A hiatus in his writing followed *Selected Poems*; *The Energy of Slaves* did not appear until 1972, *Death of a Lady's Man* was published in 1977, and *Book of Mercy* came out in 1984. His singing took precedence, and he recorded seven new albums between 1971 and 1985. His personal life underwent dramatic changes; he became a father, committed himself to Zen, and renegotiated his life with Suzanne. A number of friends and critics felt that he had compromised his artistry by moving into music, but it was music that gained him his audience.

In June 1969, *Saturday Night* magazine devoted ten pages "in celebration of Leonard Cohen." Cohen was on the cover, staring out at the reader with his large dark eyes. Type running down the left side of the cover declared, "Leonard Cohen: the poet as hero." The headline across the top read "Mordecai Richler on the Frightened WASPS of Westmount." Jack Batten, the new associate editor of the magazine, discussed Cohen's popularity as a singer among the young, and the significance of his poetry and lyrics in capturing the times. One eighteen-year-old told of a visit to Cohen's motel room, after which she remarked that, "he acts taller than he really is. I've heard other women say the same thing."

Cohen was included in a series of writers featured on thirty billboards displayed in Toronto subway stations. The brainstorm of Max Layton, son of Irving, it was an original way of promoting Canadian writing and culture. Entitled "Poetry Underground," the Cohen billboard featured a large portrait of him taken by Canadian photographer Sam Tata and the romantic lyric of "Go by Brooks," from *Selected Poems*.

During 1969 Cohen was criticized for continuing to live in Greece, following the April 1967 coup by the Greek colonels who then initiated a repressive rule. He defended himself by saying that he did not see it as "a betrayal of mankind to vacation in a country ruled by fascists . . . I had a house there, friends; I didn't consider my presence there a collaboration. It was the contrary." Two poems, both entitled "I threw open the shutters" in *The Energy of Slaves*, confront the cost to others who were there, however, and the torture they underwent. The second version ends with these lines:

> I swore by the sunlight
> to take his advice:
> remove all evidence from my verse
> forget about his punctured feet

THE SUCCESS of *Songs from a Room* in 1969 led to Cohen's decision to go on his first tour. It was exclusively in Europe, as were his 1972 and 1974 tours. Cohen didn't tour North America until November 1974, beginning in New York at the Bottom Line and ending in Phoenix at the Celebrity Theater in March 1975. He would not play in New York again for ten years.

Bob Johnston put together the band, which consisted of Charlie Daniels, Ron Cornelius, Bubba Fowler, and Johnston himself (he wanted to stay at home because he did not consider himself a keyboard player, but Cohen insisted), plus Corlynn Hanney and Sue Mussmano as vocalists. They began in Hamburg on May 4, 1970, and played six cities. At the opening concert in Hamburg, Cohen exhibited an odd showmanship by greeting the stomping German audience with a raised arm and the cry, "Seig Heil!" In Paris, he invited the ardent crowd to join him on the stage. They did, and the management called the police, although Cohen was able to control the crowd. He began the concert with "Bird on the Wire," reciting rather than singing. In Copenhagen, he led the audience out into the street and back to his hotel. In London he played before ten thousand fans at the Royal Albert Hall. A critic said that Cohen exhibited a "captivating self abasement leaving deep impressions of a sad and tortured wasteland." Cohen's peculiar melancholy earned him a loyal British audience. "Word gets around that Cohen is coming and it's a sellout, just like that," a London paper reported. "He sneaks onto the stage whilst you're still discussing how uncomfortable the seats are . . . To be alone, he tells us, is not necessarily to be lonely." Cohen had "a unique gift for juxtaposing natural speech with formal metaphor."

On July 25 the band played a festival at Forest Hills, New York, memorable for the rainy weather and poor sound, although one reviewer remarked that the "cut of his voice" was more impressive than his poetry: "Mr. Cohen sings in a dry manner, flat like a wall but textured like stucco." Another critic found that the effect wore off after a while. Dylan, unrecognized and stopped by security, came backstage to congratulate Cohen and his band on their performance. In August the group returned to Europe to play a festival in Aix-en-Provence and the Isle of Wight.

In Provence they encountered a massive traffic jam en route to the concert. Bob Johnston told Billy Daniels, the road manager, to get some horses, since most of the musicians were from Tennessee or Texas. There were horses at the stable attached to the country inn where they were staying, so they mounted up and with a guide headed through the countryside to their destination. To their astonishment, along the way they found a French steakhouse done up as a "Texas Bar." Ten cowboys and one Montreal Jew who had learned to ride at summer camp pulled in and roped their horses to the only hitching post in southern France. They marched in wearing their western garb, surprising the few patrons and fulfilling the fantasies of the owners. After several bottles of wine, they remounted and headed off to the concert. They decided the best entry would be to ride their horses onto the stage, and they did, despite Charlie Daniels' fear that that the wobbly stage would collapse. Cohen attempted a gala entrance on his white horse, which needed to be coaxed up a steep ramp; at the appropriate moment, it reared back as he saluted the crowd.

A group of Maoists in the crowd objected to paying because it reeked of capitalist domination and shouted that Cohen was a fascist. Bottles were thrown and the band thought someone had taken a shot at them, knocking out a stagelight. Cohen took the microphone and challenged the people to come on stage if they were unhappy, intimating that the singers were also armed, an expression of western bravado from a group of horse-riding musicians from the gun-totin' south. "If you don't like what you hear, come take the microphone. Until then we'll keep singing," Cohen said. The concert went on, although with difficulty. That night his backup band was named The Army.

The Isle of Wight concert on August 31, 1970, wasn't any easier. They came on at 4:00 a.m., following Jimi Hendrix, who had just set the stage on fire. The audience of three hundred thousand was exhausted. Someone had also set fire to the concession stands just before Cohen was to perform. The promoters woke up a sleeping Cohen, who first appeared in a raincoat and pyjamas, taking twenty minutes to tune up. After changing into safari jacket and jeans, he began the performance. The group played seventeen songs, mostly in 1/4 or slow time, partly the result of Mandrax. Cohen also recited three poems, slowly.

Then Cohen did a fourteen-minute encore, and Kris Kristofferson recalls that Cohen "did the damndest thing you ever saw: he Charmed the Beast. A lone sorrowful voice did what some of the best rockers in the world had tried to do for three days and failed." Kristofferson told Zal Yanofsky, his fellow musician, that that was the type of background he wanted for his own songs. "'Boss,' Zal said, 'Leonard is an angst poet. You're an alcoholic.'"

Melody Maker, the British paper, was less enthusiastic. "Leonard Cohen is an old bore who should just return to Canada which he never should have left to begin with!" Ricki Farr, a concert official at the Isle of Wight was upset about the fee Cohen had negotiated and said, "Cohen lays on this trippy thing about love and peace and all that crap. I think Leonard Cohen's a boring old crone and he's overpaid. I think he should go back to Canada."

Despite some negative feedback, the tour was a success. Part of this had to do with Cohen's realization that after years of separating himself from the world, he could join it. "I decided I couldn't live as a coward. I had to sing or I was nothing. I also started to accept guidance and to allow people to love me . . . I knew all about solitude and nothing about cohesion and unity." The *I Ching* was instrumental in this transformation. He had been studying the book of changes on Hydra, focusing on the phases of arrangement, the splitting apart and decay that occur in the world and what may affect a given moment. "The book has been a sort of teacher for me," he remarked to a journalist, and he thought that it was "time now for me and others to get together. I feel there's a great getting together in the world again . . . I want to lead the world to a new sensibility." The response of the Paris audience to his pleas for order in the midst of chaos was a sign to him that communication and unity were possible. And if suffering was responsible for leading him to where he was artistically, singing relieved him from its pain.

Accompanying him for part of the tour was his lawyer and advisor, Marty Machat. From 1969 until his death in 1988, Machat represented Cohen and looked after his recording interests. In 1973 Machat became involved in theater as well, producing an off-Broadway musical revue entitled *Sisters of Mercy, A Musical Journey into the Words of Leonard Cohen*. The show was partly funded by Columbia Records, although the company withdrew its support when Clive Davis, a Cohen fan, was ousted as president.

In Paris, the Royal Winnipeg Ballet performed *The Shining People of Leonard Cohen*, the first of several theatrical and dance productions of his work. Brian MacDonald conceived the dance, based on a group of nine love poems by Cohen recited during the ballet. Between the poems are interludes of dance, alone or with a soundtrack constructed from sound sources: laughing and words electronically distorted from the texts. A rumor circulated that Cohen was in Paris and might show up; he did not. The work was praised in the French press and in late July, it was presented at the National Arts Centre in Ottawa.

At home, Cohen received an honorary degree from Dalhousie University in Halifax, the citation stating that he had become, for many, "a symbol of their own anguish, alienation, and uncertainty" and that *Beautiful Losers* had "established him as the mouthpiece of the confusion and uncertainty felt by a whole generation." The *Globe and Mail* hailed him as "Entertainer of the Year." His intelligence and presence justified the award, the paper wrote, both more than making up for his voice. In turn, Cohen quipped that although his voice was not the finest, he did have a certain way of delivering a song.

After the tour, Cohen returned to Nashville, where he had started to record his third album, but he seemed to lose his center. As he began recording again in the studio, "absolutely everything was beginning to fall apart around me: my spirit, my intentions, my will. So I went into a deep and long depression." In addition, "I began to believe all the negative things people said about my way of singing. I began to hate the sound of my voice." His now regular use of drugs, insecurity about his work, and the unstable relationship with Suzanne were at the root of this depression. Her scorn of his work generated a distrust of her love for him. He wrote of her unpleasantness and how she blamed him for her shortcomings. "I fell in love with her imagination," he wrote, but she was looking for something else: security, success, and materialist survival. Sitting across from her in a hotel dining room, all he could think about was "familiar poison, dependence and love. . . . The fascination of her unbeauty." His marriage was becoming a prison. A period of decline and withdrawal followed, captured by the dejected tone of *Songs of Love and Hate*, his third album. "Sometimes I feel that my life is a sell-out and that I'm the greatest comedian of my generation," he told a French journalist.

> But I have to keep going. I can't remain fifteen and a virgin. So now I'm thirty-six and greedy. I'm willing to be this.
>
> I was once never able to stay in the same room with four people. Only a girl who adored me. I feel better now. The more vulgar I get, the more concerned with others I get. I'm trying to cure myself and the only way to cure myself is to take over the world.
>
> This is *my* adventure. My greatest need is to be interesting to myself.

"Suffering," he admitted, "has led me to wherever I am. Suffering has made me rebel against my own weakness." For nearly a decade he would be unable to free himself from the new pain that was about to descend on him. He tried various cures, from LSD and cocaine, to Scientology and the *I Ching*. He felt that a certain amount of suffering was educational. "You've got to recreate your personality so that you can live a life appropriate to your station and predicament."

9

T R U M P E T S A N D
A C U R T A I N O F
R A Z O R B L A D E S

THE TITLE of Cohen's third album, *Songs of Love and Hate*, reflected the double-edged nature of Cohen's life following his tour. As Zen was becoming more important to him, his relationship with Suzanne was becoming strained. They had a son, Adam, in 1972, and two years later their daughter Lorca was born. He adored his children but continued to leave to further his art as he had always done. Between 1971 and 1977 he released five albums, but only two books appeared. But his productivity did not bring popularity, and Cohen felt marginalized; his alienation and doubts increased. He thought that his voice wasn't appropriate for the material. He was depressed, and doing drugs, and there were rumors that he was about to retire. He continued to work, but his audiences dwindled and his support from the recording companies waned.

Recorded in March 1971 in Nashville, *Songs of Love and Hate* was again produced by Bob Johnston, although overdubs were added in London. Many of the songs were from earlier periods and had been reworked for the album. "Joan of Arc" had been written at the Chelsea in New York; "Avalanche" and "Dress Rehearsal Rag" dated from earlier years. Another song, "Love Calls You by Your Name," was a minor rewrite of an unpublished 1967 song, "Love Tries to Call You by Your Name." This practice of reshaping old material marked Cohen's musical career and continues with his recent albums.

"Joan of Arc" was something of an experiment for Cohen, in that he both sings and speaks the lyrics on overlapping tracks. This technique was Cohen's idea, drawn from the literary form of the palimpsest: "I had, as the model, manuscripts that you'd see with lines written over lines. I just thought it was appropriate at that moment. It's like the line of a Larry Rivers painting, you see the variations." "Famous Blue Raincoat" also appears on the album, a retelling of a romantic triangle. Originally titled "The Letter," the song outlines the dismal loss of love with no hope of recovery. Cohen based the song on a Burberry raincoat he purchased in London in 1959, later stolen from Marianne's loft in New York. Elizabeth, his London friend, "thought I looked like a spider in it . . . it hung more heroically when I took out the lining, and achieved glory when the grayed sleeves were repaired with a little leather."

His melancholic tone persisted, reflecting his unhappy situation and increasing depression. "Last Year's Man" had taken Cohen five years to finish but its theme of paralysis and decay was timely:

But the skylight is like skin
For a drum I'll never mend
And all the rain falls down amen
On the works of last year's man.

Cohen was not entirely pleased with *Songs of Love and Hate* and later commented that "with each [of my first three] records I became progressively discouraged, although I was improving as a performer."

Franz Schubert had once noted that whenever he sought to write songs of love, he wrote songs of pain, and whenever he wrote songs of pain he wrote songs of love. Cohen found himself facing the same problem. Few people responded to the relentless despair of his songs. He had been celebrated for his melancholy, but he had crossed some commercial line into depression. Cohen's critique of the album was, "the same old droning work, an inch or two forward." He also thought his voice was "inauthentic," full of anxiety and conflict, and labeled his work the "European blues."

Critics warned listeners that it was impossible to listen to a Cohen album in the sunshine. In his unpublished novel *Perennial Orgasm*, Don Lowe details the adventures of a woman named Oressia who arrives on Hydra looking for Cohen but falls into the hands of an Irish poet. His attempted seduction is thwarted by the droning of a Leonard Cohen album in the background which deflates the desire of both parties. And although his first two albums went gold in Canada with sales over one hundred thousand, his third did not. Publication of the arrangements in a songbook of the same name also failed to generate new sales.

Over the next several months, Cohen continued to perform and improve his sound as he prepared to go on tour, and he received new publicity with the release of Altman's *McCabe and Mrs. Miller*. In August 1971, Cohen formed a publishing company in London with the pop music magnate Tony Stratton-Smith, head of Charisma Records. The first book they planned, under the new Charisma Books imprint, was a selection of Irving Layton's poetry, although the book, printed from the McClelland & Stewart plates of *Selected Poems*, didn't appear until 1977. Earlier in 1971, Cohen had set up Spice-Box Books, Ltd. in England but had found that he needed a British connection to produce books effectively.

In March 1972, Cohen was back in Nashville rehearsing for a twenty-three city European tour. Two days before the band was to leave for Dublin, two singers, Donna Washburn and Jennifer Warnes, auditioned for Cohen in Studio A of Columbia Records. Warnes lived in Los Angeles but was in Nashville taping a TV show. She had heard through a secretary that Cohen was looking for backup singers. Both of their voices—especially Warnes's alto—constrasted beautifully with Cohen's. He explained to them that "the reason I need girls to sing with me is that my voice depresses me. I need your voices to sweeten mine." They were both hired.

Cohen grappled with the logistics of the upcoming tour while trying to deal with his personal problems. "I'm just reeling. Sometimes in the midst of the thing, I don't know how I do it, you know. Like I manage to get my daily life together to get this [1972] tour together. But most of the time I'm staggering under the blows. It's no doubt that I contrive these blows for myself. I think everyone is responsible for their own condition."

Cohen took a shotgun approach to his malaise; he fasted, exercised, and practised yoga and meditation. In an effort to re-establish his Montreal roots, Cohen bought a cottage on St-Dominique Street and a duplex beside it in the winter of 1972. This marked his return to Montreal, although he periodically went to Nashville to record, despite giving up his lease on the farm.

One floor of the duplex became a sculpting studio for Mort Rosengarten, another became a music studio for Cohen. Cohen made the cottage his home with Suzanne and, by September, his son Adam. He enjoyed the ethnically diverse neighborhood and three years later bought three more properties.

Bob Johnston had suggested making a film of the upcoming tour and Tony Palmer, who had made a movie about Tom Jones, was hired to direct. Cohen's lawyer Marty Machat produced. Titled *Bird on the Wire*, it premiered in London at the Rainbow Theatre in 1974 and shows Cohen performing, clowning with his musicians, and trying to pick up women. Cohen was initially unhappy with the arty look of the film and wanted a stronger, documentary texture. He spent nearly six months editing the work, shifting its focus away from visual clichés to the deeper realities of his music. Control was crucial for him, as it was in the production of his first book of poems and his first album. What Cohen wanted was a film that showed the live context of his music and his rapport with his audiences. *Bird on the Wire* did that but it also showed

Cohen emotionally wasted. He felt exposed in the film and thought that his vulnerability was inappropriate for public viewing.

Touring remained an adventure. In Vienna their instruments had been held up at the German border and weren't available for the concert. When Cohen was told of this (in the bath), he said, "Oh boy, we get to do the concert a cappella." At the theater the band asked the audience to go home and bring their instruments; after a delay, the concert began. In Copenhagen, a poor sound system upset the crowd and money had to be refunded, with Cohen himself handing out cash and dealing with disgruntled and angry fans. In Germany, where he gave six concerts, he greeted an unruly crowd at the Berlin Sportpalast with Goebbel's own fateful words, spoken on the very same spot: "*Wollt Ihr den totalen Krieg?*" ("Do you want total war?")

In Frankfurt, where he thought he played poorly, he told the following story:

> Once I was walking along in a snowstorm in New York and I came up very quickly behind a man who had a sign stuck to the back of his coat. The sign said
>> Please don't pass me by
>> I've been blinded totally,
>> But you have eyes and you can see,
>> Please don't pass me by.
>
> But when I looked at the man's face I saw that he wasn't really blind, at least not physically, and so I caught up with him at the next corner and asked him why he had that sign. He said to me, "Man, do you think I'm talking about my eyes?" so I wrote this song.

In London he again played at the Royal Albert Hall. "One got the feeling," a critic wrote, that "although the place was full to the brim, everybody sat next to an empty seat . . . you could have heard an unused tissue drop, such was the silence that followed. It was a silence, a concentration that in many ways was awful with its intensity. It was a sin to cough." Cohen left the stage, returning for the encore to thunderous applause. Surprisingly, though, he grabbed the mike and said, "I have no more songs left in me." The concerts usually concluded with

Cohen silently walking off stage, leaving his guitar and books behind.

In Jerusalem, at the Yad Eliahu Sports Palace, there was pandemo-nium when Cohen stopped mid-performance and left the stage, agitated and in tears, saying that he could not go on and that the money should be refunded to the audience. Drugs and the pressure of performing the final concert of the tour in the holy city of Jerusalem had contributed to his state. In the dressing room, a distraught Cohen rejected the pleas of his musicians and manager to return to the stage. Several Israeli promoters, overhearing the conversation, walked out to the crowd and conveyed the news: Cohen would not be performing and they would receive their money back. The young audience responded by singing the Hebrew song, "Zim Shalom" ("We Bring You Peace"). Backstage, Cohen sud-denly decided he needed a shave; rummaging in his guitar case for his razor, he spied an envelope with some acid from years ago. He turned to his band and inquired: "Should we not try some?" "Why not?" they answered. And "like the Eucharist," Cohen has said, "I ripped open the envelope and handed out small portions to each band member." A quick shave, a cigarette, and then out to the stage to receive a tumultuous wel-come. The LSD took effect as he started to play and he saw the crowd unite into the grand image of "the Ancient of Days" from Daniel's dream in the Old Testament. This image, "the Ancient of Days" who had wit-nessed all history, asked him, "Is this All, this performing on the stage?" Deliver or go home was the admonition. At that moment, Cohen had been singing "So Long, Marianne" intensely and a vision of Marianne appeared to him. He began to cry and, to hide his tears, turned to the band—only to discover that they, too, were in tears.

The high emotions soon brought the concert to an end but before they boarded the bus, Cohen and Ron Cornelius, his guitar player, walked to a wooded hillside nearby. When they turned back to look at the concert hall, a visionary light from the night sky illuminated its roof. When Cohen had first gone out to perform, he told the audience, "There are nights when one is raised from the ground, and other nights when [one] cannot raise oneself. . . . This night we can't get off the floor . . . This night my masculine and feminine parts refuse to meet each other." But in the end he triumphed; the concert was a success.

Cohen had always been petrified of touring, feeling that the risks of humiliation were too great. By the end of the tour, the tedium of travel, hotels, sound checks, rehearsals, press conferences, fans, and performances had exhausted him. To a British journalist who asked during the tour what he had been doing since 1970, Cohen replied, "Trying to maintain a balance between standing up and falling down." Cohen was never so vulnerable as he was on this tour, Jennifer Warnes recalled, opening himself up to his songs and his audiences. Working with Cohen Warnes realized that "life was art and God was music." His presence and his manner could, and often did, make the audiences weep. One of the most remarkable elements was the on-stage spontaneity of Cohen and the musicians, who would frequently improvise new songs and melodies. Warnes thought she sang badly on the tour and remembers Bob Johnston yelling at her to listen more carefully to the notes and to attend more sharply to the nuance of the material. During the tour she also recalled Cohen writing constantly, drafting an early version of "Chelsea Hotel."

One day while traveling through northern France, Warnes had showed Cohen a series of letters she had written about herself. When she was born, she was named Bernadette, but her mother later changed her name to Jennifer. Now she was writing to this earlier self, engaged in a search for her essential being. Cohen immediately thought there was a song there and began to compose; he wrote the lyrics and Warnes wrote the melody to "Song of Bernadette," which she would later record on *Famous Blue Raincoat*.

———————

DURING the spring and summer of 1972, Cohen's life with Suzanne became more difficult and his love for her was clearly faltering. He turned, once more, to drugs and mystic teachings and "to squeezing memory and vocabulary for descriptions of some ritual appetite many nights ago." He wrote, "I left you for a song above my name . . . [but] I want to stand up straighter than a promise and face the sins that make me suffer, to give up what is holding me in this painful crouch, or do anything you say." He realized that Suzanne did not love his "pious moods; you disdain my formal meditation," yet when he came home "after loving another" and then went off to write, she quietly joined him at the bar of the Rainbow on Stanley Street, "only pulling back a little as I write this down."

During this turbulent period he kept a journal in which he described, in a revealing paragraph, his process of writing:

> You ask me how I write. This is how I write. I get rid of the lizard. I eschew the philosopher's stone. I bury my girl friend. I remove my personality from the line so that I am permitted to use the word I as many times as I want without offending my appetite for modesty. Then I resign. I do errands for my mother, or someone like her. I eat too much. I blame those closest to me for ruining my talent. Then you come to me. The joyous news is mine.

In a spring 1972 interview, Cohen refers to a work he has just completed, *The Energy of Slaves*, a work that records his pain and indicates the depressive state that characterized his work for several years. Originally titled "Songs of Disobedience," which he had previously submitted and then withdrawn from his publisher, he retitled and reworked the manuscript as *The Energy of Slaves*. He explains that in the book he doesn't explicitly describe his pain because it can't be stated: "It took me eighty poems to represent the situation of where I am right now. That to me totally acquits me of any responsibility I have of keeping a record public. I put it in the book." Unhappy with the generally limited range of his material, he nonetheless felt that it represented his state of mind. He was interested in the book's reception, more so than any other book he wrote, "because I have the feeling that by making it public I may be making a mistake."

One early and sympathetic reader of the book was Irving Layton. In a December 4, 1972, note, Layton defended Cohen's position. He wrote "what alone matters are the memorable words you leave behind. For power in these one must have the strength to be weak—for this and many others to follow. One must somehow—for talent, for immortality—name the strength (courage?) to be weak in one's own way . . . God sometimes reveals his wisdom through a poet's weakness." This creed justifies much of Cohen's confessional poetry and state of longing.

In September 1972 Cohen was in London anticipating the birth of his son in Montreal when he received unexpected news: his close friend and confrere Robert Hershorn had mysteriously died in Hong Kong. The news was devastating and only partly mitigated by the call telling Cohen that his son Adam had been born. He departed immediately to welcome a son and bury a friend. Painfully, Cohen shoveled in part of the dirt on the coffin in the Shaar Hashomayim cemetery, a Jewish custom of the living honoring the dead once they are lowered into the ground. "Partner in Spirit, Laziness and love, Hershorn is now gone," Cohen lamented, adding in a notebook, "O Hershorn, first-born, first tired, first dead of anyone I knew, these ignorant papers are for you." An unpublished draft dedication to *Death of A Lady's Man*, written some four years after the death of Hershorn, enlarges his importance for Cohen, who refers to him as

> the Lion of our Youth, the Eagle of Experience, the Grizzly Bear of our Forest and the highest leaping Deer of our Imagination . . . My Pupil in Music, my Teacher in War, Addict of God, Original as an Explosion . . . Companion, Companion, Companion murdered by Mid-wives in Hong Kong, buried in Montreal snow weeks later, black and bloated, under Hasid supervision.

In 1979, Cohen remembered Hershorn in the dedication of his album *Recent Songs* with these words: "To the late Robert Hershorn, who many years ago put into my hands the books of the old Persian poets, Attar and Rumi, whose imagery influenced several songs, especially 'The Guests' and 'The Window.'" In 1994, Cohen published a prose poem entitled "Robert Appears Again," in which Cohen, stimulated by a tab of speed, holds an imaginary conversation with his friend in a Paris cafe. Admitting to him that "I can't seem to bring anything to completion and I'm in real trouble," he comically ends the meeting by castigating Hershorn for not excusing himself before "disappearing again for who knows how long."

After the birth of his son, Cohen's relationship with Suzanne became problematic. "It was a tricky time," he remembered. For help, he left Montreal and went to California to visit the Zen master Roshi at Mount

Baldy. "It began," he explained, with "a need for self-reform." He had phoned Steve Sanfield, who was now living north of Nevada City, California, and asked if he could be introduced to his teacher: "I can't get this cat out of my head. Take me to see him," Cohen said. Sanfield took him to the Cimarron Zen Center where they had tea with Roshi. The conversation was sparse but Roshi said, "Bring friend to Baldy!" Baldy was an abandoned boy scout camp in the San Gabriel Mountains that had been recently acquired by the Rinzai movement. It became the Mt. Baldy Zen Center in the spring of 1971. Cohen and Sanfield drove to the center, and then Sanfield left Cohen there. His only advice was about the Lotus position: "It's going to hurt like hell; don't move. It will just hurt worse."

It was winter and there was snow in the mountains. After three days Cohen was convinced it was "the revenge of World War II." With a Japanese teacher and German head monk named Geshin, "they had a bunch of these American kids walking around in the snow at 3:00 a.m. in sandals." The snow blew over their food in the dining hall. Cohen lasted a few weeks and then went over the wall: the regime, the mountain cold, and the discipline were too difficult; he headed for the heat of Mexico. In retrospect, he thought Roshi was a nice old rabbinical figure, but he didn't quite get what he was saying. He felt he didn't need it anyway. He ate a lot of ginseng and drove to Tijuana, then drove back to Los Angeles and called Suzanne. The two of them went to Acapulco, and their experience appears in the poem that begins "O darling (as we used to say)" in *The Energy of Slaves*:

> Even as we lie here in Acapulco
> not quite in each others' arms
> several young monks walk single-file
> through the snow on Mount Baldy
> shivering and farting in the moonlight:
> there are passages in their meditation
> that treat our love and wish us well

In Acapulco, a photo of Cohen with his Buddhist haircut, taken in a hotel bathroom, shows him glaring at the viewer, one hand holding a cigar, the other looped in a belt. The picture first appeared as an uncaptioned, rear jacket photo on *The Energy of Slaves* (1972) and was later used as the cover for his 1973 album, *Live Songs*. A second photo taken in Acapulco shows him sitting on the edge of a bathtub, looking slightly less menacing and more relaxed.

Despite his initial escape, Cohen eventually returned to Zen: "I dreamed about this, I longed for something like this. I didn't know it existed; the formality of the system, the spiritual technology was there; it was no bullshit. You *could do it* if you wanted, if you developed your will." He started to practice with some regularity, and for a time in the early seventies he became Roshi's secretary and accompanied Roshi to various Trappist monasteries where Cohen would occasionally lead the *sesshins* for the monks. Roshi's *koan* for the monks consisted of one question: "How do you realize Jesus Christ when you make the sign of the cross?"

In *The Energy of Slaves* he addressed the ambiguous problem of art no longer being able to remove him from his personal responsibilities. He was upset at the absence of creativity:

Where are the poems
that led me away
from everything I loved.

The Energy of Slaves was a difficult and troubling book that dramatically shifted from the mythology of *Let Us Compare Mythologies*, the romanticism of *The Spice-Box of Earth*, and the historical focus of *Flowers for Hitler* to a personal self-loathing and even a loathing of sex. "In many ways, I like that book the best of anything I've ever done," Cohen said in a 1993 interview, because it is one "of the strongest pieces that I've ever done." A poem summarizing his life concludes with:

Welcome to this book of slaves
which I wrote during your exile
you lucky son-of-a-bitch
while I had to contend

> with all the flabby liars
> of the Aquarian Age

There is some humor in the book, usually in the form of satire: "Come down to my room / I was thinking about you / and I made a pass at myself." He is candid about sex, describing his four months with the twenty-year-old Valentia or his time with Terez at the Chelsea or his desire for a woman he sees: "Why don't you come over to my table / with no pants on / I'm sick of surprising you." With his belated fame he can at last have "the 15-year-old girls," he could never acquire in his youth:

> I have them now
> it is very pleasant
> it is never too late
> I advise you all
> to become rich and famous

As Cohen comically admits to himself, "I am no longer at my best practising / the craft of verse / I do better / in the cloakroom with Sara." His goal is to "write with compassion about the deceit in the human heart."

In *The Energy of Slaves* Cohen introduced a theme that his later poetry, especially *Death of A Lady's Man*, extended: the failure of imagination and inspiration when love and beauty are attained. He expressed this in the ironically but aptly titled "The Progress of My Style," in which he shows why his art fails. "Each man / has a way to betray / the revolution / This is mine," he searingly admits, as he acknowledges the betrayals of his past, his love, and his art. Both poetry and love deceive him as his very identity shifts: "I have no talent left / I can't write a poem anymore / You can call me Len or Lennie now." In a 1975 interview he said of *The Energy of Slaves*, "It was like dipping all the parts into tetrachloride to clean them—I wanted to get back into my own baroque from a clean position." Introducing each poem in the book was the silhouette of a razor blade.

LIFE in 1973 was troubling on every front, as a candid unpublished auto-biographical account from that summer indicates:

> I'm thirty-eight years of age, five feet eight inches tall, a hundred and thirty-five pounds, brown hair, hazel eyes. I live in Montreal. It is the summer of 1973. Right now I have the solemn violins of the radio to accompany me. I've had [the] usual jobs. I was a popular singer for a while with my own band. I had a chance to meet a lot of girls on the road. I was very girl-crazy, after a while just cunt-crazy.
>
> I don't give a shit about your idea about human dignity because none of them ever include me. I don't care who you are and what noble form of torture you represent. You can shut this book.
>
> Don't come to me when you are sweet and cold. Come when you are nasty and warm if you want to hear a story. This is a fascinating story. It's about the fat, dead world.

By now, Cohen had an infant son and an impressive body of work but little peace of mind. He had stopped writing songs and stopped loving Suzanne. "While she suffers, I have a chance to breathe the free air and look under the flab for my body," he wrote in March. Two days later, he added, "Listening to gypsy violins, my jeep rusting in Tennessee, married as usual to the wrong woman." His relationship had deteriorated to no more than "fighting over scraps of freedom, getting even."

Live Songs came out in April 1973 to little notice. For more than a decade, it was the last of Cohen's albums to even make the U.S. charts. The album contained a range of concert songs drawn from the 1970 and 1972 tours and was uneven but spontaneous. The mood was somber, the songs full of darkness, and the cover photo haunting. The unusual liner notes by the little-known (and often institutionalized) artist and poet Daphne Richardson read in part that a transformation occurred because of "the mad mystic hammering of your body upon my body [and] your soul entered mine then and some union took place that almost killed me with its INTENSITY." She had begun communicating with Cohen while trying to publish a book of collage poems using pieces by Cohen, Dylan, and herself. Cohen found her letters engaging and often wrote to her, excusing her excesses as part of her illness.

Cohen found the intensity of her imagination attractive and her work as an illustrator appealing; he wanted her to illustrate *The Energy of Slaves*. He met her in London during his 1972 tour. A month later, he called his London agent requesting her to tell Daphne that her illustrations for his poetry book would be needed, only to learn that she had committed suicide three days earlier by jumping off Bush House in London. Cohen was mentioned in her suicide note.

The music on *Live Songs* continued the themes of *Songs of Love and Hate*. Bob Johnston again produced the album, essentially a mixing of live tapes from the two previous tours. It opens with "Minute Prologue," from London (1972), a recitation on the dissension and pain in the world that won't disappear, although music can heal any damage it causes. One of the most important songs on the album, "Seems So Long Ago, Nancy," continues the focus on death and despair and, as the liner notes explain, is about a suicidal woman from Montreal whom Cohen knew in 1961. The daughter of a judge, she had had a reckless life, sleeping with everyone and eventually giving birth to a child, who was then taken away from her. She shot herself in her bathroom. As he wrote, "In the House of Honesty / Her father was on trial / In the House of Mystery / There was no one at all."

Reaction to the album was negative. A rumor began to circulate that Cohen was going to retire from music, a rumor that upset his lawyer and record company. There was also the suggestion of suicide. In a March 1973 interview, he smoked the interviewer's cigarettes almost continuously and appeared withdrawn. He answered questions vaguely and lapsed into long, uninterrupted silences. The threat of suicide had always accompanied his morose persona and funereal songs but he later admitted, "I'm too old to commit suicide. It would be unbecoming."

The *Toronto Star* unknowingly promoted the retirement controversy, picking up an English story reporting that Cohen had quit the music business. Thinking that he was speaking in confidence following receipt of a Gold Album award from *Melody Maker* for two hundred and fifty thousand sales of his first LP, Cohen told reporter Roy Hollingworth, "I just cannot stand to remain part of the [music] business. I've reached a state when I'm just not writing anything." A week later, he enlarged on the theme of disillusionment and his decision "no longer . . . to be tangled up in the mechanisms" of the industry. The industry viewed his comments as an attack. He said that his decision had been made ten months earlier when he entered a Buddhist monastery in California. He planned to continue to write songs only "if I feel they are good."

In a later interview in the *Toronto Star*, Cohen explained the confusion about his remarks on retirement, declaring, "I never did retire. I didn't announce that. It was a completely mischievous adventure on the part of a journalist in England." The two had been discussing the state of the music business and its depressing character. "And I said, 'But I don't want to see a headline: Leonard Cohen quits music business and goes into monastery. And the next week I pick up the paper and it's been reprinted all around the world." No one was more surprised than his lawyer Marty Machat, who spent days phoning music publishers and record company executives to tell them Cohen was very much in the business. But what's to quit, Cohen added: "I mean how can I quit? I've never been in it. Nobody's making me do anything. I've done three tours, only a record every two or three years—that's not much for a singer. I've always been able to play it as I wanted. What is there to quit?"

Ironically, at the time of the controversy, his work was being celebrated. In July 1973 at the Shaw Festival, Gene Lesser, a New York director, was preparing a production of "Sisters of Mercy." Its opening led to this headline in a Canadian paper: "Bed-centered play aimed at open-minded people." Based on Cohen's songs and work, the play went to New York after its Canadian premiere and opened off Broadway at the Theatre de Lys. Clive Barnes of the *New York Times* panned it, writing that if the play was a "musical journey into the words of Leonard Cohen," as the program stated, "it is, to be frank, a journey that I would rather not have taken." Barnes also criticized the play's autobiographical element: "Unfortunately, while Mr. Cohen may very well be . . . God's final gift to women, he doesn't shape up so well as either a poet or a musician. As a poet he is cute, as a musician he is familiar." Cohen himself disliked the production.

COHEN FELT that his life was becoming a battle for survival, and the opportunity to participate in a real war was too tempting to resist. He and his family had returned to Hydra in August 1973. But to test himself and to escape the turmoil of his personal life, Cohen flew to Israel from Athens a few days before the Yom Kippur War began in October 1973, partly out of a determination to help, partly "to recover from vanities of the singing profession," and, as he wrote in the unpublished prose work "The Final Revision of My Life in Art," partly "because it is so horrible between us I will go and stop Egypt's bullet. Trumpets and a curtain of razor blades." When he arrived, he told the press that he flew to Israel to entertain troops during the conflict and "to make my atonement." He added that in the past he sided with the Arabs in their demands that Israel return territory taken by it in the 1967 war, but now he supported the Jewish state.

Cohen left Hydra and the difficulties with Suzanne. "What a burden for the woman being born to carry still-born blessings up the hill . . . I must study the hatred I have for her, and how it is transmuted into desire by solitude and distance." He felt she restrained him and curbed his success: "I never became a sign for everything that is high and nervous . . . the band ran down like an unwound music-box, too slow and too sweet. A fungus became attached to the spirit of song and high pretensions infected the gift of words." He made a pact: "I won't fuck in the Holy Land unless she is my True Wife."

At the airport he got the last seat on the flight to Tel Aviv and his attitude quickly changed:

> Nothing can stop me. My luck has changed. The girls in uniform smile at my airport style. I hate to leave them all behind. This man's traveling. I am thin again and loose. I suntan myself from within. We can fall in love now, we already have, it doesn't matter, goodbye.

Sitting on the floor at the airport with his leather bag, he felt conspicuous, and after a quick visit to the airport post office, he was stopped by a plainclothes security officer, who questioned him in the men's room about his destination. When the officer discovered that Cohen spoke some Greek and that he was flying to Israel, he was released. The unexpected expression of democratic ideals expounded by a poet in Greek convinced the police to let him go. As he waited to be searched before boarding the plane, his thoughts shifted: "I could see that certain people had recognized me. No one I wanted to fuck but some I wanted to look at naked, especially a girl whose eyes are looking at me now."

He arrived in a tense and nervous country, admitting, "I am in my myth home but I have no proof and I cannot debate and I am in no danger of believing myself . . . Speaking no Hebrew I enjoy my legitimate silence." He accepted the invitation of a married couple he had met on the flight to stay with her mother and sister in Herzliyya, a suburb of Tel Aviv. The sister immediately inflamed him, but he deflected his interest when he learned that the war was not that easily found, despite the sad news about the fighting on the radio every hour. The mother and daughter still went to the beach every day; "The war was somewhere else."

Despite his nominal pact with himself, Cohen became involved with a series of women in Israel. A tall, red-haired woman with "long, stainless steel legs" and a body he called "a sexual construction"; a Yemenite broadcaster who had interviewed him two years earlier; and a girl who recognized him in the lobby of a movie theater. One incident, he said was symbolic:

> I went immediately to the Cafe Pinoti, looking for Hanna. There was nobody on the street. I decided to quit looking for her. This event has the essential quality of my life in art.

After returning from the beach, he continued his search. "After I had showered and changed, I walked up and down the vacant blacked-out streets looking for Hanna, longing for her. Such patrols are a usual feature of my life in art."

Most of his assignations occurred in the Gad Hotel on Hayarkon Street in Tel Aviv. After checking into the Gad, Cohen heard footsteps outside his room. It was the tall and stiking woman he had just met at the desk. He heard an interior voice saying, "You will only sing again if you give up lechery. Choose. This is a place where you may begin again." Another voice countered, "But I want her . . . Please let me have her." The inner voice that won advised him to, "Throw yourself upon your stiffness and take up your felt pen." His attitude toward women remained shameless; he invited women reporters to undress for him, or at least bare their breasts during an interview.

Shortly after moving to the hotel, he went to see the singer/promoter Sholomo Semach, who was attached to the air force. Cohen wanted to volunteer, and Semach immediately lined him up with an entertainment group in the air force. Before he started, however, the Israeli singer Ilana Rovina invited him to perform one night at an air base near Tel Aviv, which he did. He then joined her group for performances in the Sinai, flying in on a Dakota aircraft. At a desert airport he stole a .45 pistol from a deserted shed, armament for the battle. Soon after his return to Tel Aviv, he had a new assignment: Cohen, Matti Caspi, and a third entertainer drove around and sang at rocket sites, tank encampments, aide stations, and army posts. They were flown by helicopter across the Suez to a former Egyptian air base, where they performed in a concrete hangar. Cohen was startled to find there a leftover Egyptian calendar and a can of mashed potatoes that had a label which read, "A Gift from the People of Canada." A helicopter arrived with wounded men, and Cohen began to weep as he stared at the bandaged soldiers. When someone told him that the troops were Egyptian, his relief disturbed him. But when an Israeli soldier gave him some Egyptian money found on a dead soldier, he could not take it and buried it in the sand.

He then drove with others toward Ismailia and General Sharon's encampment, where "tanks are the only architecture."

I am introduced to a great general, "The Lion of the Desert." Under my breath I ask him, "How dare you?" He does not repent. We drink some cognac sitting on the sand in the shade of a tank. I want his job.

Returning to the Egyptian airfield, they came under fire and were forced to take cover. Cohen fantasized: "I manage to kill an arrogant Israeli officer who has been bugging me with relentless requests to sing Suzanne. The scales are balanced. Let justice be done. I doubt if I made this up." Lurking behind his actions was this constant question: "May I entertain the notion of Personal Purity as the condition for my Task?" It was a question that he had asked of himself in Cuba as well.

The performances were ad hoc, with soldiers shining flashlights on the singers. "It was very informal and very intense," Cohen said. "Wherever you saw soldiers you would just stop and sing." Occasionally there was danger, "but you get caught up in the thing. And the desert is very beautiful and you think your life is meaningful for a moment or two. And war is wonderful . . . It's one of the few times people can act their best. It's so economical in terms of gesture and motion. . . . Everybody is responsible for his brother." War and earning a living are the only two activities that ever permit men to leave women, he added. He explains this in "My Life in Art": "Feeling good in the desert. War is ok . . . As my friend Layton said about acid on his first 'trip': 'They'll never stamp this out.'"

Before Cohen left Israel, he decided that he had to visit Jerusalem. He believed that if he walked there from Tel Aviv he would be cleansed. He quickly got lost in the outskirts of Tel Aviv, however, and found himself wandering back to Dizengoff Street, with its numerous cafes. The next day he took a bus to the Holy City, where that night at dinner, his friend Asher confronted him: "You must decide whether you are a lecher or a priest."

After a month or so, Cohen left Israel, which was demoralized because it had experienced heavy casualities in the war. He reported, however, that "people stop me and thank me here and there and tell me never to leave Jerusalem." He took a military flight to Athens but flew on to Asmara, Ethiopia, where he lived in the Imperial Hotel for a while, writing songs and re-assessing his life. Ironically, this too would become a site of war some six weeks later, when a revolution occurred. At the Imperial, he finished "Chelsea Hotel #2" and began several songs incorporating his Israeli experience: "Field Commander Cohen," for example, is about a surrealistic spy known for parachuting "acid into diplomatic cocktail parties" who returns to nothing more than "silver bullet suicides, and messianic ocean tides / And racial roller-coaster rides / And other forms of boredom advertised as poetry."

Cohen returned to Hydra to shore up the ruins of his relationship with Suzanne. But things got worse, their bitterness became more pronounced. She wanted both "passion and possession." Yet by September, the family was back in Montreal and Cohen was again a father, this time of a daughter, Lorca. They were living in the small cottage Cohen had bought on St-Dominique Street. But family life was still resistant to happiness as a journal entry confirms:

> It all breaks down for the sake of peace and it all breaks down for the sake of peace . . . it won't break down, the guilt, the intrigue, the thrones of waiting women, all in the service of fresh love. They say it all breaks down for the sake of peace.

A letter from Suzanne recounted her bitterness. She "says I took away her life and now I owe her something enormous. She wants it in a box of blood and family jewels." Cohen, however, could not "make peace with the language of love."

Despite the animosities between him and Suzanne, Cohen no longer felt that he had earned the right to sing his songs of heartache. He believed he had not suffered, not lost anyone, not experienced enough pain to justify his lyrics. A journal entry summarized his state: "It's no good if it ain't the woman that you love. Write songs but your heart will never sing." Tormenting him was an unaswerable question: "What unfreezes a man?"

10

T I B E T A N

D E S I R E

W ITH ITS EMPHASIS on suffering, Zen remained a
constant attraction for Cohen. Concentrating on
meditation and rejecting materialism, Zen com-
plemented the austerity he had pursued in Greece. "I needed so much /
To have nothing to touch / I've always been greedy that way," he sings
in "The Night Comes On." He also valued Zen's focus on the individual as the key to salvation: "If you want to see God, you must realize the
basis of your self," Roshi had proclaimed.

Cohen sought Roshi's counsel in all things, including his music. He
invited his Zen master to a recording session of *New Skin for the Old Ceremony.* The next day at breakfast Roshi told Cohen, "You should sing
sadder." Cohen felt that he lacked the courage or the ability to explore
his malaise. "I need to go deeper, always deeper," he said in 1991. One

of his attractions to Zen was that it forced him to go deeper and discover new truths about himself. It also allowed him to write with greater simplicity and purity. Although Cohen doubted the strength of his material, he did believe that from the mid-seventies through the early eighties at least his voice was true. Zen, he thought, would make his work accessible to himself.

On his earliest visits to Mt. Baldy, Cohen found the regime too difficult. But if the discipline was too much, the ideas were seductive and he perservered. During the mid-seventies Cohen made regular visits to the Zen retreat, where he immersed himself in the rigors of Zen practice. From the 3:00 a.m. rising to the hours of sitting, *zazen*, and then *sanzen*, and personal interviews with Roshi, Cohen gained the spiritual vocabulary he sought. He learned how to get rid of the baggage that prevented him from deepening his work. "When I go there," he reported in 1980, "it's like scraping off the rust."

While Zen was helping him with his work, he was still struggling with love, as a passage in *Death of A Lady's Man* outlines. In a sunlit suite of the Château Marmont on Sunset Boulevard, Cohen describes himself in the arms of a beautiful American woman, agitated and staring at the clock. His desires are fulfilled, but he is also at "the end of [his] life in art." At forty-one, love has brought death, not life, to his creativity: "Six-fifty [a.m.]. Ruined in Los Angeles . . . I want to die in her arms and leave her." The desire for women no longer satisfies him; the reality of their being possessed tarnishes his idolatry of them. "I swim in your love but I drown in loneliness." As he would later sing, "I came so far for beauty / I left so much behind / My patience and my family / My masterpiece unsigned."

A contradiction remained at the center of his life expressed by the idea of "Tibetan Desire." The phrase, appearing in *Beautiful Losers*, represents the unholy union between renunciation and longing and the difficulty in divorcing one from the other. For Cohen, they do not cancel but complement each other. Intensifying the need for denial is the determination to possess by pleasure what cannot be attained by sacrifice. The two forces interact rather than collide, creating a desperate synergy that drives his work. The spiritual feeds the physical; the physical nourishes the spiritual. Zen and passion are the twin points of this condition in which there are no victors.

Throughout the summer of 1974, Cohen attempted to resolve these issues in a new work, conceived as a novel but experimental in form. It included prose, poetry, memoir, and journals. A remarkable, unpublished document, it contained three separate divisions: "The Dictation," "Among Yellow Daisies, Summer 1975," and "Random Evidence and Subtle Visitors, 1972–1975." The sections dealt with his visit to Israel, with Hydra, and with Montreal.

He began the text in the stone basement of his Hydra home during a four-day fast and with only oil lamps to light the page. "I am growing sick in the monastery of marriage. This book is the mind of marriage," he declares at the outset. Despite Cohen's anger with both the marriage and Suzanne, it was she who helped Cohen arrange the materials of the first draft.

The text is constantly self-referential and critical of Suzanne:

Once I walked across the polished stages of all Europe. The girls waited, lined up in hallways. But you took away their beauty. You put beauty beyond my reach. Night after night you locked me against the woman of unbeauty. Bite into this one. This is where you break your teeth and amaze yourself with hopelessness.

Cohen's anger in the work grows into a rage: "Goodnight once again, you fucking plagiarists. All your stolen girlfriends don't make up for my songs' disgust under your headline names. Trees and photographs. The last night of a real poet." Cohen saw himself as trapped, while Suzanne had what she needed:

The man in chains looked down at her hair as she snuggled in his shoulder like a rifle-butt. Toward the horizon mist fumed out of the water changing clearly into the eternal shapes of comfort and poetry. I will bring thee down, I said to myself. She has given me the bullet.

In the book, Cohen revisits themes in his life, their significance and their passing. Of hypnosis, he writes, "I lost that when I was fourteen. I had it for two years. I had music for about the same time. I should turn my back on it." He thinks of falling in love again with Suzanne, "It's the least painful thing." But it doesn't happen. A letter from Roshi suggests he give up performing and touring and come to the desert to write for two years and Cohen is tempted. But his work gets progressively bleaker:

> Too early for the rainbow,
> Too early for the Dove
> These are the Final Days, this is
> The Darkness, this is the Flood.

Cohen was again returning to the inescapable theme of life versus art. One of the attractions of art was that it is equated with sex. Marriage is death.

> So the Chinese girl is unmolested
> and her life turns out okay without me,
> my slow erection unmanifested
> except within the pants of poetry.

Despite Cohen's ongoing and serious doubts, an inner confidence or artistic vanity still surfaced. "It will become clear that I am the stylist of my era and the only honest man in town. I did not quarrel with my voices."

While he was working on his memoir, his album *New Skin for the Old Ceremony* was released, his first collection of new material since *Songs of Love and Hate* in 1971. Recorded in New York, the album reflects the military experience of Israel and his constant flirtation with personal and political disaster. He reworked an early song, "The Bells," recording it as "Take This Longing." The quest for lost love pervades the album. "You got old and wrinkled / I stayed seventeen," he sings in "Is This What you Wanted?" "There Is A War" summarized Cohen's own condition rather than Israel's, one where love itself has been devalued: "I rise up from her arms, / She says, 'I guess you call this love, / I call it Room Service.'" He admits that in the past he had been easily defeated, but now he understands that to survive as an artist, he must fight.

In "A Singer Must Die" and "Chelsea Hotel #2," Cohen illustrated the links between his life and his art. These goals coincided with his renewed commitment to Zen, and the quest for purity. When his art deceived this purity, it wasn't art. What he must obtain is purity, clarity, purpose: the condition of zero.

New Skin for the Old Ceremony was enhanced by a new sound, the result of John Lissauer's production. Although Cohen lists himself as co-producer, it was Lissauer who made the difference. Cohen had first heard him in a Montreal club, playing with Lewis Furey, a Montreal friend and musician with whom Cohen would later write an opera. On the album Furey plays viola. Cohen and Lissauer talked, and then Cohen played him a number of his half-finished songs. Lissauer, he says, "has the deepest understanding of my music," and by early 1976, he and Lissauer were collaborating on new songs, something Cohen had never expected to do with anyone. On *New Skin*, individual strings, horns, and wood-winds extended but didn't overwhelm Cohen's voice. The album art created a minor controversy, however. It originally consisted of a symbolic representation of the *coniunctio spirituum*, or the spiritual union of the male and female principle from a sixteenth-century alchemical text entitled *Rosararium philosophorum*. But the arcane information on the engraving did not defuse its overt sexual imagery. In the U.S., Columbia Records thought the image was too explicit and replaced it with a photograph of Cohen on some copies, although Cohen wasn't informed of the change. In England they adjusted the wing to cover the genital area because the record company thought naked angels might offend a church-going public. Regardless of the cover, the album was not well received, failing to break into the charts in the United States and doing only moderately well in the United Kingdom, despite a promotional tour to support it. In Europe, however, it sold two hundred and fifty thousand copies in its first six weeks.

After the record appeared, Cohen and Lissauer began work on another album. Tentatively called "Songs for Rebecca," six or seven songs were recorded, but Cohen chose to kill the project, and it was never released. Only one song was salvaged, "Came so Far for Beauty," which later appeared on *Recent Songs* (1979).

In the fall of 1974 Cohen began his third and longest European tour:

thirty-three concerts in fifty days, opening in Brussels and ending in Paris. He played two concerts in Barcelona and dedicated one of the concerts to Lorca. Because Cohen was so popular in Spain, his work was almost immediately translated into Spanish. In London he concluded his concert by saying, "Thank you for remembering the songs which I wrote, all those years ago, in a room." Part of Cohen's great stage appeal was the humility he projected.

In late November 1974, Cohen began a small North American tour, performing to sold-out crowds at the Bottom Line in the Village. He was interviewed by Danny Fields who asked him why he was so popular in Europe. Cohen replied, "Maybe it's because they can't understand my lyrics." He outlined the link between his private and performing life. "When I stand on a stage, I feel I bring my private life with me there and that that's what's interesting or amusing. That's what's entertaining about me." In December he played the Troubadour in Los Angeles for three nights, and received "one of the strongest standing ovations one has ever witnessed at the club." Four encores were necessary to close out the show and, after the performance, Dylan came by.

Cohen was now spending part of his time with a woman named Lauren, a woman he called "the first lover in my new life . . . we are the beginning of an army. To whom can we offer our victory. I do bow down and kiss your nipples. Or was that the girl I saw last night [?]" He continued to tour, taking the show to Canada. He played at a psychiatric hospital in London, Ontario, and at Toronto's Massey Hall, before returning to Avery Fisher Hall in New York. The *New York Times* opened its review with: "There is a lot one could dislike about Leonard Cohen." However, the review was largely a celebration of Cohen's uniqueness: his language was imaginative and his tunes hypnotic, their repetitiveness recalling medieval music and ancient folk tunes. "If Mr. Cohen's voice is limited in its range, it is quite evocative in color."

The tour was interrupted in late 1974 to attend a recording session in Nashville for the Earl Scruggs Anniversary Special, where "Passing Thru" was recorded with Billy Joel, Joan Baez, Buffy Sainte-Marie, Ramblin' Jack Elliot, the Pointer Sisters, and Cohen.

In April he returned to Montreal to give his first concert there in four years. It was only partially successful. He performed in the small

Théâtre du Nouveau Monde, which held just over a thousand people, and projected a sense of weariness as he began the first of his two concerts with a tired smile and "Bird on the Wire." One critic wrote, "he looks like an overworked boutique owner" and complained that there was "a mechanical manner to his movements, the manner of a hospitalized hyper-depressive." He sang a second version of "Bird on the Wire" in French and did six encores.

After his tour, in the spring of 1975, Cohen returned to Hydra, newly troubled and despondent. His success and his family brought him no comfort. Writing in the cool darkness of his basement room or on the terrace, he dissected the present and recalled the past:

> It is not exactly a foam of daisies. It is something less than opulence. I remember it all as richer and yellower . . . Negotiations with the woman. Careful words. Countless adjustments to keep the balance and the floor away from your face . . . Ten years ago, I made a speech to these daisies and they are all turned toward me. It was pretty bad ten years ago, before the world knew me, but now it's a lot worse . . . Those beautiful mornings, empty of bowel and honored by amphetamine, they gone, baby, they gone . . . all this looked a lot more interesting ten years ago on acid. I addressed them [the daisies on his terrace] then in the style made popular by St. Francis.

He planned to marry Suzanne in Jerusalem, thinking this would save their relationship. But he also planned to sit an hour each day with Anthony Kingsmill and fish with Don Lowe, to go on the road again, to be "street father to the young writers in Montreal, using the harsh style," "to overthrow my life with fresh love," and:

> to teach my son that there is no light in this world. The plan to follow my true song no matter where . . . The plan to make my face noble and attractive through hard work and brave decisions. The plan for my body . . . the plan to be thin and fast and kind. My plan for you. My throne for you. My cunning toward God . . . The plan to escape. The plan not to witness.

But all of these plans remained unrealized. He was at war with himself and with Suzanne: "I am going to tune you until the string breaks . . . I have declared war on you forever and forever."

He spent his time analyzing his career as artist and lover. Memories of his life eight years ago with another woman returned and "then the obscene silence of my career, while the butchers climbed on the throne, and they hacked the veil away, and they stood there above us grinning . . . I was divided into three parts. One part was given to a wife, one part was given to money, one part was given to the daisies . . . I broke under the sentence of loneliness and the wound of my beautiful twin." Women, he told Kingsmill, have no sense of measure and are "created so much tougher and wilder than we are . . . they want to destroy the system" and their "primitive souls" become intoxicated with "the sense of shame and opportunity."

His own relationships with women had been largely on his own terms but Suzanne had demanded hostages to his future. "I gave a woman a house and babies just because she insisted," he wrote. Cohen's introspection culminated in a landscape that was simultaneously external and internal:

The moon is over the windmill. I sit here with a blanket around my shoulders. The daisies are all collapsed. It is very quiet. A dog is barking. I hope I can leave the garden soon. A clicking insect measures out a portion of the lightest breeze . . . A wave bends me over the blue table, and a dream of the mountain rolling down over the roofs and the daisies.

Cohen resolved to rebel "against Domestic Conversations," the repressive relationship that had lost its love, and the home that had lost its meaning. Referring to both Marianne and Suzanne, he wrote:

The first woman spun it around her like a skirt, faster and faster, brighter and brighter, until I fell off the edge of her hem and the next one turned the other way, dark and silent and greedy, gathering everything in, and I went into it, like a canoe into a windspout, but she was not at the center, she didn't know how to be there . . . I can't flourish the old table like a banner of order and solitude. I am here to work in the garden. I am no longer your host.

Empty, he awaited the salvation that might rescue him from this purgatory. "Without the Name, I am a funeral in the garden. Waiting for the next girl." He expanded this theme in "I Should Not Say You," a prose poem from *Death of Lady's Man*: "My heart longs to be a chamber for the Name . . . Without the Name the wind is a babble, the flowers are a jargon of longing . . . Without the Name sealed in my heart I am ashamed."

Throughout his life Cohen has preferred the more formal Leonard to any other form of address because it defines his identity as a writer. "Names preserve the dignity of Appearance," F. declares in *Beautiful Losers*. Earlier, in *Parasites of Heaven*, Cohen writes of himself that "Leonard hasn't been the same / since he wandered from his name," implying that his life in England and Greece has undermined and altered the anticipated plan of a middle-class life in Montreal. Cohen's signature, on letters, documents, or autographs, always reads, in clearly printed script, "Leonard Cohen." Yet he mocked his own formality in "The Other Village:"

When it comes to lamentations
I prefer Aretha Franklin
to, let's say, Leonard Cohen
Needless to add, he hears a different drum

The final poem of *Death of A Lady's Man* extended Cohen's self-portrait:

I am almost 90
Everyone I know has died off
except Leonard
He can still be seen
hobbling with his love

Cohen's relationship with Suzanne was deteriorating in a more graphic way than his relationship with Marianne had. "We will go back to that creek in Tennessee," he wrote, "and she will shoot me with a .22." His frustration increased: "I should have killed you in the war. I didn't know that you would turn black and play the trumpet. . . . In a corner of my heart, I planted and watered and sang to the seeds of revenge . . . the garden is ruined and this vigil is coming to an end."

Suzanne felt abandoned by Cohen, who was always either traveling or writing and had little time for her. She retaliated by acting like Cohen, staying out until 4:00 a.m. Cohen was angry and replaced Suzanne with others: Stephanie, who was sixteen, and Sherry, "who loves me for something I said ten years ago." There was "a blonde giant" named Vala who bit him all over his body, and one named Danae, who stayed with him a week at the Athens Hilton: "Did I know she was only fifteen? I thought she was only thirteen. I tried to seduce the mother and she calmed down a little." A bout of gonorrhea caught from an Australian woman required a trip to Athens and a penicillin injection but it did not deter him. While undergoing treatment in Athens, he pined for the women he couldn't have:

> Desire in Athens disordered me. I saw a woman on a motorcycle, her thigh exposed. The buttocks of the telephone operator. Stephanie somewhere in the neighborhood. The girl from Radcliff reclining on a bed of ideas where I did not join her. All this fed my hatred and I could not welcome her [his dark companion]. As soon as I came back to my blue desk, my heart welcomed her. She does not give me songs but she is the muse of discipline.

His Greek friend George Lialios said that he and Cohen had a "thirst for, and attraction to, the opposite sex in all of its varieties, and with it the dream of some ideal woman that belonged to the sphere of metaphysics rather than to reality. All of Leonard's erotic poetry bears the seal of this longing."

In a 1980 film interview, Cohen admitted that he had been completely obsessed with women ever since he could remember. As he became more well known, this obsession was reciprocated. His aura of "spiritual poverty" made women want to help him. Once, at a Montreal party Cohen approached a tall, beautiful woman with long, dark hair.

He took a piece of her hair, dipped it into his wine glass, and slowly proceeded to suck it dry. He then let it fall and walked away without uttering a word.

Awaiting another woman at the Athens Hilton, Cohen meditated on power and beauty:

To see me you must leave your consolation. You must forsake your mediocre ecstasy, your mediocre exercise of bliss. Put on your muscles and step out of the perfumed shower which has shriveled and softened you. . . . I go without a name from heart to heart, saying Courage, courage, you are already brave, knowing full well that they will die without the sight of her beauty.

By the summer of 1974 the woman from the Athens Hilton was with him in Hollywood, where Cohen realized that he "had not been denied the full measure of beauty . . . When we make love in the morning, the whole day is like coming off acid." But with such beauty came fear and the inability to create: "If I could write a song for her I could pay for this suite. . . . The table, the climate, the perfect physique for a forty-year-old artist, famous, happy, frightened."

In 1975 Cohen took a trip with Roshi to visit Zen monasteries in Japan and witnessed a monk slithering on his belly to the feet of a Zen master to present him with tea. Invited to ask the Master a question, Cohen was surprisingly silent. He remembered the beautiful calligraphy on the wall and thinking that "we didn't get this one," referring to the American bombardment of Japan and the untouched monastery. Upon returning, his religious convictions, always transient, shifted once more. "I decided to worship beauty the way some people go back to the religion of their fathers."

A reading tour of Italy to support the translation of several of his books followed. He went to Milan, then to Florence and Rome for readings and talks and was captivated by the women. In Milan there was a female doctor, and a woman named Lori; in Florence, Hugette; in Rome, Patricia. Sitting with Patricia at an outdoor cafe, he saw two doves fly toward him "in the style of the Holy Spirit descending. . . . I have been sitting in a cafe for twenty-five years waiting for this vision. I surrender to the iron laws of the moral universe which make a boredom out of everything desired. I will go back to my dark companion [Suzanne]. I don't think I will." In Rome he had a vivid fantasy about joining the Communist Party, which caused the rivers of his childhood to rise up, with snakes and sailboats, and his memory to fail as a series of ghosts spoke to him, including W.B. Yeats, "who lighted up a stick of sandalwood for my blurred soul, and the factories stamped out ten million hearts as false as mine . . . The ghosts of many crickets sang Another Man Done Gone, and little pebbles flew from my forehead against the stained glass windows of the CIA." Yet he could not write, and longed passionately for the embrace of young women. On the train from Florence to Rome, he sang into the open window but "the song could not redeem me."

Following a brief return to Hydra, and then to Montreal, Cohen headed on to California where Suzanne, Adam, and Lorca joined him. They were still trying to make the relationship work. But he wanted to escape, to write, and to sing. Roshi wanted him to move to Mt. Baldy with Suzanne and the children so that he could study with him. But Cohen felt it was the wrong time; he had work he wanted to do. By December he was back in Montreal attending Dylan's Rolling Thunder Review at the Montreal Forum. Throughout the winter he prepared new songs, and his commitment to Zen was again tested.

Columbia Records was planning to release *The Best of Leonard Cohen*, a compilation of twelve of his best-known songs, including "Suzanne," "Sisters of Mercy," "Bird on the Wire," and "Famous Blue Raincoat." Cohen had agreed to do the album because there was a new generation of listeners and because he was given complete artistic control. He picked the songs, designed the package, and insisted the lyrics be included. Cohen compiled the album in London, writing new liner notes for each song, identifying its origin. He also offered a personal critique of "Last Year's Man":

> I don't know why but I like this song. I used to play it on a Mexican
> twelve-string until I destroyed the instrument by jumping on it in a
> fit of impotent fury in 1967. The song had too many verses and it
> took about five years to sort out the right ones. I like the children in
> this version. I always wait for them if I have to listen to it.

By April 1976 he was on the road again with his most extensive European tour, to support the new album. Unsuccessful in the United States, *The Best of Leonard Cohen* was a hit in Europe, his major market in the seventies. He began the tour in Berlin on April 22 and ended in London on July 7. Roshi was lecturing in Europe at the time and appeared at the Munich concert. Backstage before the performance, he saw Cohen quickly down a tumbler of cognac and offered this observation: "Body important." A London critic remarked that the band had a definite rock quality and that a new up tempo but unrecorded song, "Do I Have to Dance All Night," was a great success. It is "surprising how he sings with so much more life outside a studio." In Paris Cohen gave four sold-out concerts with as many as twelve encores at some performances.

After the tour, Cohen and Suzanne spent the summer in Hydra, where he shared stories with Anthony Kingsmill and adventures with Pandias Scaramanga: "He told me about a whorehouse he had been to in Paris. I told him about a private club in New York." But Cohen's state of mind was fragile: "When I'm not plotting against everyone I know, or making myself look good in the eyes of the weak, my head is a din with the various commands of self-reform." He could neither write nor sing, yet he believed that "life is not perfectable, but work is." The only summer event that absorbed him was a play about the last days of Lorca written by a South African poet and performed in the lounge of a small hotel on Hydra. "Bitterly," he wrote, "I held on to my own barrenness all through the evening, doubting I would ever speak again in the old high way." However, Irving Layton's presence on the island temporarily evoked his good spirits and imagination.

Throughout 1976 Cohen increasingly found in Zen what he felt Judaism lacked: a focus on the methods of prayer and meditation. "I wanted to go into a system a little more thoroughly," he later explained. Meditation provided a respite from the turmoil of his private life. But an accident at Mt. Baldy in 1976 prevented him from sitting at any length in the *zendo*: late one night, he ran into a low wall and tore some cartilage in his knee. After treatment, it was still too painful for him to sit, so he returned to Judaism for spiritual sustenance, beginning a more deliberate, if private, study of the religion on his visits to Montreal. He prayed daily and put on *tefillin*. He made contact with several Hasidic rabbis and used

a bilingual Hasidic prayer book obtained through the Lubavitcher movement. The two religions worked in juxtaposition. "I came upon texts
and attitudes that I wouldn't have been able to understand if I hadn't
studied with my old Japanese teacher. . . . I did get one or two things
from Roshi that enabled me to penetrate, superficially, at least, the Jewish
tradition [but] without his instruction, I don't think I would have had the
attitude that allowed me to enter the tradition."

In California, Cohen continued to visit Roshi at Mt. Baldy or to get
up early to drive to the Cimarron Zen Center from the ranch house he
and Suzanne had rented in Brentwood. Anthony Kingsmill came to visit
and Bob Dylan, estranged from his wife, stayed for a while. But Roshi
increasingly commanded Cohen's life. On New Year's Eve Roshi,
Suzanne, Cohen, and Joni Mitchell met at Cohen's house, Mitchell
delayed by viewing Mae West's entrance with two bodybuilders at
Ringo Starr's New Year's Eve party, her first stop. Suzanne led the conversation to a favorite topic, sex. Cohen asked Roshi, "How do you get
rid of jealousy?" Before he could answer, Joni Mitchell said: "You quit it
like you quit smoking," and mimicked the crushing of a cigarette in an
ashtray. Cohen gave her a hostile glance, thinking perhaps that she had
intruded on Roshi's territory. But Roshi didn't seem to mind; as he prepared to leave, he hugged Mitchell and told her he wanted to move in
with her.

The appearance of *The Best of Leonard Cohen* and dropping sales led
some to think that Cohen's recording contract with Columbia had
ended. The release of his next album on Warner Brothers seemed to
confirm this, although Cohen said that he received a release to work
with legendary producer Phil Spector under the Warner Brothers label,
although the album finally came out on CBS International. Spector's reputation as a songwriter and producer came from another era. He was
responsible for the "wall of sound" that characterized "To Know Him Is
to Love Him," "Be My Baby," "River Deep, Mountain High," and
"He's a Rebel." Joni Mitchell warned Cohen about working with Spector, who she thought was difficult and past his prime. She had seen the
struggle John Lennon had had recording with him, since she had been
across the hall in the same complex at the time, recording her album
Court and Spark.

Right: Marianne Ihlen typing at the desk in Cohen's music room in Hydra. From the photograph used as the rear album cover for his second album, *Songs from a Room* (1969). Photo by L. Cohen.

Below: Cohen at the outset of his musical career. Left to right, Mimi Farina, Dave Van Ronk, Joan Baez, Leonard Cohen, Judy Collins, and Chad Mitchell on the guitar. Taken in Linda Leibman's New York apartment in 1966. Photo by Daniel Kramer.

* by Anna Marly - Hy Zaret,
MCA Mus., A Div. of MCA, Inc. (ASCAP)
All other songs
by L.C., Stranger Music Inc. (BMI)

Engineer: Neil Wilburn
Back-up: Ed Hudson

Cover design: Ira Friedlander/ Cover photo:

Columbia stereo records can be played
results. They will last as long as mono r
reveal full stereo sound when played on

Manufactured By Columbia Records/CBS,
® "Columbia" ℗ Marcas F

Above left: Suzanne Elrod in a photo from the late sixties.
Above right: Leonard Cohen performing at the Isle of Wight, August 31, 1970.

Peter Pan being read to Lorca and Adam by Leonard Cohen.

Cohen at his writing desk in his Montreal home in the early seventies with a bust of Irving Layton looking down and a series of manuscripts underneath the desk looking up. Photo by Sam Tata.

An impromptu performance in an Italian classroom undergoing
revolutionary redecoration in the early seventies.

Above left: Suzanne Elrod with her children Adam and Lorca.
Above right: Leonard Cohen under a Japanese umbrella held by a Zen monk.

Roshi, Leonard Cohen, and a Zen Monk in meditation in Japan in the mid seventies.

At the Mt. Baldy Zen Center with Roshi, his wife Haruyo Sasaki, and fellow students.

September 12, 1979. Celebrating his forty-fifth birthday on Hydra with a friend from Romania.

With Irving and Aviva Layton in Montreal under a helpful sign.

At the office. On the left, his manager, Kelley Lynch; on his right, her assistant, Sarah Rich. Photo by I.B. Nadel

Dominique Issermann photographed by Leonard Cohen.

Cohen and his banana caught by the publicist Sharon Weitz in an L.A. warehouse during the filming of "First We Take Manhattan" by Jennifer Warnes. The picture appeared on *I'm Your Man*. Photo by S. Weitz.

Stories differ as to how Cohen and Spector became partners. The liner notes on the album state that Marty Machat, who was Spector's lawyer as well as Cohen's, introduced them. According to Cohen, this occurred backstage after one of his performances at the Troubadour in L.A. Spector had uncharacteristically left his well-protected home to see Cohen, and at the show was strangely silent. Spector then invited Cohen back to his home, which, because of the air-conditioning, was very chilly, about "thirty-two degrees," Cohen recalled. Spector was also very loud, and the more people he had around him, the more wild and theatrical he became. Spector locked the door and Cohen reacted by saying, "As long as we are locked up, we might as well write some songs together." They went to the piano and started that night. For about a month they wrote (and drank) together and Cohen remembers it as a generous period, although he had to wear an overcoat almost constantly to work in Spector's freezing home.

Cohen accepted Spector's eccentricities, and found that period "very charming and hospitable." As for Spector's genius? "I thought the songs were excellent," Cohen said. In the studio, however, it was a nightmare. Spector was menacing and paranoid. "He kept a lot of guns around, armed bodyguards; bullets and wine bottles littered the floor." With Spector brandishing a bottle of wine in one hand and a .45 in the other, the atmosphere was tense. At one point Spector pointed the loaded pistol at Cohen's throat, cocked it, and said, "I love you, Leonard." Quietly, Cohen responded, "I *hope* you love me, Phil." At another session, Spector pointed a revolver at the violinist, who quickly packed up and ran out. Songwriter Doc Pomus, who was there, reported that Cohen was actually pushed aside and ignored during the sessions and that Spector was so paranoid about the tapes that he took them home each night with an armed guard.

One night, Cohen and Spector were unexpectedly joined by Bob Dylan and Allen Ginsberg, who sang backup on "Don't Go Home With Your Hard On." The night before, Cohen and Harvey Kubernik from *Melody Maker* had gone to the Troubadour for a poetry reading by Ginsberg. The next evening, Ginsberg and Dylan were eating with Ronee Blakley at Cantor's delicatessen on Fairfax when they learned that Cohen was recording with Spector at the Gold Star studios. They dropped by and before long Hal Blaine, the drummer, was directing Ginsberg and Dylan in backing vocal parts. Spector also joined in on the song. However, Dylan wasn't an influence on Cohen's songwriting for this album; as Ginsberg noted, "Dylan blew everybody's mind, except Leonard's."

The recording of the song "Death of A Ladies' Man," was indicative of the album's creation. The session began at 7:30 in the evening, but by 2:30 in the morning a complete take had not yet been made. The musicians were on double time after midnight; it escalated to quadruple time at 2:00 a.m. By 3:30 in the morning they had not even played the song all the way through yet. Spector took away the charts and prevented the musicians from playing more than six bars. Cohen sat crosslegged on the floor through most of this until around 4:00 a.m., when Spector clapped his hands and told Cohen to do the vocal. Approaching the microphone, a very tired Cohen sang the song flawlessly. Cohen has since said of the song, "It's direct and confessional. I wanted the lyrics in a tender setting rather than a harsh situation. At times that fusion was achieved. Sometimes the heart must roast on the fire like shish kebab."

Cohen expected to find Spector in his Debussy period; instead, he found him in "the full flower of his Wagnerian tempest." Personally and musically he was out of control; he locked up the master tapes of the album and mixed them without Cohen's knowledge or permission. Cohen had done only one take on the songs, what's known as a scratch vocal (a simple one-track vocal to be replaced later with a more enhanced and prepared sound) and wanted to put on different vocals, but Spector went into hiding with the tapes. He added strings, horns, and a female choir, with Cohen's groaning voice heard distantly in the mix. On "Iodine," an enormous percussive Motown styled back beat thrusts itself between the lyrics and Cohen's droning voice. "Fingerprints," which on the lyric sheet looks like a conventional, downbeat complaint, becomes a primeval hoedown with long fiddle and steel-guitar breaks. "Don't Go Home With Your Hard On" is pure burlesque, pushing the sardonic lyric to new lows by using a punchy rhythm-and-blues style horn section. Purists objected to the overproduction, which buried Cohen's lyrics.

The cover photograph showed a youthful Cohen in a white suit sitting between two attractive women in a Montreal Polynesian restaurant. One of the women is Suzanne and the other is Eva La Pierre, a French-Canadian model Cohen had met on Hydra some years earlier. Cohen disassociated himself from the album before its release in November 1977. He had initially agreed to the project because Spector liked his songs and he thought he might, with Spector's help, break through to a wider audience. "I know my work has a popular element but somehow it can't readily manifest it," he has remarked. In the press, he called the mix of the album a "catastrophe" and said that Spector had annihilated him. Cohen said he would shortly pay twenty thousand dollars to release himself from any promotion of the album. He did, however, conduct several New York interviews in the 54th Street offices of Warner Brothers to discuss the album. But in a February 1978 *Crawdaddy* interview, he was critical of Spector: "The listener could have been invited *into* the track rather than be prohibited from entering it . . . there is something inaccessible, something resistant about those tracks that should not have been there." Still, Cohen admitted that Spector was "capable of stunning melodies and production." But music, he added, "does not come out of the mansion and the kind of tyranny he wants to impose." Cohen later called the orchestrations "brilliant," although he still criticized the use of the first voice takes and secret mixing. At one point, he thought, "I should get myself some bodyguards and settle the whole affair on Sunset Boulevard." Cohen sent Spector a pair of red holsters as a comic gesture of reconciliation.

Reaction to the album was largely negative. *Rolling Stone* headlined its review with "Leonard Cohen's doo-wop Nightmare." The *Toronto Star* was less generous, declaring in large type, "Leonard Cohen is for Musical Sadists." An English paper described the union of Cohen and Spector as, "Doyen of Doom meets Teen Tycoon." *Saturday Night*, however, was more welcoming, saying the album was Cohen's "most significant step forward as a recording artist since his disc debut in 1967." The album, *Rolling Stone* pronounced, is "either greatly flawed or great *and* flawed."

In the title song, "Death of A Ladies' Man," Cohen described a powerful but destructive love:

> She took his much admired oriental frame of mind
> And the heart-of-darkness alibi
> His money hides behind
> She took his blonde madonna
> And his monastery wine
> "This mental space is occupied
> and everything is mine."

The song was a revealing coda on the death of longing, an update of his relationship with Suzanne. It was a time when "every relationship I had broke down. *Every single relationship broke down.* There was nothing left standing."

11

N E W

S C R I P T U R E

I N MARCH 1976, Cohen submitted the manuscript
for what would become *Death of a Lady's Man*,
originally titled "My Life in Art." He chose the singular rather than plural form of "lady's" to emphasize his focus on an
individual woman; for his album, with its similar title, he wanted to stress
a multitude of women that may have caused his demise. After reading the
work, one editor at McClelland & Stewart wrote, "I must say that it is
truly-to-God the most depressing thing I have read in a very long time."
But the editor did add that it was publishable and in many ways "superb."
Another editor, Lily Miller, began her report by saying that "Leonard
Cohen was one of the reasons why I came to Canada." She thought that
the manuscript marked a new phase in his work, since each significant
sequence ends with an expression of inadequacy, replacing the "constant

bragging" of his earlier work. There was a new depth of thought and self-criticism. "I suggest," she wrote, "that long discussions will be necessary to either justify or eliminate this turn of a new leaf." Miller thought that "the earlier arrogance, the more recent sense of doom and impotence, seem here to have given way to something more mellow: an acceptance of human limitations, foibles, failures—and a love which can rise out of these very weaknesses." She wanted to publish it.

The manuscript went back to Cohen for revision, and six months later he returned it, retitled "The Final Revision of My Life in Art." Plans had been made for a fall publication, and announcements and advance press galleys began to circulate. Initially, there were delays with the printers. Cooper & Beatty turned down the job "because of language in the manuscript." A second printer said that it could not meet the McClelland & Stewart schedule. A third printer, Accutext, finally set galleys for a September publication. But Jack McClelland was becoming frantic because he could not contact Cohen to finalize last-minute changes. Cohen had originally drawn illustrations for the back cover and the endpapers, but Miller had now rejected the use of Cohen's illustrations and criticized the photo intended for the front cover. She wanted a strong front cover, possibly a drawing, and a photo of Cohen on the back: "His drawings will only diminish the power of the book," she wrote in a June 1977 memo. A subsequent memo said that without Cohen's illustrations, they would be left with four blank pages. She suggested they get more poems from Cohen and, because of layout problems, four more lines for "The House." The manuscript was again revised and resubmitted in November 1976 with a new title: *Death of a Lady's Man*.

On August 10, 1977, Cohen notified Lily Miller that he was again delaying the book. In reworking it, he had written as much new material as they presently had. "He feels very excited about the new work," Miller wrote in a memo, "He feels it would add a whole new dimension to the book. However, it could not be available for another month's time . . ." Written on the bottom of the note in Jack McClelland's handwriting is the following: "This is a grim development. I am most reluctant to postpone. He called and left number. Naturally, no answer when I called back. Will do my best."

The following week a new problem emerged with the title: a prospective co-publisher objected to Cohen using the same title for his book and record album. Cohen was also "pulled apart and uptight," requiring a further delay. While McClelland told Cohen he would slow production for a while, he vented his frustration in an internal memo: Cohen "says he is re-writing the God-damn book which is nice news at this stage. . . . I should tell you this is typical Cohen, [but] we'll have to live with it. The book will be late but I don't think there is any point putting the pressure on him now."

On August 11, McClelland reported that he had spoken to Cohen in California where he said that he hoped to finish the manuscript in less than a month. "He says he is writing a 90-page commentary on the book itself. What ever the hell that means. I fear the worst." Promotion plans remained incomplete, since a fall publication was now impossible. On August 18, a telegram arrived from Mt. Baldy, announcing, "I DOUBT THAT I CAN FINISH BOOK IN 2 WEEKS OR EVEN 4 WEEKS. THERE HAS BEEN A FICTITIOUS URGENCY CONNECTED WITH THIS PROJECT FROM THE BEGINNING." Cohen told McClelland that he would simply have to wait for the finished book. McClelland replied the next day:

LEONARD THERE IS NO SWEAT ABOUT IT. MY REAL PROBLEM IS THAT WE REALLY BELIEVE YOU HAD A FINE BOOK COMPLETED AND THAT YOU ARE PROBABLY SECOND GUESSING YOURSELF UNNECESSARILY. IN ANY CASE WE WILL WAIT. BEST AS ALWAYS.
    JACK

By October, McClelland was becoming less patient. In a long and detailed letter, he told Cohen that he had been forced to make an announcement to the book trade that the volume had been postponed again. The reason for the notice was that *Saturday Night* was about to do an article on Cohen and the delay of the book. McClelland pleaded with Cohen to tell him "where we are heading so we can deal with the story." The problem is that "the whole goddamn situation is in the public arena and we have to have some answers."

The November 1977 article by Sandra Martin reviewed the situation, beginning with a November 1976 night in New York when Cohen gave McClelland the manuscript of the poems after sipping vodka and watching hockey on TV. "Christ, Leonard," McClelland was reported as saying, "*Death of a Lady's Man*! With a title like that we don't even need a manuscript." Twice since that evening, McClelland had advertised the book in his catalogue of forthcoming books and twice had withdrawn it. By June, Cohen had finished his second version and appeared at a McClelland & Stewart sales conference to promote the book and the new album. A day later he was at the Courtyard Cafe in Toronto, pulling out a tape recorder and playing a few of the tracks from the album for his friends. In mid-August, with the second manuscript typeset, and at least three magazines ready with advance reviews from galleys, Cohen called and then cabled McClelland with the request to delay. M&S stopped its promotion of the book and put aside nearly ten thousand orders for the title. McClelland defended his position by saying, "If Leonard were a normal author, I would be phoning once a week. But he always has been and always will be special."

By November 25, 1977, McClelland told editor Anna Porter that according to Irving Layton, Cohen was still working on the manuscript. There was a distinct possibility that they might not want to publish it when they saw it. The title had to be dropped from the spring list. In late January 1978, Cohen was back in Montreal. He sent a note to McClelland, telling him that he had added sixty pages to the book and had another forty to go. He expected it to be finished by the end of March. Cohen suggested a billboard campaign for the book using the sixteenth-century engraving from the cover—the same engraving used on the cover of *New Skin for the Old Ceremony*—with the words "Leonard Cohen" above and "DEATH OF A LADY'S MAN, A CURIOUS BOOK" below.

Cohen added commentaries to his work, written as though another person were viewing or judging it. Lily Miller believed that this addition added new insight and originality. A different typeface would set the commentaries apart, and they would appear on the facing pages. Since the sequence of poetry and prose remained mostly unchanged, McClelland & Stewart was able to salvage about eighty percent of the original typesetting.

Thoughts of completion, however, were premature. Throughout the summer, matters of cost, production, typeface, and paper plagued both Cohen and his publisher, with the poet frequently altering the publisher's decision. He was uneasy with the plan to issue the book in hardcover only, for a price of $10.00. His instinct suggested a $6.95 paperback. He worried about paper and rejected the sample the U.S. printer sent. If it were published in hardcover, he underlined, it should have "bulk and elegance." Concerning publicity, he wanted "a dignified treatment and a certain formality. He'd like it to be sedate." He rejected the idea of a billboard with his photo, his signature, and a few excerpts. He did not want to flaunt the personal aspect, he said. He preferred the billboard of the engraving plus the title and the statement that it was "A Curious Book." McClelland rejected the idea.

Mixed reviews greeted *Death of a Lady's Man* when it was finally published in the fall of 1978. *Books in Canada* said the work was "astonishing" in how it used the theme of poetic failure to move Cohen to "dignity and gravity." Other reviews cited a lack of talent. It was suggested that the book was simply a hangover from the poor reception the Spector album had received. In Canada, Cohen remembers, the book was "coldly received in all circles . . . dismissed almost uniformly," although he himself thought of the work as a "very leisurely and delightful kind of performance." In the United States *Death of a Lady's Man* was not even reviewed. One reason for its neglect may have been that among the literati Cohen had been largely forgotten; he had been identified as a singer and songwriter rather than a poet for too long.

During the publication delays, Cohen was also contending with his mother's illness in Montreal, his relationship with Suzanne, and his explosive dealings with Phil Spector. This meant constantly traveling back and forth between Los Angeles and Montreal. In late 1977, after the album had been completed, he moved the family back to Montreal to be closer to his mother. She died of leukemia in February 1978. *Death of A Lady's Man* is dedicated to her.

In Montreal he spent time with Adam and Lorca, feeling that children embodied an individual's resurrection. Family life, he told an interviewer, was now an important aspect of his existence. There was a period of mourning in Montreal and Cohen addressed family matters, and dealt with the estate, deciding to keep his mother's semidetached home on Belmont Avenue. But the Montreal hiatus was shortlived. Cohen decided he had to return to Los Angeles with his family to start a new recording. This time they settled in a larger house on Woodrow Wilson Avenue, high in the Hollywood Hills. In this spare, secluded home, with unobstructed views of Los Angeles from its various terraces, Cohen sought to recreate something of his environment on Hydra. He renewed his daily attendance at the Cimarron Zen Center, worked out at the Hollywood YMCA and began again to write.

In the spring of 1978 Suzanne suddenly left for France with the children, who were now six and four. Cohen was shocked. No single event had precipitated the move; it was simply the growing division between the two of them and a desire on her part to relocate and start a new life. At first Cohen felt a strange sense of elation and later commented that he was too weak for the institution of marriage. "Marriage is a monastery," he once wrote, implying that marriage enforced abstinence from other relationships on the partners, often disguised as intimacy. Marriage has become "the hottest furnace of the spirit today. Much more difficult than solitude, much more challenging for people who want to work on themselves. It's a situation in which there are no alibis, excruciating most of the time."

Immediately after Suzanne's departure, Cohen's tension and bitterness disappeared. He enjoyed the quiet and solitude and turned to old friends like Nancy Bacal, who joined him in his Zen practice and in swimming and working out regularly. He also participated in a promotional tour of his book *Death of A Lady's Man*, traveling across Canada in 1978.

In Los Angeles Cohen began to work with Henry Lewy on another album, tentatively titled *The Smokey Life*. Cohen first conceived of the album as representing the kind of life which had "the quality of smoke: fragile, and not attached to anything, but still the only one we've got. And we're leading it, without landmarks and without forms." Lewy, formerly an engineer, had been Joni Mitchell's producer for several years and had also produced Stephen Bishop, Minnie Riperton, and others. Mitchell had introduced them and suggested they work together.

One rainy afternoon, Cohen invited Lewy to listen to a rough tape of the song "The Smokey Life." Excited about the material, Lewy suggested they record it at once. He called the members of Passenger, who had been working with Joni Mitchell, and they arranged to meet at the United-Western Recording studio that evening. Roscoe Beck, Bill Guinn, and Steve Meador appeared and recorded the song with Cohen.

For the album, Cohen gave Lewy the songs and he set to work locating musicians, while Jeremy Lubbock worked on the arrangements. Paul Ostermeyer (sax), Steve Meador (drums), Roscoe Beck (bass), John Lissauer (piano), Raffi Hakopian (violin), and John Bilezikjian (oud, an eleven-string Middle Eastern instrument traditionally played with an eagle's feather) were among the outstanding studio musicians, several of whom—Ostermeyer and Meador, in particular—would continue to play and tour with Cohen over the next fourteen years. Jennifer Warnes contributed background vocals. Joni Mitchell and other musicians dropped by as well.

The 1978 recording sessions took place at A&M Records, once the studio for Charlie Chaplin. In contrast to the paranoia and frenzy of Phil Spector, a strong sense of musicianship pervaded the sessions with Lewy. Because he wanted to showcase Cohen's voice amid the striking orchestrations, Lewy had him sit in a separation booth, a small glass-walled room adjacent to the musicians where he would hear only his own voice and guitar. Cohen's voice was the dominating sound on the tracks, in contrast to the muffled voice heard on *Death of A Ladies' Man*. At the studio, Cohen was often accompanied by an attractive Mexican woman, his companion of the moment.

The album had a confident and largely acoustic style, reminiscent of *Songs from a Room*. In songs like the jazzy, "torch" quality of "Came so Far for Beauty," or the cool, sly rhythms of "The Smokey Life," Cohen was able to "wrap his voice around the words," always his goal in a song. On "The Guests" and "Ballad of the Absent Mare," however, the use of a Mexican mariachi band contradicted the near Eastern sound supplied by John Bilezikjian and his oud.

The album became an anchor for Cohen during a troubling time. It was dedicated to "Irving Layton, incomparable master of the Inner language." He also thanked the late Robert Hershorn and Nancy Bacal but his most significant acknowledgment was to his Zen master: "I owe my thanks to Joshu Sasaki upon whose exposition of an early Chinese text I based 'Ballad of The Absent Mare.'" The reference to Roshi indicated how Cohen was incorporating Zen material into his work. The early Chinese text he referred to was the "Ten Ox-Herding Pictures," also called "The Ten Bulls." At one time Cohen and Roshi worked on a translation of these texts, originally a twelfth-century set of pictures and commentary by Kakuan, a Chinese master. Traditionally, the ten bulls are ten images that represent the ten steps in the spiritual unfolding of the self. Both the song and the story emphasize a search in "the pasture of this world" for the reunification of the true self expressed through the capturing and taming of the bull. In the last two verses of "The Absent Mare," the singer unites with the horse, unconsciously joining the narrator of the "Ten Ox-Herding Pictures" to realize that there can be no separation between object and subject. He suddenly recognizes the "forms of integration and disintegration" as one, and simultaneously sees "that which *is* creating and that which *is* destroying."

The title of the album was a problem. Nancy Bacal remembers the difficulty it gave Cohen. The two of them spent an entire day working on possibilities at Cohen's home in the Hollywood Hills. When she finally did get home, there was a message from Cohen on her answering machine saying that he was unhappy with what they'd decided on and was starting all over. *Recent Songs* was finally settled on as the right title for the new album.

It was a modest success. Many thought he had returned to his old form. The *New York Times* said that *Recent Songs* provided "an ideal musical idiom for his idiosyncrasies," although the mood of the album was "strangely, even magically, uncluttered." The *Times* listed the album among its top ten records of 1979, and Larry Sloman, historian of Dylan's Rolling Thunder Review, predicted that the album would go silver, if not gold.

Before going on tour to support the album, Cohen spent several weeks on Hydra. There he celebrated his forty-fifth birthday in the company of a Romanian woman named Michelle. Cohen's love of women, one friend candidly suggested, has been the quest for a single, encompassing woman he has sought his entire life. Along the way, different women have represented different anatomical parts.

When Cohen became interested in a woman, little could stop him. Once, while in Montreal, he tried to place a long-distance call. When he announced his name to the operator, she was stunned. Before she could recover, he asked her out on a date. Lucky once, he tried again with another. He kept on with the game until one night he found himself alone in his room, dialing operator after operator, waiting for a breathless response. It did not come.

The September release of *Recent Songs* occasioned a tour which began on October 7, again accompanied by a camera crew. Rehearsals took place in London at Shepperton Studios and then the tour started in Scandinavia, moved on to France, Germany and Switzerland, before ending in Brighton, England. The tour had its difficulties, however; Cohen told an English interviewer that:

> everybody on tour has had a tiny nervous breakdown at one point or other. I don't know if it's the weather, or the tour's intensity, or the music, or the combination of the people. But everyone has had to go through a radical reevaluation of their condition on the road. We're enjoying it now because we've surrendered to it. They just carry our bodies from hotel room to airport bus, and the music manifests itself each night!

At the Berlin Sportpalast, where the group played on November 5, 1979, the strain was beginning to show. When the sound system failed, the crowd became unruly. Cohen shouted to them to be orderly and they reacted with increased hostility. Only the restored sound equipment and beginning of the music averted an ugly confrontation. In England for the last two weeks of the tour, Cohen addressed the depressing nature of his songs, telling a reporter that "the confusion of seriousness with gloominess is an inaccurate understanding. We have an appetite for seriousness and we can be destroyed as easily by mindless frivolity as we can by obsessive depression."

On his way to Australia to extend his tour, Cohen stopped in Toronto at the end of February 1980 to attend the launch of a *livre d'artiste* by the Italian Gigino Falconi, a portfolio of seven lithographs based on Cohen's poems. "He has the same kind of appreciation of women I use in my work," Cohen commented at a press conference. The questions turned to Cohen's work, particularly his recent record. "I think it's a beautiful, great thing," Cohen said. He felt he was more popular in Europe than in North America because "the market is more acceptable there. I find I get more support from the record companies in Europe. Here, the emphasis is on the quick hit. They're not concerned about an artist's past work." He referred to *Death of A Ladies' Man* as "a classic, a grotesque masterpiece," and reiterated that he worked slowly, that the process of writing never got easier. "I can't force myself, no matter how badly the company wants another record. I'm naturally protected by the slowness with which I work."

The Australian tour began on March 6 in Melbourne with four performances, continued to Adelaide, and ended in Sydney on the 14th with two shows. It was his first visit there, and he was well received. A critic said that Cohen was "destined to be the cult-figure *extraordinaire* of the eighties." Another paper described him as "the most enduring and emotionally honest poet . . . on the fringes of rock and roll." Cohen emphasized in various interviews that his work dealt not with world movements or cataclysmic change but with the self: "I never got out of my personal life," he admitted. Columbia issued a set of four of his albums as a memento of the tour and *Recent Songs* went gold in Australia, although in Canada "it didn't seem to make much of an echo." Cohen returned to Montreal to spend the spring of 1980 in the company of his children, who were visiting.

The Canadian documentary filmmaker Harry Rasky traveled with the group and used footage from the European tour for what would become a CBC film, "The Song of Leonard Cohen." Rasky showed Cohen performing in Europe and interviewed him in his Montreal home where he philosophized about his career and his attraction to music. In the film, Cohen explained his "rejection" of life on Hydra as the result of his inescapable marriage to music: "The song seized me and an appetite for reaching many people seized me. [But] when I began to make money, the quality of my life deteriorated swiftly, and even when I could afford a decent hotel room in a dark city, it compared unfavorably with a beautiful sunlit room on a Greek island." He said he now felt more rooted, less restless. He was prepared to settle in Montreal after a decade of wandering.

Much of the film was shot in Montreal and at his home across from Parc Portugal. The use of extensive family photographs deepened the feeling of an exile's return. There was, he told Rasky, "a new spirit in my work. Songs I will write will not have that elegiac quality any longer. . . . A song, or a poem, or a piece of work or even where a man is in the world—it withers if it isn't based on what is authentic and what is true."

The appearance of Irving Layton in the film confirmed the ongoing mutual admiration between the two writers. "Genius," Layton pronounced, "is seeing things exactly as they are." And Cohen, he said, was able to do that in his work. Layton linked this condition of sadness and song to that of fourteenth-century balladeers and to being Jewish, defined by him as "the gift of anxiety, of pain, of alienation, of solitude."

In the Rasky film Cohen looked healthy and fit. His performances from the 1979 tour show a polished entertainer, with more rhythm and energy in his songs. Jennifer Warnes and Sharon Robinson harmonized perfectly with Cohen's sometimes raspy voice. The tour seemed to release much of the anger and stress he had experienced over the breakup with Suzanne and the removal of his children to France.

Back in Los Angeles, Cohen taped a series of unreleased poetry readings with Henry Lewy, including one that conveyed his unhappiness at being separated from Suzanne and his children:

I wandered away from you
I bought a little electric piano.
Miles from where you live
I composed a song of farewell.
Everyone loved it.
My cup was filled to the brim.
A young Communist
Payed homage to me
with a poem entitled
Ode to the Intellectual Worker.

I made my way to Paris.
O, Paris, I said
Every little messiah
Thanks you for his loneliness.
On another occasion, I said

Paris, be strong, be nuclear
and talk, talk,
Never stop talking
about how to live without God.

It was very soon after this
that I retired to the countryside.
I installed my piano in a corner
and I cried, speak to me, speak to me,
Angel of Beauty
Speak to me
O thou comfort of the world.

─────────

WITH HIS CHILDREN GONE and his album finished, Cohen gave up the house in Los Angeles and began to spend more time in Europe, Montreal, and New York. Paris became a frequent stop on his way to Roussillon, with its ochre cliffs, and then to Bonnieux in the heart of the Luberon mountain area, where Suzanne later moved with the children. Cohen's access to the children was limited, even though he rented the house for them in Roussillon and purchased the home in Bonnieux; at one point he lived in a trailer parked outside the country house where the children stayed. Cohen and Suzanne wrangled over custody of the children and the terms of a settlement from 1978 to 1984. "On Seeing Kabir's Poems," written in 1981 at Roussillon and printed in *Stranger Music*, recalls this period.

Cohen began to study the Talmud at this time, always traveling with a copy of the text. It became a source of spiritual sustenance, always with him when he visited his children. His new circumstances meant a renewal of the now tedious vagabond life, traveling from hotel to hotel, with frequent stops at the Royalton in New York and the Cluny in Paris.

In 1979, Cohen, along with Richard Cohen and Eric Lerner, also students of Roshi, bought a house in South Central Los Angeles at a foreclosure sale. It was cheap and near the Cimarron Zen Center. Although he rarely lived there over the next five or six years, Cohen eventually made it his Los Angeles home. He didn't bother to furnish his part of the two-story house. Steve Sanfield recalls that at this time Cohen led the life of "a wandering monk," with very few possessions, and that his home was strikingly bare and simple. The kitchen was the only place to sit down, since there were no chairs in any other part of the house, only tables or cushions.

Cohen became involved with a journal Roshi wanted to start entitled *Zero*. Mixing Roshi's philosophy with contributions by creative writers, the journal appeared for several years. The title of the journal expressed Roshi's philosophy: "Zero is activity that is complete and full of good will. . . . In the state of zero there are no questions." By the third volume, the journal listed Eric Lerner as editor, Richard Cohen as associate editor, and Steve Sanfield and Leonard Cohen as contributing editors. That issue included an interview with John Cage, a collage of haiku by Allen Ginsberg, poetry by John Ashbery, an interview with Joni Mitchell, and the lyrics of several songs from *Recent Songs* by Leonard Cohen.

For Roshi, zero was the central Zen tenet, a detachment from the distractions of the self, or the absence of the self. It was the condition of positive emptiness. Only by dissolving the fixed self is one's true nature made manifest, Roshi argued. For Zen to begin, the ego self must die: "As long as we see things dualistically, we shall never see the truth." In an essay entitled "On The Nature of Zero," originally a 1979 talk at Mt. Baldy, Roshi summarized his understanding of the concept of zero: it is manifested in the practice of Zen mastery over impermanence "through realizing oneself as a sphere alternately expanding and contracting." The ultimate goal is the state of absolute tranquility where "everything is oneself." Enlightenment, Roshi said, "is the possession of two kinds of wisdom: one which looks, in a personal way, upon everything as yourself and another which looks in an impersonal way upon yourself as Zero."

Cohen spent whatever time he could with Roshi at Mt. Baldy and occasionally accompanied him to other Zen centers. Together they visited the Gethsemane Monastery in Kentucky, the former monastery of Thomas Merton. At the headquarters of the Trappist Movement in Spenser, Massachusetts, they talked with the abbot and attended Mass, observing another form of spiritual commitment. While they were there a monk confided to Cohen that every day he questioned why he was there and thought about going over the wall. Roshi believed that his monks should be a part of the world, telling them, "After you realize the mountain, go back to the world. Don't stay here too long." Roshi encouraged Cohen to play tennis and to join a nearby tennis club in Claremont. He did, but admitted that regular play did not improve his game much. As Cohen reports, "Roshi saw that I knew how to work; what I didn't know how to do was play."

Cohen's attachment to Rinzai Buddhism remained unswerving. He admired Roshi's willingness to get up at 3:00 a.m. and to meet four times a day with his students in *sanzen*, his commitment to the rigors of the *sesshins*, and his determination to teach at the various Zen centers in Vienna, Ithaca, or Puerto Rico. Roshi adapted to American ways, offering his *teishos* (lecture/sermons) in Japanese but giving *sanzen* in English. His Zen practice was considered the most vigorous in America.

Cohen's commitment to Zen, however, was never at the sacrifice of his Judaism. He told an Australian journalist that "I am not a Buddhist, but a Jew." Despite more than a twenty-five-year involvement with Zen, a religion he once described to Nancy Bacal as "for the truly lost," he has constantly affirmed his Jewishness. Cohen may criticize the lack of a meditational dimension in Judaism and devote himself physically, as well as financially, to Zen, but he has never renounced his identity as a Jew. In a 1993 letter to a Hollywood trade paper he wrote:

My father and mother, of blessed memory, would have been disturbed by the Reporter's description of me as a buddhist. I am a jew.

For some time now I have been intrigued by the indecipherable ramblings of an old zen monk. Not long ago he said to me, 'Cohen, I have known you for 23 years and I never tried to give you my religion. I just poured you sake.' Saying that, he filled my cup with sake. I bowed my head and raised my cup to him crying out, 'Rabbi, you are surely the Light of the Generation.'

IN OCTOBER 1980 Cohen began his sixth European tour, using the same musicians as the 1979 tour, although Jennifer Warnes did not join them. They started in France, where he again played to sold-out houses. In Berlin he created a controversy when he asked his fans at the packed stadium to remove the chairs. "If you see this terrible plastic, you see the dark side of our lives," he told them, an allusion to the Nazi past. Unlike the 1979 tour, which mainly featured material from *Recent Songs*, the current tour provided more of a survey of his best-known songs.

In Frankfurt, after his concert, Cohen was woken in the middle of the night by a loud knocking at his door. He opened the door to find a six-foot-two-inch blonde woman dressed only in boots and aluminum foil. Cohen nobly refused her wish to enter but she persisted and so Cohen gave in. By morning he was determined to take her with him for the rest of the tour. She declined and prepared to leave, despite his pleas and declarations of her beauty. Smiling, she said to Cohen, "One more star in my constellation," and left. The tour ended in Tel Aviv and Cohen was once more at loose ends.

A December 11 entry in a journal describes him in Room 700 of the Algonquin Hotel in New York with a chassidic prayer book, his grandfather's *tefillin* and woolen *tallit*, a box of Barton's Hanukkah candy, and a set of Hanukkah candles, all in preparation for celebrating the festival with his children. Four days later in the same journal the first draft of "If It Be Your Will" appears.

On Hydra in 1982, he met a woman who became important in his life: Dominique Issermann, a fashion photographer from Paris. Carole Laure, the Quebecois actor, and her husband Lewis Furey, had established careers in Paris, and they introduced Cohen to Issermann when she came to visit Laure on Hydra. Cohen and Issermann began a long-term relationship, characterized by maturity and a mutual devotion to work. Issermann took publicity stills of Cohen and directed two of his videos: "Dance Me to the End of Love," and "First We Take Manhattan." Cohen frequently stayed with her in her Paris apartment, writing songs and visiting his children.

Issermann stimulated a new intensity and vigor in Cohen's songwriting, marked by his strenuous efforts with *Various Positions*, his 1984 album. Her work habits influenced Cohen, who relied more on effort than inspiration. His career was faltering and Issermann became a graceful working companion who understood his anguish and commitment to his task. In his words, Issermann helped him "dig in." A period of "diligent application to this whole affair" began.

But the same pattern began to emerge. Cohen, uncomfortable in a stable relationship, found it necessary to wander as his creativity appeared to become restricted. So he spent time in New York at the Royalton, in California with Roshi, and in Montreal at his home. Dominique visited when possible and Cohen stayed in Paris when he could. He became unwilling to make space for her and her career in his life, either in Los Angeles or Montreal, and after a period of reassessment, they chose to separate. They remain close friends, however, and Issermann's photographs of him are frequently reprinted in his songbooks, in his concert programs, and on French postcards. She anchored his life in the eighties and became an important creative force. An inscription on his album *I'm Your Man* reads, "All these songs are for you, D.I." Issermann was a crucial, if little recognized, figure in Cohen's recovery from depression, the redirection of his musical career, and the renewal of his spiritual life.

On Hydra in the winter of 1981–1982, Cohen began to work on the libretto of an opera for which Lewis Furey would do the music. Variously titled "Merry-Go Man, "The Hall," "Angel Eyes," and finally *Night Magic*, Cohen actually thought of it as a ballet. The title derived from the name of a popular nightclub in Old Montreal named *Nuit Magique*. It was run by a friend of Cohen's named Bob Di Salvio, who had first heard the phrase in Van Morrison's song "Moondance." A back room at the club was named *Les Beaux Ratés*, "the beautiful losers." Cohen described *Night Magic* as a cabaret opera about a broken-down Montreal singer who has his wishes granted, "a combination of Brecht and Disney." The plot involved a music hall star named Michael who was preparing a show that would revive a run-down theater named the System, the same theater used by Cohen in *Beautiful Losers* and the name of an actual Montreal movie house. In the course of one night, three female guardian angels visit him, and one falls in love with him. A series of songs on the clash between art and life result.

The work was a musical pastiche that reflected Cohen's renewed interest in regulated form. He wrote the entire opera in Spenserian stanzas.

This Renaissance verse structure, first used in the epic *The Faerie Queen*, consists of nine lines, eight five-foot iambic lines, with the ninth, an iambic line of six feet. Cohen felt he needed to locate himself in a literary tradition in order to give his work resonance.

The opera was filmed and starred Nick Mancuso, Carole Laure, and Frank Augustyn. Furey directed, composed the music (Cohen wrote the lyrics), and supplied the voice for the songs which were lip-synced by Mancuso, a gifted dramatic actor but not a musical star. Carol Laure played the enamored angel. Robert Lantos and James T. Kaufman produced.

The film opened at Cannes on May 17, 1985. *Variety* complained that the music and lyrics were "reminiscent of the sixties era . . . [but] as tuneful as the score is, it lacks the necessary power to grip the listener." The choreography, said *Variety*, was in the style of TV extravaganzas. Coordinated with the film release was a double-album soundtrack recording distributed by the French division of RCA with a slightly different cast from that of the film. Cohen and Furey won a Juno for best music score in 1985 for the music to the "rock opera."

COHEN had an idea for a short film, initially based on the experiences of a hotel and his song "The Guests." Produced by Barrie Wexler, "I Am a Hotel" was intended for the Canadian pay-TV network, C-Channel, but when the network collapsed and Cohen twice threatened to pull out, Moses Znaimer and City-TV stepped in to complete the production (he is listed as executive producer) with CBC-TV and the Canadian Film Development Corporation assisting with funding.

No one involved really had any experience with rock videos, though. Wexler and Cohen watched various examples at City-TV, settled on a budget of two hundred and fifty thousand dollars, and started to plan. Several months later Cohen returned to Toronto and told Barrie Wexler that he wanted out of the planned video production, explaining that he couldn't write a music video in his present state of mind (he was working on a book of psalms). That was a Saturday night, Wexler remembered, and he had promised to deliver a script for the video by Monday morning.

He persuaded Cohen not to give up, and they worked all night. With the help of the Toronto writer Mark Shekter, they put together a thirteen-page treatment. In the interim, singer David Blue had died in New York (Cohen gave the eulogy at the funeral) and Cohen named the production company "Blue Memorial Video" in his honor since Blue had portrayed Cohen onstage in Montreal at the Centaur Theatre production of "The Leonard Cohen Show."

Wexler and Znaimer lined up the King Edward Hotel for the shooting, set to begin in April 1983. In the meantime, Cohen had gone to Roshi's New Mexico Zen center, where he could make only one fifteen-minute telephone call a week. The day Wexler was to sign the deal with C-Channel, Cohen telexed to say he had changed his mind, that he would refund the money, and that the project had to be postponed or canceled. Znaimer told Wexler to find Cohen and make him change his mind. Unable to contact him, Wexler went to C-Channel and signed, despite the telex from Cohen in his pocket. He couldn't speak to Cohen for four days and when he could, he was able, during their fifteen-minute conversation, to convince him to participate, although Cohen wanted to be written out of much of the video.

Four days before filming, Cohen arrived in Toronto, the day the newspapers were saying C-Channel was going to fold. Wexler bought a copy of every Canadian newspaper at the King Edward Hotel's newsstand where Cohen was staying so he would not learn of the channel's collapse. Wexler and Znaimer worked through the night to re-finance the project. Three CBC executives were dining together that night and between the first course and dessert, Wexler was able to convince one to come to City-TV's offices to hear his pitch. That evening Wexler got a call approving the money. The Canadian Film Development Corporation also came through in record time to help finance the film.

Filming took six days. It was a thirty-minute surreal drama, a pastiche of fantasy, song, and dance woven around five sets of lovers (including Cohen) who meet at a grand hotel. Five songs narrated the drama, opening with "The Guests" and moving to "Memories," "Gypsy Wife," "Chelsea Hotel," and finally "Suzanne." The sequences were shot in both black and white and color. Skating champion Toller Cranston, dancer Ann Ditchburn and the National Ballet's founder Celia Franca all appeared in the video. Cohen described the film as "a kind of carousel, you just see figures moving in and out, and their stories unfold, they find what they want." There is no dialogue, only the songs and body movment. Wexler explained that what they tried to do was make the singer almost incidental to the dancing, acting, and music. During an interview after the shooting, Cohen said that hotels had always been his natural habitat, "My personal life is such that there's nowhere else to *go*. Where does a guy *go*?"

When Cohen saw the film, he hated it. Some scenes had to be reshot, and more money was needed. Additional sequences, especially for "Suzanne," were added by the post-production director, Don Allen. Editing was a long and stressful process, but when Cohen saw the final product, he was thrilled. The film was broadcast on May 7, 1984, and beat out entries from thirty-two other countries to win the Golden Rose award at the 24th International Montreux Television Festival. It also received a special mention in the Critic's Choice category. Critics praised the work and saw a transition in Cohen's work from the erotic and experimental to the traditional, with worship and redemption as the new focus. Cohen, Wexler, and Znaimer suggested that their next video would be an adaptation of *The Favorite Game*, but it has never been made.

Cohen realized that one "must assume an alarming flexibility," and that projects undertaken without structure could sometimes succeed, while those that were planned could fail. He recognized that he was an inflexible man for the most part. "I like to get up at 3:00 a.m. to the sound of a bell . . . Flexibility for me is a position I'm hounded into—and I don't like it." Order, structure, and discipline were his strengths.

———————

AS HE APPROACHED FIFTY, Cohen felt he needed to re-evaluate his direction once more. He was at last ready to "get down to a Jew's business." The spiritual quest came in part from an inability to do anything else. "I was silenced in all areas. I couldn't move. . . . It was the only way I could penetrate through my predicament." What he discovered was "the courage to write down my prayers. To apply to the source of mercy . . . I found that the act of writing was the proper form for my prayer."

His efforts resulted in a book of psalms first titled *The Name*, then *The Shield*, and finally *Book of Mercy*. Asked to describe it, Cohen cryptically claimed the book is either "inspired or it isn't; it either rings true or it doesn't. I think it does . . . I'm happy for being able to write it because the writing of it, in some ways, was the answer to the prayer." But Cohen was hesistant to have the material published; he felt it was risky because it was so unlike his last book, *Death of A Lady's Man*.

Book of Mercy was published by McClelland & Stewart in April. "It came from an intense desire to speak in that way," he said of the odd form, "And you don't speak in that way unless you feel truly cornered, unless you feel truly desperate and you feel urgency in your life. . . . I also wanted to affirm the traditions I had inherited." In the book, Cohen follows the Old Testament practice of numbering rather than titling the psalms. The book contains fifty psalms, marking Cohen's age. Like the biblical psalms, the psalms in *Book of Mercy* deal with longing and self-abnegation; "Broken in the unemployment of my soul, I have driven a wedge into your world, fallen on both sides of it. Count me back to your mercy with the measures of a bitter song, and do not separate me from my tears." He also recorded several of the psalms with a string quartet in a Los Angeles studio in 1984. Henry Lewy engineered the recording, but it was never released.

Critics were unsure what to make of the book, a position similar to Cohen's: "It's a tricky thing to publish a book like this. I really don't know what section of the bookstore it should be in . . . It's not a quarrel, it's not an argument, it's not theology; it is just an asking." Some wondered how the poet who appeared to possess such venom in *Death of A Lady's Man* could now possess such spiritual love. Others felt that it added another dimension to Cohen's work. In July 1985, he won the Canadian Authors Association Literature Prize for lyrical poetry for the book, receiving five thousand dollars, although the recognition didn't affect his anxiety: "Everyone is in some kind of fix. Writing is my trade, and I treat my fix that way. When I'm feeling good about my work, I call it my vocation; when I'm feeling ordinary about it, I call it my trade."

Book of Mercy was mystical, spiritual, and indulgent, displaying none of the lyricism of his early work or the anger of his later. The focus of his longing was no longer a woman, but a desire to find spiritual fulfillment.

Prayer, he acknowledged, was not in. "We're such a hip age. Nobody wants to affirm those realities. It doesn't go with your sunglasses," he explained to one critic.

The reawakening of his Judaism in the eighties took another form as he transposed Hebrew prayer into his songs. "Who by Fire" is based on the Hebrew melody for the prayer "Mi Bamayim, Mi Ba Esh" sung at the Musaf or noontime service on Yom Kippur. "If It Be Your Will" was also borrowed from Jewish prayer, originating in a phrase from the Kol Nidre service on Yom Kippur eve where, just before the listing of sins, the petitioner cries, "May it therefore be Your will, Lord our God, and God of our Fathers, to forgive us all our sins, to pardon all our iniquities, to grant us atonement for all our transgressions." The melody for Cohen's song is derived from the synagogue song.

———————

Various Positions was the musical counterpoint to *Book of Mercy*. Cohen acknowledged that he had really started to slave over his songwriting. Until 1983, he could write more or less on the run, or at least on the tour buses, in the hotel rooms, in the airplanes, in bed. What altered his attitude from working hard to giving everything to his craft was a growing sense of mortality as he approached fifty. "I had no idea how hard the task was," he told an interviewer in 1993,

> until I found myself in my underwear crawling along the carpet in a shabby room at the Royalton Hotel unable to nail a verse. And knowing that I had a recording session and knowing that I could get by with what I had but that I'm not going to be able to do it.

He was broke, he had a lot of financial obligations, and he felt his career had more or less evaporated. But he perservered: "I bought my first synthesizer and I started working in a way that I have never worked before," Cohen said. "I had always worked hard, but I really threw myself into this. The work was very intense, very clear." In 1993 he explained this new intensity in a characteristically laconic, yet ironic manner: "I don't know why, but something happened to me ten years ago. When things got really desperate, I started to cheer up." Around 1984, the alternative rock scene began to rediscover his music when Sisters of Mercy and Nick Cave started to do cover versions of his songs. "The initial thing had passed," Cohen said. The mainstream audience was dwindling, but the alternative culture was tuning in to his work.

On hearing *Various Positions*, Bob Dylan commented that Cohen's songs were becoming more like prayers. For this album, his first in five years, Cohen also relied on extensive backup vocals. One of the reasons for the album's success was producer John Lissauer, who had assisted on *Recent Songs*. He created a unique sound that reflected the spiritual feeling Cohen wanted to convey. His song "The Law," possibly referring to the Torah, reinforced his realization of a powerful and long-lasting set of principles that must control the behavior of men and women. The law has frequently called him but he had not responded until recently: "I left everybody / But I never went straight."

But religion didn't dominate the record. "Coming Back to You" is something of a country and western song, narrating the determination of the lover/worker/prisoner to return to a woman, despite her transgressions. "Dance Me to the End of Love" marks his return to love from hate, from the breakup with Suzanne to the new joy with Dominique. One of the most troubling songs on the album, and perhaps the most autobiographical, is "The Night Comes On." In five verses Cohen rewrites his life, beginning with his mother, his childhood fears, and her death. The 1973 war in Israel and the peace following is linked to his father's death. He also alludes to his unhappy marriage with characteristic clarity:

> We were locked in this kitchen
> I took to religion
> And I wondered how long she would stay
> I needed so much
> To have nothing to touch
> I've always been greedy that way.

"If It Be Your Will," with Jennifer Warnes singing harmony, made for a haunting conclusion to the album.

Cohen had recorded the album in New York for CBS but they decided not to release it in the U.S. It was released in Europe, where it was felt his European audience was more adaptable. But in the U.S., tolerance for Cohen's already uncommercial style was being stretched with an album of religious themes. *Various Positions* made the Top Ten in Spain, Portugal, and Scandinavia, and fared modestly well in England. In the U.S. it was finally released by Passport Records, a division of JEM records, but only a few thousand copies were pressed.

Cohen told an interviewer that his audience in North America had dried up, although in Europe it had remained loyal. Europeans appreciated "people who can't sing but whose voices are connected to the heart. . . . In the secret chambers of my heart, I consider myself a singer; on good days, I consider myself a stylist."

Cohen said that he couldn't really mount tours in North America because his record company was not behind him. During the seventies and into the eighties, the company seemed to release his records in secret. He referred to the CBS building in New York as "the Tomb of the Unknown Record." When the interviewer asked Cohen what occupation he would list if he were filling out an application, Cohen replied, "Sinner."

Depressed at the lackluster reception of his work, Cohen returned to touring. On May 5, 1985, he played Carnegie Hall, his first New York concert in ten years. A month later he performed at the Wiltern Theater in Los Angeles, where he referred to himself as "an old veteran of the rainbows, rambling on in his invisible trench." Dressed in black and playing a black acoustic guitar, Cohen sang new compositions like "Dance Me to the End of Love," and a rollicking "Diamonds in the Mine." Afterwards, Bob Dylan, Joni Mitchell, and Al Kooper visited him backstage to congratulate him.

The 1985 tour was his most extensive, encompassing Europe, North America, Australia, and Israel. In Poland, SOLIDARITY, the independent trade union that would shortly oust the dictatorial Polish government, asked him to perform and he discovered he was something of a hero to the movement. He declined, however, because of the band's fear of the political tension that might suddenly surround the concert and their tour. When he arrived, he received a note from Lech Walesa, the trade unionist who won the Nobel Peace Prize in 1983 and would later become president of the country. A pirated double cassette from one performance circulated as *Cohen in Warsaw, 22 March 1985* with twenty-one songs from the concert.

Between January and July Cohen performed seventy-seven concerts. Women, he said, were what kept him sane on the road. Otherwise, it was just hotel rooms, the bus, and bad food.

12

P L A S T I C

A L G E B R A

BACK IN LOS ANGELES Cohen became involved in a fresh project: an album of his songs recorded by Jennifer Warnes. She and Cohen had remained close since the days when she had sung background vocals for his band. He had even provided "deep rescue" for her in 1974 when her boyfriend was murdered. "Leonard made sure I wasn't going to sink," she said. When her solo career began to flag, she asked Cohen if she could join him on the new 1979 tour. He discouraged her from singing back up because it might impede a solo career but Warnes said she needed to write and the tour would allow her to do that. "Leonard's tours are catalysts for change," Warnes said, "and whatever is bubbling underneath comes up and you go through it on tour . . . the tour always pushed people to their next spot." The reason? There was "too much fire."

In 1984, Warnes and Cohen were walking around his neighbor-hood—she had been a guest in his house for several months—discussing the AIDS crisis, which was just reaching the public. No longer could people be casual about sex; an iron door had shut. "This is horrible," she confided to him. "What are people going to do; they won't stop loving each other." "Well, honey," he responded, "there ain't no cure for love." "I think you should write something about that," she replied. Several weeks later, he called and said, "I wrote you this song and it's called 'Ain't No Cure for Love.'"

It was Warnes and Roscoe Beck of Passenger who first had the idea of Warnes making a record exclusively of Cohen songs. At first, Cohen was skeptical of the project, but Warnes was confident: "*I* knew that I saw something within the songs that he didn't." The major record companies disagreed and quickly turned down the proposal. It looked as if the project would die until they met the executives at Cypress Records who decided to take a chance. Throughout 1986, recording sessions took place in Los Angeles, with Cohen flying out from Montreal, where he had been living, for a four-month stint to assist with production and the adjustment of lyrics. On "First We Take Manhattan," which he had recorded before he gave the song to Warnes, he rewrote the bridge several times because she disliked the two stanzas that begin with "And I thank you for those items that you sent me, the monkey and the plywood violin." Warnes also sings a different middle and concluding verse to "Ain't No Cure for Love." Cohen would often appear unannounced at the recording studio, glaring at Warnes through the glass until he felt she got the phrasing of a particular lyric right. But Warnes always felt she sang better when he was there.

After one session in the late spring of 1986, Cohen and Warnes went out for dinner at Mario's in Hollywood and she asked him about the album cover. On a napkin he rapidly sketched a torch held by two hands and the phrase "Jenny Sings Lenny." But Cohen's title and drawing weren't used; instead, the album was released as *Famous Blue Raincoat*, with the image of a battered blue raincoat on the front. Cohen, of course, preferred the torch and two hands.

The album was a hit, reaching number eight in the United States; for seven weeks it held a top spot in England, and went gold in Canada.

One critic said *Famous Blue Raincoat* had made Cohen's voice respectable again in America. "It has been conclusively established that I do not know how to sing," Cohen said, "but, like the bumblebee who defies the laws of aerodynamics, I persist . . . and I soar."

Famous Blue Raincoat demonstrated a wide musical range, from the pulsating guitar work of Stevie Ray Vaughan on "First We Take Manhattan," to the oddly grating voice of Cohen in duet with Warnes on "Joan of Arc" and the lyricism of Warnes on "Came so Far for Beauty." With sales of over 1.5 million, the album was a commercial success and got radio play. Several critics have suggested that without this album Cohen's re-emergence on the American scene could not have occurred, but Warnes never believed the album overshadowed Cohen or his singing.

What Warnes found so remarkable in Cohen's songs was their ability to "pry open your heart with a crowbar." Cohen changed the way she regarded music. His singing and its effect on his audiences was "the place where God and sex and literature meet . . . I've never known anyone with more courage to go where all of us are afraid to go." And she always recalls Cohen's remark that the divine, not the devil, can be found in the details: "Your most particular answer will be your most universal one," he once told her. She felt that his songwriting ability was unparalleled:

> Because of Leonard's facility with language and his sense of his place in the culture and his respect for traditional literature, he builds a lyric in such a way, whether it's use of interior rhyme or an eternal quality to the language, that the songs he writes beckon the soul with just the configuration of the lyric.

And Cohen found Warnes' sound extraordinary: "Her voice is like the California weather, filled with sunlight. But there is an earthquake behind it. It is that tension that I think defines Jennifer's remarkable gift." He often refers to her as the most underrated singer in America and has said that "if you want to hear what a woman is thinking, if you want to hear what a woman sounds like in 1992, listen to Jennifer Warnes."

At a Los Angeles warehouse to watch the filming of the Warnes' video "First We Take Manhattan," Cohen was photographed by publicist Sharon Weisz in his dark glasses, charcoal gray pin-striped suit, and white T-shirt, eating a banana. For him, the image was precise and revealing:

> Sharon showed it to me later and it seemed to sum me up perfectly. 'Here's this guy looking cool,' I thought, 'in shades and a nice suit. He seems to have a grip on things, an idea of himself.'

The only thing wrong, of course, is that he was caught holding a half-eaten banana.

> And it suddenly occurred to me that's everyone's dilemma: at the times we think we're coolest, what everyone else sees is a guy with his mouth full of banana . . . .

He admired the photo so much that it became the signature image for his 1988 hit album *I'm Your Man*, and the poster image of his 1988 world tour.

DURING the production and release of *Famous Blue Raincoat*, Cohen kept active by writing, traveling between the east and west coasts, trying his hand at acting, and giving readings. A cameo role in the television series *Miami Vice* as the head of INTERPOL drew more on his presence than his acting, and most of his scenes ended up on the cutting room floor. His role was praised but he was eventually fired, his lines rewritten for another actor. From March through May 1986, he did several readings, including one at New York's Carnival of the Spoken Word.

He sang on a compilation album to honor the fiftieth anniversary of the death of Lorca entitled *Poetas en Nueva York*. His contribution, "Take This Waltz," was recorded in September 1986 in Paris; a month later he participated in a celebration of the poet's work in Granada. In the house near Granada where Lorca was born, Cohen starred in a CBS video of his song, hopping like a kangaroo and then standing on his head for nearly four minutes. "I thought we should do something wilder, surreal [because] that's what Lorca brought us—surrealism." For his translation of the Lorca poem that became "Take This Waltz," he reportedly worked one hundred and fifty hours. During the filming, a Japanese tourist asked Cohen if he was a famous Spanish actor. "No, I'm a famous nobody," he replied.

In New York, another musical based on his work appeared: *Sincerely, L. Cohen*, put on by the Medicine Show Theater Company in June 1987. Directed and arranged by Barbara Vann, it grew out of a popular set of readings of his work done in New York in 1986. Cohen assisted in the selection of material, and the success of the production marked the renewed interest in his work; he had re-emerged, and journalists noted that although Cohen might have been out of fashion, he was never far from the scene. *Chatelaine*, a Canadian women's magazine, voted him one of the "Ten Sexiest Men in Canada" that year.

Roshi continued to animate his life. An anniversary gathering was held for him at the Biltmore Hotel in Los Angeles on October 4, 1987, marking Roshi's twenty-five years in America. To commemorate the event, *The Zen of Myoshin-ji Comes to the West* appeared in a limited edition of two hundred numbered copies. In pictures and prose, it told the story of Roshi's life as the child of farmers, his arrival in America, his efforts at establishing a vibrant school of Rinzai in America, the success of his teaching, and the many centers then in existence in California, New Mexico, Texas, New York, and Puerto Rico. Cohen participated in the production of the book and the gala evening.

———————

COHEN EXPERIENCED intense depressions as he struggled with the songs for *I'm Your Man*. His relationship with Dominique was faltering. His depression was recurrent and he retried a variety of solutions from the past: travel, Zen, sex, drugs, Judaism, exercise. This time he read a book titled *The Positive Value of Depression* and consulted the work of the mystical Hasidic rabbi Nahman of Bratslav, who treated depression as a "holy condition." But recording the album became a difficult process. "It broke down a lot," he said, "I had to leave it many times and I spent a lot of money and my judgments were all wrong. In the middle of recording, I realized that the lyrics were all wrong, and they'd already taken a year or two to write." Cohen went into the studio with what he thought were finished songs, but "I couldn't get behind the lyrics, even though they had taken months and sometimes years to finish. Although they had a certain integrity, they didn't represent me accurately enough. I couldn't find a voice for them. So I had to start over almost every song." This album, he explained, was more holistic than the others, possessing a unified vision, although it had been recorded in Los Angeles, Montreal, and Paris.

The work had paid off. The album shot to the top of the charts in England when it was released on February 14, 1988, and it was nominated for album of the year in both England and the U.S. It remained number one for seventeen weeks in Norway and for almost as long in Spain. Sales in the United States, however, were low, despite an enthusiastic critical response. He was outside the commercial system. "Everything is public and the commercial institutions are now the landscaping of this public world," Cohen said. "There's nowhere else for you to exist . . . Unless you are in the system here, you don't exist." CBS Records awarded Cohen a Crystal Globe award, reserved for performers who have sold more than five million albums overseas. At the ceremony, Cohen commented that "I have always been touched by the modesty of their interest in my work." *I'm Your Man* helped restore Cohen's commerical appeal and re-invent the sixties' bohemian as an eighties' hipster.

The album opens with "First We Take Manhattan," originally called "In Old Berlin." It plays with certain geo-political ideas then in the air, he explained to an Oslo interviewer: extremism, terrorism, fundamentalism. They are all attractive positions because they lack ambiguity; such dogmatism is always seductive, he added, because of its "total commitment to a position without any qualifications, without any conditions . . . there is some kind of secret life we lead in which we imagine ourselves changing things, not violently, maybe gracefully, maybe elegantly in a very imaginative way and with the shake of a hand. The song speaks of longing for change, impatience with the way things are, a longing for significance; we deal in the purest burning logic of longing." Two years later, he referred to the song as a "demented manifesto," although he also reported that it became so popular in Athens that people were greeting each other in Greek by saying, "First, we take Manhattan," the other person replying with "Then we take Berlin!"

"Take This Waltz" was an elegant rendition of the Lorca poem originally recorded on *Poetas en Nueva York*. Expanding the images and adding a stronger, surrealistic element to the original poem, Cohen augmented the verse with music. The poem as song becomes a metacommentary on the deathly tradition it possesses, clarified by the refrain: "This waltz, this waltz, this waltz, this waltz. With its very own breadth of brandy and Death. Dragging its tail in the sea." Lorca sought "to get at the dramatic depths of the ballad and set them into action." The basis for such evocation are the slow movements which "ought to be the plastic algebra of a drama of passion and pain." Lorca's phrase "plastic algebra" is pure Cohen, an expression he could have made up. To a Spanish journalist Cohen said that Lorca's transcendental vision taught him that poetry can be pure and profound, as well as popular.

"Jazz Police," the most unorthodox song on the album, was Cohen's response to his band's effort to introduce augmented fifths and sevenths to their playing. He policed such jazz intrusions, although he admits that he wasn't sure of the lyric's meaning and grew to dislike the conceit. But he left it on the album because "it caught the mood of this whole period . . . this kind of fragmented absurdity." "I Can't Forget," with its limpid language, "started off as a song about the exodus of the Hebrew people from Egypt. As a metaphor for the journey of the soul from bondage into freedom." It started that way, "but in the studio I couldn't handle it and couldn't sing about a burden being lifted since mine hadn't." Originally called "Taken Out of Egypt," which took months to write, it had to be recast, beginning with the question "What is my life?" "That's when I started writing that lyric: "I stumbled out of bed / I got ready for the struggle / I smoked a cigarette / And I tightened up my gut."

"Tower of Song" is the keynote work on *I'm Your Man*. With it Cohen wanted to "make a definitive statement about this heroic enterprise of the craft" of songwriting. In the early eighties he called the work "Raise My Voice in Song." His concern was with the aging songwriter, and the "necessity to transcend one's own failure by manifesting as the singer, as the songwriter." He had abandoned the song, but one night in Montreal he finished the lyrics and called an engineer and recorded it in one take with a toy synthesizer. Jennifer Warnes added some vocals and Cohen attempted some "repairs," which was difficult since there were only two tracks. It was intitially felt that the quality was too poor and the musicality too thin. Warnes, however, "really placed it, putting it in the ironic perspective it needed; she was a real collaborator on it more than anything she ever did—and she's done wonderful things for me but this was the most wonderous thing she ever did for me, this doo-wop kind of perspective; she really illuminated the song with that contribution," Cohen said.

The revised song contains a classic Cohen opener, both self-reflexive and comic, positioning the singer in a new-found posture: "Well, my friends are gone / and my hair is grey. / I ache in the places / where I used to play. / And I'm crazy for love / but I'm not coming on. / I'm just paying my rent every day / in the Tower of Song."

When he had written the song and completed the album, Cohen realized for the first time that he was an entertainer: "I never thought I *was* in showbiz." Until then, he had held on to the notion of being a writer: "Now I know what I am. I'm not a novelist. I'm not the light of my generation. I'm not the spokesman for a new sensibility. I'm a songwriter living in L.A. and this is my record."

His own tower of song was the second-story study of his modest Los Angeles home, where he kept a fax machine, an electronic keyboard/synthesizer, and a computer on an oversized, roughly cut wooden table. He quickly adjusted to using a computer: "They say that the Torah was written with black fire on white fire. So I get that feeling from the computer, the bright black against the bright background. It gives a certain theatrical dignity to see it on the screen." The keyboard/synthesizer allows him to "mock up" his songs with various accompaniments to test their musical possibilities.

Supporting the April release of the single "Ain't No Cure For Love," Cohen sent a note to the CBS sales reps that read, "I don't really know how to do this, but I hear you'll be working my record, so here's two dollars." His joke was prompted by the publication of Fredric Dannen's *Hit Men*, exposing the shoddy dealings of the record industry and the importance of payola. Reaction to the album was positive; it was hailed for its accessible sound and incisive lyrics, "a sardonic last call from a ravaged *roué*." The month the album was released Cohen began a forty-one concert European tour.

Rehearsals for the tour were grueling and several days spent on perfecting one song was not uncommon. Often Cohen would complain that "it doesn't sound like music." Arrangements would change quickly and new approaches would be tried. A backup singer, for example, suggested a funkier version of "First We Take Manhattan," replacing the Euro-Disco sound Jennifer Warnes used on *Famous Blue Raincoat*. It worked and Cohen used it. He constantly reminded his singers and musicians that "what you have to go for is honesty, not complication." By honesty he meant an openness to the music and to oneself that would transcend even a flawless technique.

Reaction to his European performances was strong. Playing in smaller halls meant that the band was in some cities for two or three nights, allowing publicity to build and the people to swarm. Once on a ship leaving Denmark for Sweden, Cohen was besieged by groups of teenage girls screaming for his autograph. He acceded to each request. In Iceland, he was received by the president, who held a reception in his honor. The band included two new vocalists, Perla Batalla and Julie Christensen. Batalla had performed with the Motels, Cheap Trick, and Ted Nugent; Christensen had a gutsy sound drawn from years of singing with L.A. jazz and rock bands. John Bilezikjian played oud; Bobby Furgo, violin and keyboards; Bobby Metzger, guitars; and Steve Meador, drums. Tom McMorran assisted with keyboards, and Stephen Zirkel with bass and trumpet. Roscoe Beck was the musical director.

In December 1988, Cohen was disturbed by the unexpected death of Roy Orbison, just as his career was reviving with the Traveling Wilburys. A few days later a memorial was held in the lobby of the Wiltern Theater in Los Angeles. Cohen and Jennifer Warnes attended. Orbison had become the musical signature for Cohen's 1988 tour. In rehearsal Cohen would tell the band to "make it like Roy Orbison would do it," which led to an onstage joke, "Orbisize this song." The musicians had a picture of Orbison pasted into their chart folder.

Cohen's North American tour included the Théâtre St. Denis in Montreal, where, after his second performance, he met privately with former prime minister Pierre Trudeau. Afterwards, Cohen told reporters that they discussed "what you have to do to get a good review in this town," alluding to his mother's comment concerning his 1971 performance in Montreal when he failed to get a single positive notice.

Cohen's voice, like Dylan's, had long been the subject of jokes and imitations. In "Tower of Song" Cohen defused criticism by deadpanning, "I was born like this, / I had no choice, / I was born with the gift / Of a golden voice." In concert, cheers and applause greeted his ironic declaration. It was the unmusicality of his voice, which makes his phrasing flat and his ability to shift registers impossible, that led to his becoming a songwriter. "I think if I had one of those good voices, I would have done it completely differently. I probably would have sung the songs I really like rather than be a writer . . . I just don't think one would have bothered to write if one could have really lifted one's voice in song. But that wasn't my voice. This is my voice." A new self-confidence, if not happiness, began to seep through his persona of darkness. "I've come a long way compared to the kind of trouble I was in when I was younger. Compared to that kind of trouble, this kind of trouble [the difficulty of songwriting] sounds like peace to me . . . I'm a lot more comfortable with myself than I was a while ago. I'm still writing out of the conflicts and I don't know if they'll ever resolve."

A 1988 BBC film, "Songs from the Life of Leonard Cohen," capitalized on his renewed profile. It combined concert footage with an interview, early film clips, and documentary footage from Hydra. The film lacked a unifying narrative, but it showed a much more relaxed and confident performer than the one seen in the 1972 film "Bird on the Wire."

Cohen also performed on *Austin City Limits*, a one-hour concert filmed in Austin, Texas, for PBS television and appeared on David Sanborn's late-night show in New York where he did a memorable duet with Sonny Rollins. When Rollins began a sensational saxophone solo on "Who By Fire," Cohen turned his back to the camera to admire the jazz great. Taking advantage of his popularity, CBS/SONY reissued all of Cohen's albums on CD, making *Various Positions* widely available for the first time and his earliest work accessible in the new digital format. At the age of fifty-four, Cohen was becoming a rock star.

IN 1989 Cohen's work appeared as the centerpiece of a celebration of fifty years of Canadian Poetry in English at the National Library of Canada in Ottawa. The title of the exhibit was "Let Us Compare Mythologies," and references to Cohen appeared throughout the catalogue. The opening paragraph described Cohen's first book and its centrality to the exhibit's theme, the title chosen "as a tribute to Leonard Cohen and to all poets who have enriched Canada's literary heritage over the last half century." Cohen's writing, the catalogue stated, "links two vital periods in the history of modern poetry in Canada," the period of the 1940s when the work of Raymond Souster, Irving Layton, and Louis Dudek opened Canadian poetry to international influences, and the 1960s when poet and audience were united through performance. That was a time when "poetic voices became intensely personal," challenging traditional forms. A later section highlighted Cohen's "romantic lyricism" and explained his move into popular music as "both natural and inevitable given his lyrical and accessible style."

Despite the success of his album and recent honors, Cohen's personal life continued to be plagued by unhappiness. Various women arrived and left. Sean Dixon, whom he first met at Rock Steady, the L.A. recording studio where he mixed *I'm Your Man*, spent a good deal of time with him and became a friend. He spent time with Claudia Kim and later with an Egyptian woman from Paris. His romantic world was framed by his breakup, reconciliation, and final separation from Dominique Issermann, and he was again depressed. A female friend attributed his inability to sustain a long-term relationship to his basic mistrust of and deep anger at women, originating, perhaps, with his mother, who tried to control him with tears and guilt and food. He was still bitter over his breakup with Suzanne, who had initiated a lawsuit staking financial claims (she already had a house in France and custody of the children). The suit was dismissed in court, but added to his mistrust of women.

Cohen was always in need of a relationship but each relationship was conducted on his stringent terms. He required commitment but couldn't always offer it in return. He wanted intimacy, but he also wanted freedom. He was depressive and vulnerable and used his charm like a switchblade. Zen and romance, or Zen and Prozac, or Zen and whatever temporarily exorcised his demons. But they always returned. Throughout the eighties Cohen continued to use drugs but they had taken the form of antidepressants and legitimate pharmaceuticals. There have been times when he could not get out of bed, when the storm in the brain, as William Styron described it in his book *Darkness Visible*, overtook him. Of his depression, Cohen said, "That's what it's all about. Every day, every morning I face it, I try to deal with it." He has resisted control, especially by women, and has not lived with a woman since Suzanne left. Some stay for a while, but none move their things into his home, nor does he move into theirs. He cannot commit himself to anyone but Roshi.

At those moments when "he has no psychic skin," he needs his private space. Sean Dixon recalls that in 1990 and 1991, when he was writing "The Future," "Democracy," and "Waiting for the Miracle," she would often force him to leave his synthesizer to go out for food, but the company was not always pleasant. "We would go out to lunch a lot and he would sort of sit there like a little zombie, mumbling to himself. And then he would recite lyrics now and then." When she would bring him the news that Communism was falling, or that the Berlin Wall was going down, or that the president of Romania had been deposed, he would say, "It's hell, darling; you have no idea of what's going to happen. It's going to be very dark. Very bad things are going to come out of this. Believe me." Dixon was exasperated: "Leonard, you just can't get happy about anything!"

When he read her the opening verses of "The Future," she told him they were appalling. "You can't say things like that!" she exclaimed. But he didn't listen, and gradually, she agreed with his point of view. As he predicted, "*Things are going to slide in all directions / Won't be nothing / Nothing you can measure anymore.*" After completing the lyrics to a song, he would occasionally go to the mini-studio at the Record Plant to experiment with the sounds and possibilities. And when he was fighting with a lyric, he would often ask anyone to help. Dixon remembers her contributon to "Waiting for the Miracle." A line in the final verse read "If you're pressed for information, / That's when you've got to play it dumb." She thought "pressed" was too mild and suggested "squeezed." He liked the change and incorporated the word.

Cohen's work was interrupted in 1990 by his son's serious car accident in Guadaloupe. Adam Cohen had to be airlifted to a North York,

Ontario, hospital, where Cohen virtually lived for three months. The injuries were major, involving broken ribs, fractured vertebrae, and a damaged hip. The hiatus slowed Cohen's normally stately artistic crawl to a halt, but after his son had recovered, Cohen returned to Los Angeles, eager to continue working.

Around Christmas of 1990, Cohen began his highly publicized winter-spring romance with the actress Rebecca De Mornay. Cohen says he first noticed De Mornay during a visit in the late sixties to the Summerhill school in England. He recalls a strikingly beautiful five-year-old girl who turned out to be De Mornay. She recalls that she first heard him sing when she was ten, when her mother played her one of his early albums. De Mornay went on to become tremendously adept as an athlete with skills in Tae Kwon Do, a Korean martial art, as well as horseback riding. After high school in Australia, she enrolled in Lee Strasberg's Los Angeles acting institute and then continued her studies with Francis Ford Coppola at his Zoetrope Studios. She debuted in Coppola's *One From the Heart*. Cohen was properly introduced to her in Paris in 1986 at a party given by Robert Altman and they became friends. By December 1990, they had begun a romantic relationship which lasted for more than three years, their twenty-eight-year age difference apparently no barrier.

De Mornay had been in the movie business for almost ten years before she became a star with *The Hand that Rocks the Cradle*, appearing in *Risky Business*, *And God Created Woman*, and *Backdraft* before earning attention from her role as the disturbed and violent nanny in the 1992 hit. Previously involved with Tom Cruise, De Mornay had also been married for a short time to a Los Angeles screenwriter. Cohen's fans were startled to see him escorting De Mornay to the 1992 Academy Awards and his name suddenly appearing in numerous gossip columns. De Mornay accompanied him on his travels and video shoots and observed his recording sessions. She was eager to please, although many in Cohen's inner circle felt she was always scrutinizing Cohen's actions and behavior with his friends, especially his female friends. He credited her as co-producer of one song on his 1992 album, *The Future*, and he dedicated the album to her as Rebecca "coming forth," referring to a passage from Genesis. "Leonard is one of the most down-to-earth people I've ever met," De Mornay has said. "He never feels the party is somewhere else."

In an uncharacteristically cute celebrity moment, Cohen interviewed her for *Interview* magazine:

> De Mornay: Do you want to know what the best thing is about you
>   interviewing me?
> Cohen: No.
> De Mornay: It's . . .
> Cohen: I guess I do.
> De Mornay: . . . that you're the only interviewer who won't ask what
>   the exact nature of my relationship is with Leonard Cohen.
> Cohen: I would like to know. Let's start with that question.

When Cohen was later asked about the contradictions of his brooding lifestyle and his involvement with a high-profile actress, he answered, "Solid-gold artists would *kill* for this kind of anguish." By November 1993, however, their relationship had changed; he told a journalist earlier that summer that "Rebecca got wise to me and I'm not with her anymore . . . but Rebecca and I will always be friends in some kind of way. We were engaged but we're not engaged anymore."

Through his bouts of depression, Cohen retained a sense of humor. Perla Batalla sent him a personal ad from a San Francisco weekly that asked for a man who could combine the passion of Leonard Cohen with the rawness of Iggy Pop. Cohen had recently met Pop at a recording session, and when he showed him the ad, they decided to send a photo of the two of them to the female inquirer with their phone numbers.

Cohen's business arrangements by this time were complicated, partly because his lawyer lived in New York, while he was living in Los Angeles. For a time he rented out the downstairs of his house and lived upstairs in a sparsely furnished flat. Nearly ten years after buying the house, Cohen decided that he was ready to furnish it. He gradually acquired some rugs, tables, and chairs, a sign that he at last was feeling settled. In 1991 Kelley Lynch, a former legal assistant to Marty Machat, moved to Los Angeles and soon became Cohen's manager, as he shifted his business affairs to California following the death of Machat. The proximity of his business did not interfere with the completion of his new album, although the word chaos often described the situation around him as he prepared for a 1993 tour as part of the album's promotion.

His office, like his home, is furnished sparely, though it is suffused with light, which pours through large curved windows on the second floor and falls on the whitewashed wooden floors and large wooden tables. Greek or oriental rugs are scattered on the floors, but each of the four principal rooms has only a worktable, chair, and phone. The walls are white and bare. One office has a series of filing cabinets, and the fax and typewriters are tucked into a former pantry. Cohen's own office at the back is equally spare, remarkable only in the contrast between the large wooden table/desk and his high-tech, ergonomic chair. On the first floor, an untuned piano sits alone in the former living room. On the wall is a large gold, red, and yellow banner with four brown squares, representing the four noble truths of Buddhism. Cohen designed the banner for Roshi's eighty-fifth birthday.

COHEN'S SONGS were enjoying a renaissance, covered by other artists and being used in movie soundtracks. The Neville Brothers had a hit with "Bird on a Wire" in 1990, the year that Goldie Hawn and Mel Gibson starred in a comedy of the same name. "Everybody Knows" and "If It Be Your Will" appeared in the movie *Pump Up the Volume*, starring Christian Slater. Concrete Blonde sang "Everybody Knows" for the movie. A tribute album entitled *I'm Your Fan* featured a series of alternative bands performing Cohen's songs. The House of Love sang "Who by Fire," The Pixies did "I Can't Forget," REM performed "First We Take Manhattan," and Nick Cave sang "Tower of Song." The project had been initiated by Christian Fevret, editor of the influential French rock magazine *Les inrockuptibles*. Cohen was flattered by the attention and impressed with the original arrangements. They presented his songs to a younger generation of listeners.

Others could more lyrically convey his melodies, although not necessarily his substance. Buffy Sainte-Marie, Joe Cocker, Joan Baez, Neil

Diamond, Diana Ross, Jennifer Warnes, and Johnny Cash had all covered his songs. Suzanne Vega has repeatedly acknowledged his influence on her work. The release of a third tribute album, *Tower of Song*, further confirmed his influence as a songwriter.

On March 3, 1991, Cohen was inducted into the Juno Hall of Fame, the Canadian equivalent of the Grammys. "I am trying to stay alive and raw to the voices that speak to me," he stated after the presentation by his friend and founder of MuchMusic, Moses Znaimer. "If I had been given this attention when I was twenty-six," Cohen said, "it would have turned my head. At thirty-six, it might have confirmed my flight on a rather morbid spiritual path. At forty-six, it would have rubbed my nose in my failing powers and have prompted a plotting of a getaway and an alibi. But at fifty-six—hell, I'm just hitting my stride and it doesn't hurt at all."

In April 1991, he was honored with an even more prestigious award, appointment as an Officer of the Order of Canada. At his investiture on October 30, 1991, he was celebrated as:

> one of the most popular and influential writers of his generation whose work has . . . made Canadian literature familiar to readers abroad. Images of beauty, despair, outrage, and tenderness are found in his lyrical poetry and prose, whose themes of love, loss and loneliness touch a universal chord in us all.

That same month, Cohen was a surprise guest at a salute to Irving Layton that took place at the International Festival of Authors in Toronto. His appearance was a well-guarded secret because he did not want to upstage Layton. When he appeared, Cohen told the audience that "exposure to [Layton's] work moves us. . . . This is the tonic, the elixir. I salute the aching and triumphant impeccability of your life." Layton complimented Cohen on his fabulous timing. Three years later he admitted that Cohen's songs could still make him cry—not because they moved him but because he knows he will never write anything so beautiful. Cohen, Layton emphasized, "has never been disloyal to his genius."

13

M Y   S E C R E T

L I F E

C OHEN COULD SEE the flames from South Central Los Angeles reflected in his kitchen. The 1992 riots skirted his life, destroying the grocery store, musical supply store, and electronics store that he patronized. "From my balcony I could see five great fires. The air was thick with cinders [but] having been writing about such things for so long, it was no surprise." Los Angeles has always seemed an odd city for Cohen. He had grown up in the tight urban community of Montreal and spent time in seclusion on Hydra; L.A. offered the advantages of neither. It was a disembodied sprawl with a gift for the superficial and a civic amorality. The air was bad and the film industry had spread its corrupt charm, but the winters were mild. Jack Kerouac had described the city as a place where "those soft California stars . . . are lost in the brown halo of the huge desert encampment L.A. really is." But it had certain advantages; there were musicians and studios. And there was Roshi.

Cohen lived close to the Cimarron Zen Center. There, and at the Mt. Baldy Zen Center, Cohen continued his study of what he called "a training in self-reform." Cohen redefined himself to suit his context. "It's very dangerous for someone to describe themselves as a poet. I just think I'm a songwriter living in L.A. and, as Serge Gainsbourg said of himself, I'm kind of a pseudo-poet. I like that."

In a recent poem, "The Mist of Pornography," Los Angeles served as a backdrop:

> When you rose out of the mist of pornography
> with your talk of marriage and orgies
> and I was a mere boy of 57 trying to make a fast buck in the slow lane
> and it was ten years too late when I finally got the most beautiful girl
> on the Hollywood hill
> to go with her lips to the sunless place
> and the art of song was in my bones
> and the coffee died for me and I never answered any phone calls
> and I said a prayer for whoever called and didn't leave a message
> and this was my life in Los Angeles[.]

In an earlier poem, "My Life in Art," he had a similar feeling about the city's gift for destruction. "Six-fifty. Ruined in Los Angeles. I should start smoking again. I want to die in her arms and leave her."

In the *Los Angeles Times* Cohen described himself as a committed songwriter who rarely ventured out into the maelstrom of the city, although he observed it constantly and found in it a healthy level of discomfort. He thought the incongruities of the city were fascinating: through Zen and the Cimarron center, L.A. was the source of his spiritual life; through the music and record business, it was the source of his popularity.

Geologically and politically unstable, Los Angeles was the harbinger of the next millennium, a perfect backdrop for his album *The Future*, Cohen's first in four years. Originally titled "Busted," the record was to be recorded in Montreal, but when he started to work in Los Angeles with

Jennifer Warnes again as a backup vocalist for "Democracy," he saw the value of staying there to do the entire album. Musicians from the 1988 tour contributed, notably Bobby Metzger, Steve Meador, and Bobby Furgo.

"Democracy" was culled from more than eighty verses that had been written over the past several years. Don Henley performed the song at the MTV ball in Washington celebrating the January 1993 inauguration of President Bill Clinton. "Closing Time," with its hoedown feel, received radio play, but had the same difficult genesis. Cohen had recorded another version of the song, the result of wrestling with the verses for over two years, but he came "to the painful decision that I hadn't written it yet." He put down several tracks but felt he "couldn't get behind the lyric." He dumped the tracks and started over in March 1992 with a new melody and verses.

"Anthem" was borrowed from Kabbalistic sources, especially the sixteenth-century rabbi Isaac Luria. It was one of the most difficult songs Cohen had ever written, taking almost a decade to complete. He recorded it three times, with one version for *Various Positions* and another for *I'm Your Man*, mixed with strings, voices, and overdubs. It was finished, he explained, "but when I listened to it there was something wrong with the lyric, the tune, the tempo. There was a lie somewhere in there, there was a disclosure that I was refusing to make. There was a solemnity that I hadn't achieved." Only when he reworked it for *The Future* did he "nail it." Songwriting begins for him not in the form of an idea, but in the form of an image. He explained:

> the way I do things is that I uncover the song and discern what it's about through the actual writing of it. Every song begins with that old urgency to rescue oneself, to save oneself. And it's quite a powerful gnawing at the spirit. It's not at all evident at the beginning of the process what it [the song] is about.

Shaping the album is a darkening view of the political and moral developments of contemporary history, broadening the usual focus from his own despair. The title song, "The Future," was originally called "If You Could See What's Coming Next" and underwent extensive revision, occupying almost sixty pages in Cohen's notebooks.

The album sold over one hundred thousand copies in Canada in its first four months, earning platinum status, and the video for "Closing Time" won a Juno award for best rock video of 1994. It featured a boozy Cohen in a honky-tonk club, Toronto's Matador, singing:

And the whole damn place goes crazy twice
and it's once for the Devil and it's once for Christ
but the Boss don't like these dizzy heights
we're busted in the blinding lights
of Closing Time

Rebecca De Mornay partly directed and re-edited the video.

Cohen worked hard to promote the album, giving interviews, sharing his anguish over the songs with journalists and the public. At the Toronto launch party for the album, he signed a white leather shoe offered to him with his name and words borrowed from *Beautiful Losers*: "magic is afoot." In the video accompanying "The Future," Cohen was filmed standing in water which rises past the knees of his well-tailored suit. "A pessimist is someone who is waiting for it to rain," he has said. "But I'm already soaked to the skin." On March 21, 1993, Cohen won another Juno, this time for best male vocalist. In accepting Cohen said, "Only in a country like this with a voice like mine could I receive such an award."

In April of that year, after six weeks of rehearsals on the large sound stage at The Complex in Los Angeles, Cohen toured to support the album, playing twenty-eight concerts in Europe. Unlike the '88 tour, Cohen played larger halls, often stadiums or ice rinks, which created sound and recording problems. Soundchecks were problematic and the audiences often didn't fill the vast halls. Cohen was also suffering neck and shoulder pain which made traveling and performing more difficult. De Mornay joined him for part of the tour.

A North American tour followed. Allen Ginsberg attended the show at New York's Paramount Theater and remarked on Cohen's "gritty realistic voice . . . and the elegant ease of irony with which he thanked overzealous screamers and demanders in the audience—the language bitter, disillusioning like a practiced (Buddhist) Yankee-Canadian, always surprising." At the Vancouver concert Cohen was interrupted when he sang "let's do something crazy," from "Waiting for the Miracle." From the back of the Orpheum Theatre a woman's voice cried out, "Yessss, Leonard." After the laughter died down, he repeated the line, and the woman again responded. A third attempt brought the same response, even more longingly shouted. Cohen strolled upstage with the mike, and looking into the darkness, said, "There is nothing like an idea whose force does not diminish with repetition."

He was listed second among the top ten live performances in Boston in 1993, after Peter Gabriel. The *Boston Globe* wrote that "Leonard Cohen wrapped the most exquisite, sad poetry around exquisite chamber rock at the Berklee Performance Center." After the tour and the hype and the publicity, Cohen had had enough. He canceled a proposed tour of Eastern Europe in favor of some rest and spiritual renewal, beginning his most intense and sustained involvement with Roshi.

In September 1993, an hour-long special on his work, "The Gospel According to Leonard Cohen," was aired on CBC Radio with a long interview recorded in Montreal. Then, on October 5, 1993, it was announced that Cohen had won a Governor General's Performing Arts Award for his contribution to Canadian music. Presentation of the ten-thousand-dollar award was made in Ottawa on November 26 by the Governor General of Canada with a gala tribute to Cohen and the other winners the following evening at the National Arts Center. One of the highlights of the gala was dinner with the acclaimed Quebec singer Gilles Vigneault, also a winner, and a third guest, Pierre Trudeau, whom Cohen had long admired for his leadership during difficult times. That fall, Cohen and Trudeau both had books on the bestseller lists.

The attention and tributes created a curious blend of melancholy and satisfaction for Cohen. "I feel like a soldier," he said just hours before receiving his award. "You may get decorated for a successful campaign or a particular action that appears heroic but probably is just in the line of duty. You can't let these honors deeply alter the way you fight. If you do, I think you are really going to get creamed in the next battle. And I do feel like I am on the frontline of my own life." When asked what these honors meant to him, Cohen laughingly answered, "The implication is—*this is it!*" But he welcomed the tributes in his own country: "It is agreeable to have this recognition."

Coinciding with the Governor General's award was the release on November 13, 1993, of his long-awaited collection of poems and songs, *Stranger Music*. It was a book that had been in the works since the mid-eighties. Jack McClelland had long urged Cohen to assemble a collection of his best work. In a 1989 video that Adrienne Clarkson made for CBC television, Cohen is shown at his kitchen table selecting works with her and joking that it should be called "Everything I'm Not Embarrassed By." At other times, it was to be titled "New Selected Poems" and, later, "If the Moon Has a Sister, It's Got to be You, Selected Poems and Songs." *Stranger Music*, its final title, is a many-sided pun. It ironically refers to the nature of his writing and music and also alludes to the music publishing company he started up in the late sixties after "The Stranger Song" on his first album.

The original cover for the book was to be a "primitivist, protuberant purple *derrière*," set against a tomato-red background. Instead, his publisher chose a moody but evocative black and white photograph of Cohen. He had trouble determining the content of the book; in addition to poems, he wanted it to contain his songs, or at least a good part of them. By 1990, he had done all the work and "came up with three books: a short book, a middle-sized book, and a long book. I established this index, and the long book was prepared. It's done, it's finished, but at a certain point I lost interest in the project. I thought it should have a preface. I thought it should have something else besides the poems and the songs, and then I became distracted with other matters."

Cohen later admitted that another cause for delay was that he "could never get around to confronting the various dismalities that were presented [to] me, just the meagreness of the whole thing [the book project]." He turned to his friend Nancy Bacal to assist him, admitting that he didn't know where to begin. For months the two worked daily to select, revise, cut, and restore texts. His goal, according to Bacal, was to "select the pieces that express the place he finally got to rather than the road taken there." He wanted to eliminate the poems of searching or what he called "the messy ones." He also wanted works of simple but refined language. Then Rebecca De Mornay became involved, often arguing for inclusion of the so-called "messy" works, which demonstrated not the finished precision of his best writing but items that spilled over with emotion and feeling.

Late night sessions, debates, and numerous faxes went back and forth among Cohen, Bacal, and De Mornay until the manuscript was finished. In his words, he wanted

> a book that was a good, entertaining read from beginning to end. I tried to weed out the lyrics that didn't stand up as poems, and weed out the poems that didn't stand up on the page. I can never actually give up, so I keep moving words around. I don't alter things substantially, but there are nuances that change, expressions that I can no longer get behind, and phrases that my voice doesn't wrap around easily.

The final text of the book provides a chronological selection of his work, incorporating poetry, prose, and song. Noticeably absent, however, are any passages from *The Favorite Game*, his most autobiographical novel, perhaps an indication of his self-protective nature, even at this stage of his career. He also de-emphasizes the Montreal aspect of the collection, leaving out most of the poems about the city in favor of those dealing with foreign locales. The original selection from *Beautiful Losers* avoided sex, but then he realized it had to be there, since it was an essential component of the novel. The most widely cited text is *Death of A Lady's Man*, reworked and in some cases re-ordered from the original book, with new headings for some sections. Cohen himself has said that he is happiest with this version of the work, for he at last made the book "coherent," ridding it of a great deal that could not be penetrated in the original text.

Albums are only partially represented—"Dress Rehearsal Rag" from *Songs of Love and Hate*, "Heart with No Companion" from *Various Positions*, "Jazz Police," from *I'm Your Man*, and "Be for Real" from *The Future* all missing. Some notable poetic works one would expect to see are also not present—for example, "Go by Brooks," "Out of the Land of Heaven," and "The Bus." There are also some curious textual changes: the original version of "The Escape" was untitled in *The Energy of Slaves* and featured the line "I'm glad we ran off together." In *Stranger Music* he elaborates this to read "I'm glad we got over the wall / of that loathsome Zen monastery." The poetic forms of three songs—"Suzanne," "Avalanche," and "Master Song"—are replaced by their recorded versions. There is a section entitled "Uncollected Poems," with eleven works ranging from 1978 to 1987 and written in Paris, Mt. Baldy, Hydra, and Montreal. This section caused some disagreement among the three editors, and two works were excluded from the finished manuscript, one dealing with Robert Hershorn.

Jack McClelland was now acting as Cohen's agent and he had to convince Doug Gibson, now publisher of McClelland & Stewart, that Cohen preferred informal agreements. In lieu of a contract, a letter of agreement was drawn up and Gibson accepted it, although he stipulated that the volume was to be a "major new book by Leonard Cohen with a heavily autobiographical slant, i.e., a lengthy introduction and a central text that contained his finest poems." By January 1990, however, Cohen had lost interest in the project and his son's accident in September of that year further delayed the book.

The matter of an introduction remained contentious. Cohen wanted a short statement and Gibson was pushing for an autobiographical essay. Disagreements slowed progress, while song lyrics were added. Everyone was becoming impatient. By August 1991, a proposed twenty-thousand-word introduction was dropped, although Gibson thought it would be the key selling point of the book. He suggested a less formal piece, perhaps "reflections on his career, reflections on his life . . . think of this as a riff; introductory by virtue of its placement in the book." Cohen still refused, choosing to keep the book clean, free from any introductory declaration.

Nevertheless, *Stranger Music* provides the most comprehensive single-volume collection of poems and lyrics now in print. It is important because most of his poetry has been out of print for years. For a younger generation of fans, his activity as a writer was a surprise; they were startled to learn that he wrote anything but songs. The volume reaffirms the union between poet and songwriter, which Cohen never separated. Cohen himself thought of the book as a sort of poetic autobiography: "I tried to eliminate poems that suffered from those youthful obscurities and rambling intoxications of language, poems that really didn't stand up. I wanted my better poems to be around. What is here are the poems that survived my scrutiny. In any case, it's selected poems, not collected poems."

Reaction to *Stranger Music* was positive, although there were quibbles over the failure to print every song and every poem (the only volume to come close to a full publication of his lyrics is the dual language, *Leonard Cohen, Canzoni da una stanza*, edited by Massimo Cotto [Milan, 1993]). The book quickly went to number four on *The Globe and Mail* national bestseller list and a second hardcover printing was necessary.

The book was also published in a limited edition: one hundred and twenty-five signed and numbered copies, specially bound and elaborately presented in a clamshell box which contained three signed, limited-edition prints drawn by Cohen. Even priced at three hundred and fifty dollars each, the books quickly sold out. The sudden reappearance of his earlier works in paperback prompted him to comment that "it's very agreeable at fifty-eight to see these books you wrote at twenty-five, twenty-eight. I'm delighted. You do have that sense of vindication of people who were really misunderstood in their time and then re-discovered." His reputation as a professional depressive, he felt, wasn't entirely warranted. "I'm really not all that morose. But you get nailed with something and every time they call your name up on the computer it reads 'depressed and suicidal.' I'm probably one of the few people that actually have jokes and a few light moments in their songs and poems."

Following the necessary publicity for *Stranger Music*, Cohen largely withdrew from public life to spend time with Roshi and act again as his principal secretary. This meant a grueling schedule, not only in the daily activities at Mt. Baldy but in the visits Roshi made to various Rinzai Zen centers in New Mexico, Puerto Rico, Vienna, and upstate New York.

In July 1994, Cohen came to New York to spend a day shooting the video of "Dance Me to the End of Love" from his new release *Cohen Live*. In between takes and re-takes, he visited his sister Esther and her husband Victor, who was suffering from a deteriorating illness. He extended his stay to be with them; within a month Victor had died.

Cohen Live featured performances from his 1988 and 1993 tours, mixing new versions of old songs. Cohen felt that this album represented "the final pages of a chapter" that began with *Various Positions* and continued with *I'm Your Man* and *The Future.* "These are old songs refashioned," he said. "The voice has deepened after fifty-thousand cigarettes." The critical reception was mixed. *Time* magazine wrote, "This glum, melancholy collection should be dispensed only with large doses of Prozac."

After the promotional tour for the live album, Cohen concentrated on Zen and his writing, admitting that the quiet of the monastary was only occasionally disrupted by the sound of his composing on his electric keyboard. And occasionally a glass: "I only drink professionally," he told one interviewer in late 1993, "I don't practice meditation anymore. I practice drinking. My Zen master gave up trying to instruct me in spiritual matters but he saw that I had a natural aptitude for drinking."

Cohen narrated *The Tibetan Book of the Dead* for the National Film Board of Canada, lending his authoritative voice to the project. Barrie McLean, co-producer and director of the NFB film, first asked Cohen to revise the original narration, which had been prepared for the Japanese version. Cohen declined, recommending Douglas Penick, a Buddhist expert, who rewrote it. Cohen then recorded the narration for the two-part film, the first entitled "A Way of Life"; the second, "The Great Liberation." A co-production between NHK Japan, Mistral Film, France, and the National Film Board of Canada, the film was a remarkable portrait of life in the Himalayas and the rituals of Buddhist practice. In the film, monks read the *Bardo thodol*, or *Tibetan Book of the Dead*, to the dying and then reread it during the forty-nine days after physical death to assist the consciousness in choosing the right path. Roshi believed the book to be "a Tibetan fairy tale" and Cohen partially shared his view. "I respect the book and I respect the tradition," he said, "but it's not the one I'm studying in. But fairy tales have within them deep truths, even if they are expressed as paradoxes. . . .the major advice [in the work] is to view all things that happen to you as projects of your self. Not to run from them but to embrace them, and that is always valuable." When asked himself if he was afraid of death, Cohen answered that it's not the event that is worrying, it's the preliminaries: "the event itself seems perfectly natural."

His musical profile had rarely been higher. He appeared on Elton John's record *Duets*, singing Ray Charles's "Born to Lose" with John, and "Everybody Knows" had been used on the soundtrack of Canadian filmmaker Atom Egoyan's *Exotica*. "I'm Your Man" was featured in Nanni Moretti's Italian film *Caro Diario* and "Waiting for the Miracle," "Anthem," and "The Future" were all on the soundtrack of Oliver Stone's controversial film *Natural Born Killers*. Johnny Cash covered "Bird on a Wire" on *American Recordings*.

In honor of Cohen's sixtieth birthday on September 21, 1994, a book of poems, analyses, and appreciations of his work was published. Titled *Take This Waltz*, it included contributions by Joan Baez, Judy Collins, Louis Dudek, Allen Ginsberg, Kris Kristofferson, Jack McClelland, Phil Spector, and Jennifer Warnes. Otherwise, his sixtieth birthday, spent flying to Vienna with Roshi, passed with little attention: "I was ready to pass it off as another irrelevant occasion." But the congratulations offered by numerous friends and well-wishers forced him to reconsider it. Months after the event, he began to understand its significance:

I remember when I was about forty-five going into a *sanzen* with Roshi and his saying, 'Your generation is finished.' And it was such refreshing news. For somehow when you grow up in North American underground culture, you always feel you're representing the cutting edge and that you speak for the young and you speak for the alternative. . . . Forget it, Leonard, you're not that any more. Look at yourself. It was refreshing news. It's for the young. . . . So it was with the 60th birthday, although I had been prepared to ignore it, as I ignored all my birthdays. There was something about it that was indisputably connected with the threshold of old age. It was a landmark of some kind in my own tiny little journey.

As soon as I absorbed it, I was able to relax in a way that I had never relaxed before because I really thought, well, it was okay, it is the end of one's youth so to say. . . . In this culture you can extend it, you really can extend a personal vision of your own youth up to the age of sixty and then there is something indisputable about the end of youth; now you can begin something else. Well it is the threshold of something else.

A poem published in June 1994 articulated some of these feelings:

On the path of loneliness
I came to the place of song
and tarried there
for half my life
Now I leave my guitar
and my keyboards
my drawings and my poems
my new Turkish carpets
my few friends and sex companions
and I stumble out
on the path of loneliness
I am old but I have no regrets
not one
though I am angry and alone
and filled with fear and desire.

In June 1995 *Dance Me to the End of Love* was published, a book that merged the lyrics to his song from *Various Positions* with twenty-one images by Henri Matisse. Musically, he thought of preparing an album of fourteen short songs, none more than three minutes in length. One song was recorded, "I Was Never Any Good at Loving You," but he quickly realized that he had "a ponderous mind that seems to need eight or ten stanzas to uncover the idea of the song." The project was put aside.

In August 1995, *Tower of Song*, his third tribute album, appeared. More of a mainstream effort than *Famous Blue Raincoat* or *I'm Your Fan*, the album contains performances by some of the most acclaimed singers in pop music: Billy Joel, Tori Amos, Sting, Bono, Elton John, Peter Gabriel, Suzanne Vega, Don Henley, Jann Arden, Willie Nelson, and Aaron Neville. Grateful for the effort, Cohen remarked that "I am very very happy when anybody covers any of my songs. My critical faculties go into immediate suspension. . . . Whatever good things happen to my songs are deserved because they're not casually made." In appreciation, Cohen sent silver letter openers to each artist on the album.

The novelist Tom Robbins wrote the liner notes, summarizing

Cohen's life in this fashion: "A quill in his teeth, a solitary teardrop a-squirm in his palm, he was the young poet prince of Montreal" who found direction in language and song. As rock music weakens and "the sparkle curtain has shredded," Cohen sits "at an altar in the garden, solemnly enjoying newfound popularity and expanded respect." His lyrics, Robbins muses, "can peel the apple of love and the peach of lust with a knife that cuts all the way to the mystery." Cohen's voice, he concludes, was "meant for pronouncing the names of women. Nobody can say the word 'naked' as nakedly as Cohen."

The appearance of the album led to reassessments of Cohen's work. His insistent pessimism had become the new reality; the world had caught up to Cohen's vision. An essay in *Time* in the fall of 1995 entitled "In Search of Optimism" featured Cohen and *The Future*, using his line from "Anthem," "there is a crack in everything, that's how the light gets in," as a sign of a new philosophy that allowed many to see promise in the treacherous landscape (which literally occurred in 1994 when a Scottish clergyman attributed his survival in a snowslide to his singing Leonard Cohen songs the entire night).

In an interview with Anjelica Houston that fall, Cohen articulated his optimistic view of love which, despite his personal defeats, he still believes is lasting. Although we don't know what to do with it, "when [love] can be assimilated into the landscape of panic, it is the only redeeming possibility for human beings. . . . We actually lead very violent, passionate lives and I think that we're hungry for insights into this condition."

Amid the publications and the albums, Cohen's involvement with Roshi intensified. In 1993 he moved permanently to the isolated monastary, living in a sparsely furnished, two-room cabin, his only comforts a synthesizer, a small radio and a narrow cot. He eats, prays, and studies with the monks. Despite the meager surroundings, there is a richness of creative spirit, and a pattern emerges that originated in Cohen's youth. Once his life becomes too cluttered, he moves to an empty room. He removes the debris and starts over again, seeking a clean slate that the bohemian life of Montreal, the remote island of Hydra, and the isolated forest of Mt. Baldy have variously given him. Spiritually, this parallels a shift from the ornate elements of Judaism to the austere practice of Zen; physically, it parallels his change from the dark suits and hip L.A. look to the simple monk's robes he dons when he arrives at Mt. Baldy. The sun-glasses, however, often remain. For Leonard Cohen survival means rein-vention and simplification. "Nowadays my only need is to jot everything down. I don't feel that I am a singer, or a writer. I'm just the voice, a living diary."

At the monastery Cohen cooks, does repairs, and looks after Roshi, as well as participating in the daily rituals of Zen. He travels constantly with his teacher and assists with the administration of five new centers, including one in Montreal called Centre Zen de la Main, which opened in the summer of 1995 in The Plateau, his old neighborhood.

His relationship with Roshi has a playful complexity to it. Cohen has joked that his principal role has been to introduce Jewish food into Roshi's diet and that Roshi's has been to introduce Cohen to drinking. But it deepens when he expresses his admiration for Roshi's incorpora-tion of the spiritual with the sensual. "With him," Cohen has said, "there's no sense of piety divorced from the human predicament." More recently, Roshi has decided to study red wine under Cohen's tutelage.

At Mt. Baldy, discipline and hardship reign, and Cohen rises at three a.m. and walks to the meditation hall in the snow. "I love it, man. Every-thing's perfect. It couldn't be worse. I've always been drawn to the volup-tuousness of austerity . . . [but] I'm working on a song while I'm sitting there." The life is worth it. When asked what Roshi and Rinzai Zen con-tributed to his work and life, Cohen unequivocally answered, "Survival."

Cohen explains his involvement with Zen as the fulfillment of what he understands as his priestly calling. He has made the symbolic decision to follow Buddha's precept that at the age of fifty you renounce your possessions and walk about the world with only a bowl. "For me, it hap-pened ten years later," he noted. He has considered writing a commen-tary on the first verse of Bereshith (Genesis) emphasizing his view that the world was created out of chaos and desolation.

In 1994 Cohen summarized the importance of Zen to him by what it does not do:

[Zen] has a kind of empty quality. There is no prayerful worship. There's no supplication, there's no dogma, there's no theology. I can't even locate what they're talking about most of the time. But it does give you an opportunity, a kind of version of Hemingway's "A Clean Well-Lighted Place." It gives you a place to sit that is quiet in which you can work these matters out.

In 1992 Roshi celebrated thirty years of teaching Zen in America. A commemorative book entitled *The Great Celebration*, containing an interview with Roshi and a *teisho*, as well as a survey of Rinzai-ji centers, was published to mark the occasion, and his eighty-fifth birthday. Cohen and Kelley Lynch organized the commemoration in Los Angeles and oversaw publication of the book. Cohen also designed an emblem for the front cover. In the summer of 1995, he marked the occasion of Roshi's thirty-three years of teaching in America by arranging a day of song and prayer at the Cimarron Zen Center.

Just as 1977 marked the "death of a lady's man," in the 1990s Cohen sees his relationship with Zen changing. A proposed omnibus collection, encompassing notebooks and poems from his archive, will have a section of new poems tentatively entitled "The Collapse of Zen." The proposed title of the entire volume, "The Book of Longing," suggests a possible shift in his personal practice of Zen after Roshi dies. With his teacher aging, his own position may alter, continuing what has been the defining characteristic of his career: movement, change, reinvention—the assumption of various positions in an effort to locate a vantage point from which he can operate in his quest for *kensho*, the experience of seeing into the true nature of things.

For almost thirty years, Zen and Judaism have interacted to provide a method for Cohen to deal with his spiritual life and public career. His life embodies the Zen view that harmony with the universe can only occur if each thing/event is allowed to be freely and spontaneously itself. This aspect of Zen belief, that immediate experience makes contact with the absolute, is part of the koan of *Mu*, or nothingness, which teaches that being is nothingness, and parallels the genesis of Hasidism in the *ayin*, or naught. Hasidic thought stresses knowing the absolute through direct religious experience rather than through theology or doctrine. Only through a concentrated focus on individual truth can one comprehend spiritual happiness. Discipline, integrity, spirit, and generosity—all ingredients of Zen—form the essential lexicon of Leonard Cohen. They establish a basis not just of action but of belief that Judaism, Zen, music, writing, and learning have reaffirmed.

Women are the source of Cohen's pain and loss: "the crumbs of love that you offer me / are the crumbs I've left behind," he sings. He longs "for the boundaries / of my wandering" but still leaves. He has been largely defenseless against the beauty and energy of women, writing

I'll rise up one of these days,
find my way to the airport.
I'll rise up and say
I loved you better than you loved me
and then I'll die for a long time
at the centre of my own dismal organization,
and I'll remember today,
the day when I was that asshole in a blue summer suit
who couldn't take it any longer.

For all his despair, Leonard Cohen has led a life of unfettered romance, largely free of obligations or responsibility. It has been bolstered by faith and pitted with depression. In the late summer of 1995, Cohen observed that his life didn't much interest him. "I find that my life has become so much my own I don't have an objective view of it any more . . . the things that happened to me I don't look at objectively any more. They're cellular." Mastering his life has allowed him at sixty-two to enjoy it for the first time. Things from the past no longer get in his way; although he has not attained all he has desired, he is now able to see more clearly what is necessary to take him closer to his goals, aided in the last twenty-five years by his study of Zen.

On the wall of Cohen's sunlit Los Angeles study is a Kabbalistic amulet or *kame'a*. It is the image of an open, ornate hand with golden Hebrew lettering inscribed on the palm and inside each of the fingers, which are surrounded by Hebrew texts of mystical importance and encompassed by a large silver "H" (pronounced "hey" in Hebrew). One of the prayers contains forty-two words, the initials of which form the secret forty-two-letter name of God, while the six initials of each of its seven verses form additional Divine Names.

Has this holy object warded off misfortune? Has the shrine to Catherine Tekakwitha, the Canadian saint-in-waiting, a few feet away in his kitchen, prevented disaster? Did the *zendo*, once located on the ground floor of his home, provide the meditational path he long sought? He would likely deny the individual power of any of these talismans and the worlds they represent, just as he would deny that he is happy. Like many of us, Cohen is unsure of what steps are necessary to secure one's psychic and spiritual health. Yet the ability to love, write, compose, and practice both Zen and Judaism are for him the best protection against all that might father disorder. For Cohen, mastering the dawn as well as the night is a triumph.

BIBLIOGRAPHY

POETRY

Let Us Compare Mythologies. Toronto: Contact Press, 1956.
The Spice-Box of Earth. Toronto: McClelland & Stewart, 1961.
Flowers for Hitler. Toronto: McClelland & Stewart, 1964.
Parasites of Heaven. Toronto: McClelland & Stewart, 1966.
Selected Poems, 1956–1968. Toronto: McClelland & Stewart, 1968.
The Energy of Slaves. Toronto: McClelland & Stewart, 1972.
Death of A Lady's Man. Toronto: McClelland & Stewart, 1978.
Book of Mercy. Toronto: McClelland & Stewart, 1984.
Stranger Music: Selected Poems and Songs. Toronto: McClelland & Stewart,
    1993.
Dance Me to the End of Love. Poem by Leonard Cohen. Paintings by Henri
    Matisse. ed. Linda Sunshine. New York: Welcome Books, 1995.

FICTION

The Favorite Game. New York: Viking Press, 1963; Toronto: McClelland
    & Stewart, 1970.
Beautiful Losers. Toronto: McClelland & Stewart, 1966.

DISCOGRAPHY

Songs of Leonard Cohen. Columbia CL 2733, 1968.

Songs from a Room. Columbia CS 9767, 1969.

Songs of Love and Hate. Columbia C 30103, 1971.

Live Songs. Columbia, KC 31724, 1973.

New Skin for the Old Ceremony. Columbia KC 33167, 1974.

The Best of Leonard Cohen. Columbia ES 90334, 1975.

Death of a Ladies' Man. Columbia 90436, 1977.

Recent Songs. Columbia, KC 36364, 1979.

Various Positions. Passport, PCC 90728, 1984.

I'm Your Man. Columbia, FC 44191, 1988.

The Future. Columbia-SONY, CK 53226, 1992.

Cohen Live. Columbia-SONY, CK 80188, 1994.

TRIBUTE ALBUMS

I'm Your Fan. Warner Music, 17 55984, 1991. Contributions by Ian
   McCulloch, John Cale, Nick Cave, REM, and others.

Famous Blue Raincoat. Cypress Records, 1986. Jennifer Warnes.

'Tower of Song': The Songs of Leonard Cohen. A&M Records 31454 0259 2 1995. Contributions by Sting, Elton John, Peter Gabriel, Bono, Aaron Neville, Billy Joel, the Chieftans, Jann Arden, Willie Nelson, and Suzanne Vega.

ACKNOWLEDGMENTS

I FIRST ENCOUNTERED Leonard Cohen after his performance at the Royal Albert Hall in London in May 1993. It was a brief, polite, backstage meeting, and his manner, despite exhaustion, was typically fastidious. We spoke little, and after I mustered the courage to ask him to sign my program, I left. But walking back to my place, I suddenly realized I never asked him any of the questions I had long wanted to know. This biography, written after a period of exhilarating interviews, travel, reading, and research, attempts to answer some of those unasked questions. It has benefited from the constant support of Leonard Cohen, who has made himself available to my often inconvenient requests and not only encouraged me to speak to numerous friends but allowed me to visit his homes in Montreal, Hydra, and Los Angeles. I am deeply grateful for his cooperation and paradoxical reminder: "Don't let the facts get in the way of the truth." And if he occasionally exclaimed "news to me!" when we reviewed the manuscript in an isolated cabin at the Mt. Baldy Zen Center (where he spent the day cooking "the best fucking stew you'll ever eat"), he never dissuaded me from seeking the truth and presenting it honestly.

I must acknowledge, as well, what I can only call the astonishing cooperation of a series of individuals who have been life-long friends of Leonard Cohen. Their openness and honesty in sharing with me the life of someone they clearly honor is a testament to his importance in their lives. Their helpfulness in supplying information about events, dates, and names to one whom they've never before met, one who has constantly asked details about someone as private as Leonard, was an unexpected pleasure. Whether it was in an outdoor bar in Hydra, a rundown office at the Chelsea Hotel, or a well-known delicatessen in Montreal, people have repeatedly offered to help me tell this story. If this book could not have been written without the assistance of Leonard Cohen, neither would it possess any of its possible merit without the contribution of his many friends. What I have attempted in return is to convey in some way the integrity of the man who has always acted from the heart and been aware that the opposite of despair is joy.

Among those who have assisted me most generously, Kelley Lynch, Leonard's manager, and Nancy Bacal, his close friend, stand out. On numerous visits to Los Angeles, they have not only made themselves available but also provided me with remarkable insights into Leonard's career and life, while easing my access to information. Despite the pressures of managing and endless interruptions at the office, Kelley Lynch always found time to explain, suggest, and assist me when I needed help, and I thank her. Nancy Bacal has been, from our first meeting, supportive, helpful, and encouraging. She not only provided remarkably articulate views of Leonard's character but generously shared with me her own special powers of writing and understanding. Joan Lynch and Sarah Rich, both at Leonard's office, have also helped in countless ways. One other individual close to Leonard cannot be overlooked: his Zen teacher, Joshu Sasaki Roshi. To be in the company of Roshi, whether in the *zendo* at Mt. Baldy or at a restaurant in Los Angeles, is a remarkable experience and his incisive perspective on Cohen remains essential for any grasp of Cohen's life. Roshi clearly demonstrates that even through silence there is understanding. Esther Cohen kindly permitted me a glimpse into the family life, while Adam and Lorca Cohen assisted me in various indirect and direct ways.

Others in Los Angeles who have contributed begin with Perla Batalla.

A backup singer with Cohen on the 1988 and 1993 tours, Perla in many ways facilitated this project following our meeting at the first Leonard Cohen conference ever held in Canada. She, and her husband Claude, also provided important comments on Leonard's sense of performance and the nature of the touring life. Jennifer Warnes took time from a busy studio session to talk with me and explain with patience the musical challenges of Leonard's songwriting and nature of his career; Henry Lewy, producer, shared with me many stories of making records and touring with Leonard; Sean Dixon, Sheila, and the staff at Ocean Recording Studios also helped. Yafa Lerner and Steve Sanfield, both in California, provided me with singular and essential portraits of Leonard's early life and involvement with Zen. Eric Lerner, formerly of Los Angeles, also contributed helpful information on Leonard's days in California.

Two other performers were generous with their time: Judy Collins and Joni Mitchell. Each described important moments in their careers associated with Leonard and were able to clarify various movements in his life. Judy Collins repeated for me the earliest steps in Leonard's career, whereas Joni Mitchell shared numerous memories of Montreal, New York, and Los Angeles with me over a late summer lunch on the Sunshine Coast of British Columbia.

People were equally forthcoming in Toronto and Montreal. Jack McClelland allowed me to intrude upon his wonderful retreat at Lake Muskoka; Beryl and Giza Schiff made sure I would not languish in Toronto; and Doug and Janet Fetherling, early promoters of the book, insured I would have a detailed understanding of Leonard's literary past. David Mayerovich provided me with stories of camp life and was helpful with a wonderful photo from Pripstein's camp, made available from Eleanor Levine, while Roz and Eddie Van Zaig generously recalled life in the Cohen family on Belmont Avenue. They also permitted me to include an important photograph, and I thank them. Danielle Trembley, formerly of City-TV, also assisted, as did Gerald L'Ecuyer of BRAVO TV. David Kaufman provided not only remarkable photos but glimpses of historical moments long forgotten. Florence Pripstein outlined, in often comic detail, life at her father-in-law's summer camp. Winfried Siemerling kindly shared with me an edited copy of an important talk by Cohen, as well as his general knowledge of

Cohen's writing. Avie Bennett, publisher of McClelland & Stewart, kindly permitted me access to the firm's archives.

In Montreal, two memorable afternoons spent with Irving Layton reminded me of his vigorous grasp of Canadian poetry and his contribution to its evolution. He also conveyed to me some remarkable perspectives on Leonard's development as a writer. Louis Dudek was also generous in remembering many moments of Leonard's McGill past and kindly let me examine his presentation copy of Leonard's first book. Morton Rosengarten, Hazel Field, and Charles Gurd, three of Leonard's Montreal friends, allowed me to explore details from his youth and recent past with them. Nancy Southam elaborated various key moments in Leonard's Montreal life, while Ruth Wisse clarified aspects of Leonard's days at McGill. Freda Guttman gave me a sense of Leonard's early literary and social interests. Vera Frenkel recounted assorted moments in his emerging career. Edgar Cohen, now in his eighties, cheerfully recalled life with Leonard and various incidents that determined his vocation as a poet. Edgar's son, Andrew Cohen, also contributed a number of lively insights into the more recent family history of the Cohens. Joseph and Joanne Ronsley, formerly of Montreal, stimulated my interest in understanding the city's cultural and culinary life. Sam Tata, a Canadian photographer of remarkable talent, permitted me use of several outstanding photos and conveyed an amusing sense of Leonard in the 1970s to me, while Hugh Whitney Morrison clarified the life and times of "Marita." Michael and Rhona Kenneally of Montreal provided hospitality when it was most needed, and Steve Goldstein introduced me to the geography of Montreal, especially the old city, and allowed me access to his outstanding international collection of Cohen records and tapes.

Bob and Joy Johnston and Charlie Daniels contributed immensely to my understanding of the Nashville years. Their sense of Leonard as an evolving musician, fashioning a style that merged country and western with folk, has helped me in grasping the progress of his music. John Cale also assisted, with directions as much as detail. The Franklin, Tennessee, Fire Station #2 and the Williamson County Deeds Office were both instrumental in assisting me in finding Leonard's farm. Sister Mary Colman of the Sisters of Mercy Convent, founded in 1866 in Nashville, is also to be thanked. In New York, Stanley Bard of the Chelsea Hotel narrated for me its unusual past, while outlining its unique present and allowing me to tour several floors.

On Hydra, a marvelous group of *raconteurs*, friends, and passers-by assaulted me with details of Leonard's time there. Demetri Gassoumis was especially helpful, although I am still recovering from a bone-jarring donkey ride shared with him to the Prophet Elijah monastery high above the port. But idyllic afternoons spent at the sunlit Moita bar in the company of Demetri, Brian Sidaway, and Gunther and Lilly Bohr more than made up for the mountain ride and confirmed for me that often the most rewarding research is conducted far from traditional archives. Don Lowe, cornered at a bistro in Kamini at one in the morning, was also a helpful source who kindly lent me various works-in-progress dealing with island life. Pandias Scaramanga and George Lialios, both of Athens, but with roots in Hydra, were immensely helpful. Dominique Issermann in Paris assisted with several photographs.

In Vancouver, Leonard Angel, Herbert Rosengarten, Sandra Djwa, Dr. Mark Fisher, Dr. Sid Katz, and Rabbi Mordecai Feuerstein furnished sources, medical advice, and spiritual commentary. Robert Silverman rehearsed for me the misadventures of Montreal youth and life at Prip-stein's summer camp. Stephen Scobie shared with me from the beginning a thorough knowledge of Cohen's career, his detail exceeded only by his grasp of the complete works and life of Bob Dylan. James McClaren gladly allowed me access to an extensive catalogue of tapes and concert material that was invaluable, while Michael Pacey graciously allowed me access to the correspondence between Irving Layton and Desmond Pacey. Alan Twigg, journalist, Peter Buitenhuis, critic, and Lewis Rosenbloom, retired clothier from Sherbrooke, Quebec, who did business with the Freedman Company, all helped in various ways. Tom Northcott, singer, was wonderfully generous in educating me in the art of the recording studio and the possibilities of re-interpreting Leonard's songs. Pamela Dalziel provided continuous support and remarkable tolerance for my obsession with this project, although at an early stage in the research it was she who received an inscription from Leonard that took me another six months to earn.

My children, Dara and Ryan, have not only supported but partici-pated in this project from the beginning. Their involvement was total;

one evening my daughter—at the time seven—impatiently asked, after my by now habitual summary of the book, "Is it information or story?" I tried to explain that it was both, without one necessarily toppling the other. My son took a different tack. Frustrated at my efforts to assist him with a limerick, he suddenly smiled and without hesitation said, "Call Leonard! He'll know!" We didn't, but redoubled our attempts. My mother, Frances Sofman Nadel, has become an eager student of Leonard Cohen, although she often wondered if my own life had been subsumed by his. My late father, Isaac David Nadel, would have taken pleasure in the detail and determination to get the story right.

Among the archivists of Leonard Cohen's career, Robert Bower in New York and Yvette Hakze in the Netherlands are pre-eminent. Both have assisted repeatedly with details, information, and encouragement. Robert, in particular, provided me with numerous sources otherwise unavailable and graciously presented me with a rare copy of *Beautiful Losers*. His enthusiasm for the project has been continuous; his knowledge of Leonard's career incomparable. Through her editorship of *Intensity*, shared with Bea de Koning, Yvette has kept a worldwide network of Cohen fans informed of his latest activities and past achievements. Even in the final months of this project, she assisted with new sources and information that was much valued. Jim Devlin in Sheffield, England, has for more than ten years maintained an important Cohen newsletter and is to be thanked for supplying me with various items that have clarified numerous events in Cohen's concert life. Christof Graf in Germany has provided many useful details and photographs from his own archive, and I am grateful. Soheyl Dahi has, through a friendship that began on a wintry day at the Calgary airport with a description of the charms of Hydra, constantly kept me up to date on the latest Cohen events and discoveries. He has also been a research assistant extraordinaire, generously providing me with essential materials and continual support.

Larry Hoffman has been an energetic and supportive literary agent, and I am indebted to him for his promotion of the project from the first. Doug Pepper of Random House has been a concerned and enthusiastic publisher who, from the beginning, recognized the importance of this project, and, to his credit, saw the value of doing it right, rather than rush it to completion. Nancy Flight has been an outstanding editor whose good humor masked her astonishment at my first-draft confusions and other lapses of reasonable prose. She also reminded me that biography in practice differs from theory, and prevented me from committing further offenses to the reader in the name of detail. Don Gillmor and Tanya Wood have also brought their editorial skills to the manuscript when it was most needed.

Finally, my thanks to the University of British Columbia Social Science and Humanities Awards Committee for support to initiate this project; to Patrick Dunn, David Truelove, and Patrick Patterson of the University of British Columbia's Interlibrary Loan division; to Kathleen Garay, Curator of the McClelland & Stewart archive at McMaster University; to Richard Landon, Librarian of the Thomas Fisher Rare Book Library at the University of Toronto and Mrs. Edna Hajnal, Curator. Bruce Whiteman, head of the Rare Books division of the MacLennan Library, McGill University, and author of an early bibliography of Cohen, has also been of great assistance.

NOTES

The following abbreviations have been used for frequently cited titles; initials followed by date indicates an interview.

Books

BaL	Ballet of Lepers
BCQ	Beauty at Close Quarters
BL	Beautiful Losers
BM	Book of Mercy
DLM	Death of A Lady's Man
ES	The Energy of Slaves
FG	The Favorite Game
FH	Flowers for Hitler
FR	The Final Revision of My Life in Art
LCM	Let Us Compare Mythologies
PH	Parasites of Heaven
SBE	The Spice-Box of Earth
SM	Stranger Music
SP	Selected Poems, 1956-1968

Albums

BLC   Best of Leonard Cohen
CL   Cohen Live
DLSM   Death of a Ladies' Man
IYM   I'm Your Man
LS   Live Songs
NS   New Skin for the Old Ceremony
RS   Recent Songs
SFR   Songs From A Room
SLC   Songs of Leonard Cohen
SLH   Songs of Love and Hate
TF   The Future
TS   Tower of Song
VP   Various Positions

Archives and Sources

C   Columbia University
MCM   McClelland & Stewart Archive, McMaster University
NYT   New York Times
UT   Leonard Cohen collection, Thomas Fisher Rare Book Library, University of Toronto
LCA   Leonard Cohen Archive

Introduction

1   "tolerated": LC 11/14/94
"part wolf and part angel": Anjelica Huston, "Leonard Cohen," *Interview* (November 1995) 90.
"the grocer of despair": "Field Commander Cohen," *NS*; also, Steve Lake, "The Grocer of Despair," *Münchner Stadt Zeitung* 14 (1987) 28–29.
"poet laureate of pessimism": Richard Guilliatt, "At Times his Life Has Been Dark," *Sunday Times* (12 December 1993) 62.
"the prince of bummers": Leon Wieseltier, "The Prince of Bummers," *New Yorker* (26 July 1993) 41.
"music to slit your wrists by": Nancy Southam, "A Flash of Genius," *Toronto Star* (20 August 1988) 10.
"Thank God Sylvia Plath": "Love Me, Love My Gun Barrel," *New Musical Express* (23 February 1980) 24

2 "moody amorousness": Elysa Gardner, "Leonard Cohen," *Rolling Stone* (5 August 1993) 28.

"There is a confusion": "Love Me, Love My Gun Barrel," *New Musical Express* (23 February 1980) 24.

"In punishment": *On the Genealogy of Morals*, tr. Walter Kaufmann and R.J. Hollingdale (NY: Vintage Books, 1967) 67.

"A Zen Man": Joshu Sasaki Roshi in Steve Sanfield, "The Inner Passage," *Zen and Hasidism*, compiled by Harold Heifetz (Wheaton, Ill.: Theosophical Publishing House, 1978) 229.

"I am formal": Leonard Cohen to Vince Scelsa, "Idiot's Delight," WXRK-FM (NYC) 6/13/93.

"I have to do a lot": LC to VS 6/13/93.

"at the very center": LC 4/20/95.

3 "just the Beacon": LC 4/20/95

"the thing you place": LC 4/20/95.

"Keeping things": LC 4/20/95

"what I admire": BCQ 349

4 "I like to include": LC to Peter Gzowski, CBC Radio 11/18/92

"Each book": *The Gateway* [University of Alberta] (2 December 1966) C4.

"has led me": LC 5/10/94

"I want no attachments": BCQ 354

"Far from flying": BL 95-96

Chapter 1

6 "deprivation is the mother": FG 26

"What was it like": FG 24

"His father's death": FG 24

"what happens when": FG 3

"I've been digging": *People* 13 (14 January 1980) 55.

"nourished all the sleepers": FG 68

"heroic landscapes": FG 68.

7 "all the English reticence": FG 21-22

8 "My son, Leonard": EC 10/23/94

"Let him go on": BCQ 29

"the persecuted brother": FG 22

"He died ripe for": BCQ 36

"most dreamy spiritual influence": *People* 13 (14 January 1980) 56.

"had the flair": RVZ 7/19/94

11 "past that happened somewhere else": FG 124-5

13 "He'd read it again": Michael Benazon, "Leonard Cohen of Montreal" [interview], *Matrix* 23 (Fall 1986) 52.

"He swam in it": LC 12/29/94

"because I wanted": *Matrix* 52

14 "Religion structured": LC in Christian Fevret, "Comme un Guerrier, An Interview with Leonard Cohen," *Throat Culture* #3 (1992) 22. (The interview originally appeared in the French magazine *Les Inrockuptibles*.)

15 "a fat man": BCQ 31

"walked ahead": BCQ 32

"part Catholic": Mark Rowland, "Leonard Cohen's Nervous Breakdown," *Musician Magazine* (July 1988) 106.

"Christianity": Rowland, *Musician Magazine* 106.
17 "would continue the story": BCQ 27
"there was repression": LC in L.S. Dorman and C.L. Rawlins, *Leonard Cohen, Prophet of the Heart* (London: Omnibus, 1990) 27-28.
"huge .38": FG 15
"I loved the magic": BL 163
18 "the gun proved": FG 16
" I didn't feel": "Comme un Guerrier" 22
"No one looks": UT Notebook
"always left on one": LC in Dorman 49
19 "my uncle Horace": *Matrix* 51
"I knew how to address": *Matrix* 51
"professionals in suffering": LC in Dorman 362
20 "World famous orator": *Westmount High School Yearbook* (1951) 23.
"swam in a Jewish world": LC 12/29/94
21 "to go into a system": *Matrix* 53
"he wanted to touch": BCQ 214
"there [was] some tangent": BCQ 57
22 "calling on his dead father": BCQ 357
"a history of injustices": BCQ 357
"a ferocious instrument": BBC Radio 7/8/94
"I'm a lot better": BBC Radio 7/8/94
23 "led me into the racket": LC in *Toronto Star* (18 October 1986) G3.
"Through the Arch": Lorca, *Collected Poems*, ed. Christopher Maurer (NY: Farrar Straus Giroux, 1991) 681.
"Am I to blame": Lorca, *Collected Poems* xxv.
24 "I was sitting down": LC in Michael Harris,"Leonard Cohen: The Poet as Hero: 2," *Saturday Night* (June 1969) 30.
"I wanted them": LC in Susan Lumsden, "Leonard Cohen Wants the Unconditional Leadership of the World," *Weekend Magazine* (12 September 1970) 25.
"It is my domain": "Murray Park at 3 a.m.," UT.
"in stone plazas": "Murray Park," UT.
"You [an early love] brought": "Murray Park, UT.
25 "to think of themselves": BCQ 87
26 "homemade songs of protest": *People's Song Book* (1948; NY: People's Artists, 1956) 6.
"developed a curious notion": "The Partisan," Album Notes, BLC (1975).
"Through my interest": LC, National Public Radio, 5/1/1985
27 "There were no cries for help": LC in "Comme un Guerrier," *Throat Culture* 37.
28 "especially beautiful thighs": "Fragments of Prose, 1952–56," UT
"She moved with": "Prose, 1952–56," UT
"A smothering sense": "Prose, 1952–56," UT
"has something to do with": "Prose, 1952–56," UT
"I have never loved": "Prose, 1952–56," UT
29 "I have never thought": "Prose, 1952–56," UT
"love generally": "Prose, 1953–56," UT
30 "life was purely": LC, "Comme un Guerrier," *Throat Culture* 37.
"I nursed you": Freda Guttman 8/11/94
"always feeling like": Nancy Bacal 2/18/94
"He seemed": FG 8/11/94
31 "contain and survive": NB 2/18/94

Chapter 2

33 "If you did things right": NB 2/18/94
34 "paying off old debts": LC in Harris, "LC: The Poet as Hero: 2," *Saturday Night* 27.
"limitless space": NB 2/18/94
"ineffectual shower curtains": LC, "Nomination Speech," LCA.
35 "My colleague has promised you": LC, "Address" (February 1956), UT.
37 "CIV/n: not a one-man job": Pound in a letter cited by Louis Dudek in "Louis Dudek," *Contemporary Authors Autobiography Series* 14 (1991): 132; also see Louis Dudek, "Black Mountain Contact, CIV/n Tish, A Memoir," *Sagetrieb* 7 (Spring 1988) 42.
"a vital": "Canadian Culture," *CIV/n, A Literary Magazine of the 50's,* ed. Aileen Collins (Montreal: Vehicule Press, 1983) 129.
"forced to write": *CIV/n:* 129
"For Kulchur's sake": *CIV/n:*129
38 "Last night": IL in Elspeth Cameron, *Irving Layton* (Toronto: Stoddart, 1985) 204.
"standing for maximum awareness": Ezra Pound to Louis Dudek in *Dk/ Some Letters of Ezra Pound,* ed. Louis Dudek (Montreal: DC Books, 1974) 102.
"Leonard N. Cohen": *CIV/n:* 126.
"secret undulations": *CIV/n:* 112.
"swarmed the shadows": *CIV/n:*112.
39 "savage integrity": LC to Vin Scelsa, "Idiot's Delight," 6/13/93.
"voluntarily studying": Phyllis Webb, "Tibetan Desire," *Take This Waltz, A Celebration of Leonard Cohen,* ed. Michael Fournier and Ken Norris (St. Anne de Bellevue, Quebec: The Muses' Company, 1994) 183.
"got battered about": Webb, *Take this Waltz:* 184.
40 "That's where my life": LC in *Matrix* 54.
"the more restrained": LC in *Matrix* 54.
"warm and wonderful": LC in Sandra Djwa, *The Politics of the Imagination: A Life of F.R. Scott* (Toronto: McClelland & Stewart, 1987) 288.
41 "What race will read": Irving Layton, "Prologue to the Long Pea-Shooter," *CIV/n:* 187.
"One can get tired": Northrop Frye, "Letters in Canada: 1951," *University of Toronto Quarterly* 21 (1952): 255.
"with a happy / screech": LC, "For My Old Layton," *FH* 37.
42 "I taught him": LC in Dorman 57.
"always seemed to leave": Don Owen, "Leonard Cohen: The Poet as Hero: 3," *Saturday Night* (June 1969) 31.
"poised on a rope": IL, "Foreword," *The Tightrope Dancer* (Toronto: McClelland & Stewart, 1978) 9.
43 "in a car full of women": Doug Jones in Djwa, *The Politics of the Imagination: A Life of F.R. Scott* 280.
"*You have discovered*": *McGill Yearbook* (1955)
44 "I yearned to live": LC in Paul Williams, "The Romantic in a Ragpicker's Trade," *Crawdaddy* (March 1975) 54.
"He knew": BCQ 198
"slow and reluctant": LD letter to author 7/20/93.
"the sentimental late-romantic": LD letter to author 7/20/93.
45 "To Louis Dudek": LD's copy of LCM; cited with permission.
"Leonard always had": LD in Dorman 55.
"I was fortunate to see him": LD address, McGill Convocation "But Leonard": LD address, McGill Convocation 6/16/92.

"He has won through": LD, "Address," McGill Convocation 6/16/92.
46 "I want to continue": "Prose Fragments, 1952-1956" (27 December 1956) UT.
   "I know all about": "Prose Fragments" (27 December 1956) UT.
   "strive for folk-song": "Prose Fragments" (27 December 1956) UT.
47 "The moon dangling": LCM 54.
   "It's been downhill": LC in Michael Freeman, "Leonard Cohen," *Venue* (Winter
      1994) 58.
   "Mostly what I was": LC in Freeman, "Leonard Cohen," *Venue* (Winter 1994) 59.
   "Breasts, in my mind": Untitled ["I thought I'd seen a lot of things,"] "Prose Frag-
      ments, 1952-56,"[1] UT.
   "Women who have popularity": "Prose Fragments" [1] UT.
   "Layton would at once": "Prose Fragments" [2] UT.
48 "dark southern slope": "Prose Fragments" [2] UT.
   "And at that moment": "Prose Fragments" [3] UT.
49 "I am change": LC 10/24/95.
   "Our song led us to the ovens": LC 10/24/95.
   "The nightmares": PH 13.
   "I merely step": PH 13.
50 "In principle": LC, Black Notebook (March 1967), LCA.
   "which is famous": LC, 1981 Luberon Journal, LCA.
   "My personality": LC in "Newsletter," *Leonard Cohen Information Service* 1 (16
      December 1984) 1.

Chapter 3

51 "passion without flesh": "It Swings Jocko," SBE 24.
   "love with no climax": "It Swings Jocko," SBE 24.
   "I feel lonely": Columbia Notebook (7 November 1956) UT.
52 "He was lying under": John Walsh, "Research, you understand. . . Leonard
      Cohen," *Mojo* (September 1994) 58.
   "a certain kind of genius": LC to Vince Scelsa, "Idiot's Delight," 6/13/93.
   "really spinning": LC to Vince Scelsa, "Idiot's Delight," 6/13/93.
   "I was always only on the fringe": *Mojo* (September 1994) 58.
53 "UNINTERRUPTED AND UNREVISED": Jack Kerouac, "Introduction," *On The
      Road* [Norwegian ed.], *The Portable Kerouac*, ed. Ann Charters (NY: Viking,
      1995) 481.
   "This magazine intends": *The Phoenix* 1 (April 1957) [1].
   "Riverside Church": "Notebook, ca. 1956," UT.
54 "durable, disciplined and athletic": FG 137.
   "old rules of light": FG 171.
   "the scene the heart": FG 136.
   "about her body and her beauty": FG 140.
   "I'd no sooner forget you": White Notebook (September 1961), UT.
55 "Reader": White Notebook (September 1961), UT.
   "I would appreciate": LC to Esther Cohen, 13 July 1961, UT.
   "Your report": EC to LC, ? November 1961, UT.
56 "Let's run away": LC to Anne Sherman, ? December 1961, UT.
   "Don't worry about me": LC to Canada Council, 2 June 1961, UT.
57 "Must we find": "Priests 1957," SBE 78.
   "Now Leonard Cohen": IL to Desmond Pacey, 18 October 1958.

"What will become": DP to IL, 29 October 1958.

"Layton, when we dance": "Last Dance at the Four Penny," SBE 71.

58 "Work, fine work": "A Hundred Suits from Russia," UT [3].

"one day": "A Hundred Suits," UT [3].

"One hundred": "A Hundred Suits," UT [4].

"My grandfather came": *A Ballet of Lepers*, TS. ca. 1957, UT [1].

59 "Defeated he stood": BAL, UT [59].

"each of us had": BAL, UT [60].

"Flee from this place": LC 5/12/94.

"I had a clock": LC in Winfried Siemerling, "Interview," *Take This Waltz* 168.

"How sad and beautiful": BAL, UT [61].

60 "It happened": BAL, UT [67].

"We are not mad": BAL, UT [68].

"learn betrayal": BAL, UT [74].

"to learn shame": BAL, UT [74].

"probably felt": IL in Cameron, *Irving Layton* 277.

61 "Don't worry": Vera Frenkel 3/2/95.

"torment on the bed": VF 3/2/95.

"Leonard always needed": VF 3/2/95.

"a red fire hydrant": Al Purdy, *Reaching for the Beaufort Sea* (Maderia Park: Harbour Publishing, 1993) 221.

"within a slight": AP 222.

"sad Duke of Windsor": IL to DP, 29 June 1957.

62 "we had lots": IL to DP, 29 June 1957.

"on the threshold": "Goodbye Old Rosengarten," TS ca. 1958, UT [1].

"He's currently": IL to DP, 13 February 1958.

"but Cohen": IL to DP, 13 February 1958.

"It was written": LC tape 8 April 1958.

63 "I wonder": LC tape 8 April 1958.

"Well, ah, this": LC tape, 8 April 1958.

"the nightclub poets": Morley Callaghan, "Holiday Weekend in Montreal," *Maclean's* (30 August 1958) 42.

"is a kind of": MC 44

"a waiter placed": MC 44.

64 "Whatever I have written": Untitled, June 1958, UT [1].

66 "Edgar, I had no choice": LC quoted by EC 10/23/94.

"not even capable": LD, "Patterns of Recent Canadian Poetry" *Culture* 19 (December 1958) 412.

"obscure cosmological imagery": LD *Culture* 412.

"as stupid as it is false": IL to DP 26 January 1959.

"the Canadian poet": IL in Louis Dudek, Irving Layton, Raymond Souster, *Cerberus* (Toronto: Contact Press, 1952) 45.

67 "the fires": LC in IL to DP 8 June 1959.

"Klein chose to be": LC, "Loneliness and History," ed. Winfried Siemerling, *Take This Waltz* 147.

"a certain Hebraic sense": LC *Matrix* 45.

"His fate": LC *Matrix* 45.

"I was always more": LC *Matrix* 45.

68 "Dear Mr. McClelland": LC to Jack McClelland 5/5/59, UT.

"I think": JMCCL 7/23/94.

"too slight": Claire Pratt to LC, 7/15/59, UT.

"no other poet": CP to LC, 7/15/59, UT.

69 "I have bought": LC to CP 7/21/1959, UT.

"Please understand": LC to CP 7/21/59, UT.

"inner-directed adolescents": LC to CP 7/21/59, UT.

"Thank you": LC to CP 7/21/59, UT.

"Can't take it anymore": IL to DP 6/8/59. Written in June, Layton reports Cohen's proposed decision to change jobs in September.

70 "to liberate spiritual energy": LC, "Comme un Guerrier," *Throat Culture* 58.

"thanks to drugs": LC, "Comme un Guerrier," *Throat Culture* 58.

"enough Anglo-Saxon dignity": IL to DP 19 November 1959.

"An All-Season Haiku": LC, TS, fall 1959, UT.

Chapter 4

72 "As long as you": LC, "Comme un Guerrier," *Throat Culture* 59.

"She is partly": LC, "Comme un Guerrier," *Throat Culture* 59.

"London is welcoming": LC, "Comme un Guerrier," *Throat Culture* 59.

"permanent advisor": LC, "Comme un Guerrier," *Throat Culture* 59.

73 "very lovely": LC to Esther Cohen 18 April 1962, UT.

74 "until by sheer weight": BCQ 1.

"I'm glad the book": LC to CP, 27 March 1960, UT.

"I wouldn't like": LC to CP, 27 March 1960, UT.

75 "the only copy": LC to JMcCL 28 August 1960, UT.

"I said to myself": LC, "Comme un Guerrier," *Throat Culture* 59.

"I suppose": IL to DP 15 February 1960.

76 "wild and naked perfection": Henry Miller, *The Colossus of Maroussi* (1941; NY: New Directions, 1958) 55.

78 "six deal tables": Charmian Clift, *Peel Me a Lotus* (London: Hutchinson, 1959) 15.

"in a wild spate of words": Clift, *Peel* 60.

79 "horseshoe-shaped": George Lailios to author 12 September 1994.

"the actors": GL to author 12 September 1994.

"Bet between LC": "Bet between LC and George Johnston," 16 October 1961, UT.

80 "a lot of writing": Cynthia Nolan in Garry Kinnane, *George Johnston, A Biography* (Melbourne: Thomas Nelson, 1986) 158.

"Pull up your sex": LC 5/10/94.

"Forget the Grace": "Fragment from a Journal," SM 386.

81 "He exposed": Don Lowe, *Kingy* (unpub.) 44.

"I don't think": DL, *Kingy* 48.

"living in a past century": GL to author 12 September 1994.

82 "origins are truly": GL to author 12 September 1994.

"I used to sit": LC, "Journal," 17 May 1966, UT.

83 "It wasn't just": LC, BBC 7/8/94.

"Marianne is perfect": LC to IL, 21 April 1963, UT.

"the incarnation of the European woman": Charles Gurd 7/12/94.

"the way she inhabited": LC, BBC 7/8/94.

"Marianne and I": LC, BBC 7/8/94.

"There was a woman": LC, "Comme un Guerrier," *Throat Culture* 59.

84 "Leonard was unique": NB 12/29/94.

"You could not own": NB 12/29/94.

"It has a huge terrace": LC to Masha Cohen, 3 August 1961, UT.

85 "I wander through": LC to EC, ? October 1961, UT.

"But they came back": LC to EC, 3 August 1961, UT.

"It is like receiving": LC to MC, 18 October 1961, UT.

"having this house": LC to Wog [Daniel Kraslavsky], 19 December 1961, UT.

"The years are flying": LC to ?, 16 December 1961, UT.

"The primitive circumstances": FR 29.

86 "the first Hebrew": LC 5/11/94.

"everything you saw": LC, "Comme un Guerrier," *Throat Culture* 59.

"You knew everything": LC, "Comme un Guerrier," *Throat Culture* 59.

"There's sun all over": LC to IL, 8 December 1961, UT.

"There's something in the light": LC in Michael Ballantyne, "Poet-Novelist Reflects on the Quebec Scene," *Montreal Star* (26 October 1963) 2.

87 "Hydra — you can't live": LC 10/24/95.

"all the old potent guilts": LC to "My dear friends," (15 December 1960) UT.

"Since hearing the news": LC to EC, 15 December 1960, UT.

"It took me some time": LC to Maryann Greene 16 February 1961, UT.

"I have finished": LC to Jake and Stella Pullman, 19 December 1961, UT.

88 "a protracted love-affair": LC to DP, 23 February 1961, UT.

"every event described": LC to JMCCL, 12 October 1960, UT.

"wanted to tell about": LC to JMCCL, 12 October 1960, UT.

"He managed to offend": LC to JMCCL, 9 March 1962, UT.

"I will always consider": LC to JMCCL, 9 March 1962, UT.

"miserable . . . behalf": LC to JMCCL, 8 December 1961; 26 July 1962, UT.

"a book without alibis": LC to JMCCL, 4 July 1963, UT.

89 "perhaps its only value": LC to Seymour Lawrence, 29 October 1961, UT.

"my work limps along": LC to EC, 29 October 1961, UT.

"It doesn't matter to me": LC to JMCCL, 2 November 1961, UT.

"absolutely beautiful writing": anon., Sheila Watson to LC, 29 January 1962, UT.

"too long": SW to LC, 8 May 1962.

90 "Three in the morning": LC to friends, 15 ? December 1960, UT.

"Except for this tiny": LC to Bim, 17 February 1961, UT.

"We did it simply by": LC in *Canadian Theatre Review* 14 (1977) 54.

"macabre, compelling thing": IL to DP, 11 December 1960.

Chapter 5

91 "I am wild": LC to Anne Hébert, ? January–February 1961, UT.

"I had this mythology": Tom Chaffin, "Conversations from a Room," *Canadian Forum* (August/September 1983) 10.

92 "the day you left": CP to LC, 27 March 1961, UT.

"The island": FGL to parents, 5 April 1930, *Poet in New York*, tr. Greg Smith and Steven F. White (NY: Noonday Press, 1988) 255.

93 "presence urgently requested": LC 5/11/94.

"I was Upton Sinclair": LC 5/11/94.

"Your mother's worried": LC 5/11/94.

95 "This is no time": IL to DP, 15 April 1961.

"Just think": LC to JMCCL, 18 April 1961, UT.

96 "It's going to be": LC 5/11/94.

"to see a socialist revolution": LC to Victor Cohen, 9 November 1962, UT.

97 "I'm one of the few men": LC to VC, 9 November 1962.

"deep interest in violence": *Ladies and Gentlemen . . . Mr. Leonard Cohen* (NFB film), 1965.

"The city was Havana": "The Famous Havana Diary," TS, UT 1.

"I enjoyed her": "The Famous Havana Diary," TS, UT 4-5.

"oppressive and repugnant": LC to VC, 9 November 1962, UT.

"Power chops up": LC to Cork Smith, 1 September 1963, UT.

98 "a tragic figure": IL to DP, 4 May 1961.

"Communism is less sinister": LC to Lonie?, 4 September 1961, UT.

"Dorian Grayish": IL to DP, 13 May 1961.

"Leonard Cohen, 27": dustjacket, SBE.

99 "For you": "The Genius," SBE 87.

"probably the best": Robert Weaver, "Leonard Cohen's *Spice-Box* Presents Sombre Vision," *Toronto Daily Star* (10 June 1961) 29.

"The Lean and the Luscious": David Bromige, "The Lean and the Luscious," *Canadian Literature* 10 (Autumn 1961) 87-88.

100 "easily the most promising": Desmond Pacey, *Creative Writing in Canada* (1952; New edition, revised and enlarged, Toronto: Ryerson, 1961) 247.

"There isn't a single": IL to DP, 12 April 1962.

"Psychologically, I think": IL to DP, 12 April 1962.

"His passport was": LC to Robert Weaver, 20 May 1961, UT.

101 "Your purity": "Alexander Trocchi," FH 47.

"yield profits": LC to Canada Council, 2 June 1961, UT.

"distance is essential": LC to Canada Council, 2 June 1961, UT.

"I remind them": LC to Shaar Hashomayim Hadassah, 11 June 1961.

"they weep most of the day": LC to EC, 13 July 1961, UT.

"that makes": LC to EC, 13 July 1961, UT.

"rooted on the rock": LC to EC, 13 July 1961, UT.

"his Gothic insincerities": LC, dustjacket, *The Favourite Game* (London: Secker & Warburg, 1963).

"Thank god for": LC to JMCCL, 18 August 1961, UT.

102 "I gather the Greek wines": IL to DP, 28 August, 1961.

"dig deep": LC to JMCCL, 18 August 1961.

"I chose a lonely country": "For E.J.P.," FH 69.

"you just felt good": LC in "Comme un Guerrier," *Throat Culture* 59.

"there is my beautiful house": LC to RW, 22 November 1962, UT.

"Of men the sky demands": "Here Was the Harbour," PH 45.

103 "everywhere is going Communist": LC to EC, 7 October 1961, UT.

"My abandoned narcotics": "Indictment of the Blue Hole," FH 19.

"Is there anything emptier": "The Drawer's Condition," FH 16.

"I've smoked": LC to Madeleine ?, 12 November 1961, UT.

104 "In this part of the planet": "We are getting to know the police better," TS 1965, UT [3-4].

"I write a year's verse": LC to John B. Oakes, ? October 1961, UT.

105 "the next book": LC to CP 18, September 1961, UT.

"It's so simple": "For Marianne," FH 52-53.

"seems to have endured": LC to IL, 8 December 1961, UT.

"Lead me into families": "For a long while," PH 51.

"Something in the air": LC to EC, 18 April 1962, UT.

106 "I've been working on": LC to EC, 18 April 1962, UT.

"it's so melancholy": LC to EC, 22 April 1962, UT.

"Eating and kissing": LC to Stephen Vizicenzy, 27 April 1962, UT.

"Norway is blonde": LC to RW, 14 May 1962, UT.

"I can be seen Twisting": LC to RW, 14 May 1962, UT.

"Strange to find myself": LC to Yafa Lerner, 16 December 1961, LCA.

"This is the same novel": LC to Peter Dwyer, 31 January 1962, UT.

107 "be interested in publishing": LC to JMCCL, 6 March 1962, UT.
 "it's the kind of chutzpa": LC to Rabbi Samuel Cass, 6 March 1962, UT.
 "London is horrible": LC to RW, 6 March 1962, UT.
 "Over the two years": LC to Daniel Kraslavsky, 10 March 1962, LCA.
108 "twice as slowly": LC to Madeleine ?, [10?] March 1962, LCA.
 "terrified of waking up": LC to Madeleine ?, [10?] March 1962, LCA.
 "fight for some tiny": LC to Madeline ?, [10?] March 1962, LCA.
 "I feel I've lost": LC to Madeline ?, [10?] March 1962, LCA.
 "There are a million things": LC to Marianne Ihlen, 10 March 1962, LCA.
 "I long for you": LC to Marianne Ihlen, 10 March 1962, LCA.
109 "just as I always": LC to MC, 10 March 1962, LCA.
 "the things which are given": LC to MC, 10 March 1962, LCA.
 "the secret of my triumph": LC to MC, 10 March 1962, LCA.
 "I want to tear": LC to IL, 23 March 1962, LCA.
 "Too bad because": LC to EC, 26 March 1962, LCA.
 "beautiful book": LC to EC, 26 March 1962, LCA.
110 "What a joyless farce": LC to EC, 26 March 1962, LCA.
 "It's the first time": LC to EC, 26 March 1962, LCA.

Chapter 6

112 "in the last six thousand years": LC to MC, 20 May 1962, UT.
 "My house is big": LC to MC, 20 May 1962, UT.
 "Buying this house": LC to MC, 30 May 1962, UT.
 "She's a little overwhelmed": LC to EC, 29 June 1962, UT.
 "all the old chaos": LC to Madeleine ? 30 June 1962, UT.
113 "nothing sounds any good": LC to Roland Gant, 26 July 1962, UT.
 "I don't intend to open": LC to EC, 13 August 1961, UT.
 "whom I had never spoken to": LC to EC, 30 April 1963, UT.
 "I've greeted people": LC to EC, 2 July 1963, UT.
114 "intolerably touristic": LC to EC, 2 July 1963, UT.
 "It is hard to be": LC to Renee Rothman, 2 July 1963, UT.
 "eliminated a kind of self-conscious": LC to RG, 26 August 1962, UT.
 "I think I have": LC to George Dickerson, 30 October 1962, UT.
 "One day I found": LC to GD, 30 October 1962, UT.
 "anyone with an ear": LC to IL, 15 October 1962, UT.
115 "Has the world": LC to RW, 22 November 1962, LCA.
 "coffin-colored room": LC, "Luggage Fire Sale," *Partisan Review* 36 (Winter 1969)
    91.
 "*change is the only aphrodisiac*": "Luggage Fire Sale," *PR* 92.
 "a couple of women": "Luggage Fire Sale," *PR* 91.
 "and a complete suntan": "Luggage Fire Sale," *PR* 91.
 "sweetest aspect": "Luggage Fire Sale," *PR* 92.
 "Cultural crises": LC, unpub. report, [1962], LCA, [3].
 "It's a perfect little machine": LC to IL, 26 February 1963, UT.
116 "[Yeats] has had": LC to CS, 10 May 1963, LCA.
 "Tell all your gold friends": LC to CS, 22 May 1963, LCA.
117 "The photograph is of": LC to CS, 7 July 1963, LCA.
 "I haven't been to sleep": LC to SW, 15 February 1963, LCA.
 "a first novel": JMCCL to LC, 31 May 1963, MCM.
 "a third novel": LC to JMCCL, 4 July 1963, UT.

"I will write a book": LC, to JMCCL, 4 July 1963, UT.

118 "a beautiful book": JMCCL to LC, 31 May, 1963, MCM.
"one of the great dangers": JMCCL to LC, 31 May, 1963, MCM.
"I've never written easily": LC to JMCCL, 4 July 1963, UT.
"will speak to nobody": LC to JMCCL, 4 July 1963, UT.
"I accept the hemlock": LC to CS, 10 May 1963, LCA.
"a fairly original study": LC to CS, 1 September 1963, LCA.
"best creative periods": LC to EC, 12 Nay 1963, UT.

119 "prose poems": LC to CBC, 12 June 1963, UT.
"I gave my mental health": LC to Marian McNamara, 6 September 1963, C.
"So many of my values": LC to CS, 1 September 1963, LCA.
"Because you are Leonard Cohen": JMCCL to LC, 22 August 1963, MCM.
"feeling as you do": LC to JMCCL, 9 September 1963, UT.
"I know this book": LC to JMCCL, 9 September 1963, UT.
"they've been staggered": JMCCL MCCL., 9 September 1963, UT.

120 "This is a manuscript": anon. to LC, ? October 1963, MCM.
"This poetry is full of": anon. to LC, 14 August 1963, MCM.
"immature": ? to LC, 14 August 1963, MCM.
"With scorn, love, nausea": CP to LC, 13 August 1963, MCM.
"I was ambushed by fifty": LC to JMCCL, 29 March 1964, UT.
"The title is": LC to JMCCL, 29 May 1964, UT.
"with my face for tits": LC to JMCCL, 2 September 1964, UT.

121 "The whole point": LC to JMCCL, 16 August 1964, UT.
"Note on the title": FH [iii].
"I don't profess": JMCCL to LC, 11 September 1963, MCM.
"has made me and the book": LC to JMCCL, 1 March 1965, UT.

122 "The Mediterranean": LC to IL, 6 August 1963, UT.
"Well, you know": "So Long, Marianne," SLC.
"I had the woman I loved": "The Price of This Book," DLM 168.
"a violent disintegration": LC to CS, 6 September 1963, UT.

123 "what I want from people": LC to CS, 6 September 1963, UT.
"The further a writer": LC to CS, 4 August 1963, UT.
"A tall blonde girl": LC to IL, 1 September 1963, UT.
"Lots of French lesbians": LC to EC, 31 August 1963, UT.
"from a sexual point of view": LC to EC, 31 August 1963, UT.
"I threw open the shutters": ES 10–11.

124 "there were thousands of poems": LC, *English Poetry in Quebec*, ed. John Glassco (Montreal: McGill University Press, 1965) 42.
"a self-authenticated speaking": IL, *EPQ* 30.
"The mass magazine": LC, *EPQ* 63.

125 "were never lovers": LC in Barbara Amiel, "Leonard Cohen says that to all the girls," *Maclean's* (18 September 1978): 58.
"Suzanne takes you down": "Suzanne," SLC.
"And Jesus was a sailor": "Suzanne," SLC.
"compassionate attention": LC, "The John Hammond Years, Pt. 12," CBC Radio (October 1986).
"Now Suzanne takes your hand": "Suzanne," SLC.

126 "Most of my songs": LC, "The John Hammond Years," CBC.
"uncovering the lyric": LC, "The John Hammond Years," CBC.
"TV stations pay me": LC to "Dear People," 11 December 1963, UT.
"I was mailing a letter": LC, 11 December 1963, UT.
"this Sunday": LC, 11 December 1963, UT.

"Poet-Novelist Says": "Poet-Novelist Says Judaism Betrayed," *Canadian Jewish Chronicle* (10 January 1964) 3, 15 carried a report of the meeting. The edited talk appears in *Take This Waltz*, 143-153.

127   "Draw me with a valuable sign": "Foreign God," PH 74.

128   "please quit soon": LC to Earle Birney, 21 February 1964, UT.

"the distinction between": LC to Ann Caffin, 21? February 1964, UT.

"there's something about the West": LC to AC, 21? February 1964, UT.

"Vancouver is": LC to AC, 21? February 1964, UT.

"fairly triumphant": LC to MMCN, 29 March 1964, UT.

"Most of all": LC to "Dear People," ? February 1964, UT.

"liturgy, a big confessional oration": LC to Phyllis Webb, CBC TV, 29 April 1966.

"in the country": LC to "Dear People," ? February 1964, UT.

"new novel, PLASTIC BIRCHBARK": LC to JMCCL, 2 September 1964, UT.

129   "the whole system collapsed": LC, "Comme un Guerrier," *Throat Culture* 60.

"Leonard Cohen": *Time* 84 (6 November) 1964: 16.

130   "the reading-tour": LC to JMCCL, 1 March 1965, MCM.

"torn on the conflicts": LC to MMCN, 29 March 1964, UT.

"You're coming to your goal": *Montreal Star*, 13 July 1963, 1.

131   "in ten years": LC to "Dear People," ? February 1964, UT.

"I have made a commitment": LC to George Johnston, ? February 1964, UT.

"embodied in her own life": LC in Winfried Siemerling, "A Political Constituency that Really Exists, "*Take This Waltz* 161.

132   "We have among us adepts": LC, "We are getting to know the police better," 1965 [2-3], LCA.

"and if it gets by": LC to JMCCL, 1 March 1965, MCM.

133   "written the Bahgavad Gita": LC to JMCCL, 20 March 1965, UT.

"BEAUTIFUL LOSERS": LC, UT.

"You have been": BL 149.

"a man is writing this": BL 102.

"how to treat": LC to MMCN, 27 April 1965, C.

"As far as the prologue": LC to CS, 10 July 1965, LCA.

135   "my fast has been": LC, prose fragment, 1966? UT.

"Canada with the Maple Leaf": anon., 30 December 1965, MCM.

"honest-to-God": Leslie Fiedler, 17 January 1966, UT.

"It astounds and baffles": JMCCL, 15 June 1965, MCM.

136   "for a brief period": LC to JMCCL, ? August 1965, MCM.

"Fiend of the Kaballa!": LC to JMCCL, ? August 1965, MCM.

"the book I hold": LC to JMCCL, ? August, 1965, MCM.

"exhibitionism I argued off": LC to JMCCL, ? August 1965, MCM.

"Canadian critical opinion": LC to JMCCL, ? August 1965, MCM.

"if you can get": LC to JMCCL, ? August, 1965, MCM.

137   "Driven by loneliness and despair": LC, prose fragment, 1965, UT.

"I lost my only carbon": LC to MMCN, 4 August 1965, C.

138   "Live forever": telegram to LC, 29 March 1966, UT.

"a fantasy wrapped": Robert Fulford, "Leonard Cohen's Nightmare Novel," *Toronto Star* (26 April 1966) 27.

139   "the story concerns": Miriam Waddington, "Bankrupt Ideas and Chaotic Style," *Globe Magazine* (30 April 1966) 17.

"i give the book of Cohens": bill bissett, "!!!!," *Alphabet* 13 (June 1967) 94.

"it's the best thing": LC in S. Lumsden, *Weekend Magazine* (12 September 1970) 24.

"most of the people": JMCCL to George Renison, 21 April 1966, MCM.

"because you": JMCCL to LC, 9 May 1966, MCM.

"calling it": JMCCL, to LC, 9 May 1966, MCM.

140 "It is pleasant to think": Robert Fulford, "Leonard Cohen, the TV Star," *Toronto Star* (28 July 1966) 31.

"I thought it was time": Fulford, *Toronto Star* (28 July 1966) 31.

"is no substitute": "These notebooks," PH 61.

"So you're the kind": "So you're the kind of," PH 11.

"How can I use the gull's": "The stars turn," PH 40.

Chapter 7

141 "bounded out of the room": S. Djwa, *The Politics of the Imagination, A Life of F.R. Scott* 290.

142 "Do you know": Sid Katz 12/24/95.

"In hindsight": LC in William Ruhlmann, "The Stranger Music of Leonard Cohen," *Goldmine 19* (19 February 1993) 13.

"I felt very much": LC in Williams, *Crawdaddy* (March 1975) 55.

143 "Once I hit": LC, *Goldmine 13*.

"rich in character": LC 5/11/94.

"iron regard": LC 5/11/94.

"on a lot of involuntary trips": LC, "Idiot's Delight," 6/13/93.

144 "Once upon a time": LC concert tape, Amsterdam, 30 October 1980.

"Are you looking for someone?": LC, Oslo Norway, 2/13/88.

145 "She had this deep": LC, "Idiot's Delight," 6/13/93.

"I finally got it right": LC, "Idiot's Delight," 6/13/93.

"KILL COOL": LC in *Mojo* (September 1994) 58.

146 "professionaly tortured": VF 3/2/95.

"I am so impatient": LC, Journal (March 1967) LCA.

147 "Everything serves his work": Yafa Lerner 12/17/94.

"the perfect Aryan ice queen": LC in Scott Cohen, "Leonard Cohen," *Yakety Yak* (NY: Simon and Schuster, 1994) 164.

"I saw this girl": LC, October 1974, in D. Thompson, *Beyond the Velvet Underground* (London: Omnibus, 1989) 29.

"macabre face": David Antrim in 1966 in Thompson, *Beyond* 30.

"the screeching ugliness": Paul Morrissey in Thompson, *Beyond* 31.

"secret marriage": Richard Goldstein in Thompson, *Beyond* 17.

"in those days": LC in Thompson, *Beyond* 29.

148 "I was lighting candles": LC, *Mojo* (September 1994) 58.

"Terrible day": LC, Journal, 15 March 1967, LCA.

"poet maudit ca. 1890": LC, Journal, 15 March 1967, LCA.

"It's a pity if": LC, prose fragment, UT [1].

"the creator of the Black Photograph": LC, prose fragment, UT [1].

149 "My work among other things": LC, prose fragment, UT [2].

"perplexed by her conversation": LC, "Comme un Guerrier," *Throat Culture* 61.

"Completely disregarded": LC in Robin Pike, "September 15th 1974," *Zig Zag, The Rock Magazine* 5 (October 1974) 48.

"I put my hand on": *Mojo* (September 1994) 59.

150 "Once in my room": LC in Thompson 29.

"She said she loved": LC in *Goldmine 13*.

"I'm really in the middle": LC in "The John Hammond Years," CBC Radio, October 1986.

"Roman Catholicism, Buddhism, L.S.D.": LC in Gaby Goliger, "Leonard Cohen,"

Echo 1 (16 December 1966) 13.

"just speak from the center": David Kaufman, one of the three visiting students, reporting Cohen's statement 1/12/96.

151 "You got it, Leonard": LC in "The John Hammond Years," CBC.

"hypnotic effect": John Hammond, "The John Hammond Years," CBC.

"Leonard set": John Hammond, "The John Hammond Years," CBC.

"Leonard, we know": Walter Yetnikoff in *Goldmine* 20

152 "a compassionate lapse": LC, "The John Hammond Years," CBC.

"Leonard always needed": John Hammond, "The John Hammond Years," CBC.

"pillows of sound": John Hammond in *Goldmine* 14.

"linear, should be smooth": LC in *Goldmine* 15.

153 "The songs and arrangements": LC, SLC.

"unguessable": Buffy Sainte-Marie, "Leonard Cohen, His Songs," *Sing Out* 17 (1967) 16.

"It's like losing": Sainte-Marie, *Sing Out* 16.

154 "lost in New York City": LC, "Notes," BLC.

"What do you think?": LC 11/14/ 94.

155 "I sort of felt": LC in Jack Hafferkamp, "Ladies and Gents, Leonard Cohen," *Rolling Stone* (1972) rpt. in *Songs of Love and Hate* (New York: Amsco Publishing, 1972) [2].

"the stories of the street": "Stories of the Street," SLC.

"It was the only time": LC, *Mojo* (September 1994) 59.

156 "our most sophisticated singer": LC in Rowland, *Musician* (1988) 98.

Dylan as Cohen: *Yakety Yak* 13.

"Well, I think": LC in Adrienne Clarkson, "Leonard Cohen, A Monster of Love," *Take This Waltz* 25.

157 "pace runners": Joni Mitchell 8/26/ 94.

"the extension of our friendship": LC 11/14/94.

"They showed me the film": LC, *Yakety Yak* 165.

"James Joyce is not dead": "Cohen Overwhelms Listeners With Prose, Poetry, and Song," *Introspectrum, Buffalo State University* (11 April 1967) [1].

"I cannot sing unless": Sid Katz 12/24/95.

"guitar playing": Sid Katz 12/24/95.

158 "None of you guys": Marty Machat, *Goldmine* 11.

"strictly an underground celebrity": William Kloman, "I've Been on the Outlaw Scene Since 15," *NYT* (28 January 1968) D21.

"on the verge of": *NYT* (28 January 1968) D21.

"When I see a woman": *NYT* (28 January 1968) D21.

"I wish the women": *NYT* (28 January 1968) D21.

159 "have a pathological tone": *NYT* (28 January 1968) D22.

"rediscover the cruxcifixion": *NYT* (28 January 1968) D22.

"on the alienation scale": Donal Henahan, "Alienated Young Man Creates Some Sad Music," *NYT* (28 January 1968) II: 21. "Pity": *Maclean's* (February 1968) 72.

"Cohen suffers": Richard Goldstein, "Beautiful Creep," *Village Voice* (27 December 1967) 18.

160 "the environment": LC in Alastair Pirrie, "Cohen Regrets," *New Musical Express* (10 March 10973) 66.

"I never married": LC, *Musician* 98.

"The thing died very quickly": LC, *Musician* 98.

"What is Scientology?": JM 8/26/94.

"Did you ever go clear?": "Famous Blue Raincoat," SLH.

161 "My new laws": "Why I Happen to be Free," FH 60.

Chapter 8

164 "had catlike characters": Lailios to author 9/12/94.

"God, when I see": LC in Barbara Amiel, "Leonard Cohen says that to All the Girls," *Maclean's* (18 September 1978) 58.

"I fear we are to be": LC 5/11/94.

"Leonard, don't say": LC 5/11/94.

"to make us laugh": LC, *People* 13 (14 January 1980) 57.

166 "Diamonds in the Mine": SLH

"I moved there": LC, "Comme un Guerrier," *Throat Culture* 62.

"As long as someone": Suzanne Elrod, *People* (14 January 1980) 57.

167 "I leave to several": LC, "The Pro," *Nashville Notebook of 1969*, LCA; also see "The Pro," DLM 187.

"What do you want?": Bob Johnston 10/29/94.

"a musical bodyguard": Charlie Daniels 11/3/94.

168 "to make his voice": BJ 10/29/94.

"Leonard has always had": BJ 10/29/94.

"The voice is uncertain": LC, "Notes," BLC.

"created an atmosphere": LC, *Goldmine* 16.

"read the Zohar": LC, Journal [1969], LCA.

"Sometimes I need you naked": "You Know Who I Am," SFR.

169 "seems to return me": LC, "Notes," BLC.

"Like a bird": "Like a Bird on the Wire," SFR.

"I would stare out": LC in Paul Zollo, "Leonard Cohen, Inside the Tower of Song," *SongTalk* 3;2 (1993): 31.

"three guys": *SongTalk* 3:2: 31.

170 "Who are you?": LC in Paul Williams *Crawdaddy* (March 1975) 52.

"Forget everything I said": *Crawdaddy* 52.

"not only serious": Vincent Canby, "McCabe and Mrs. Miller," *NYT* (25 June 1971) 17.

171 "delivered sotto voce": John Simon, "An Appalling Plague has been Loosed on Our Films," *NYT* (19 September 1971) II:13.

"like Villon with frostbite": *Time* (25 January 1993) 57.

"Show me": Steve Sanfield, "The Inner Passage," *Zen and Hasidism*, ed. Harold Heifetz (Wheaton, Ill." The Theosophical Publishing House, 1978) 223.

172 "Nice song": LC in Sanfield, *Zen and Hasidism* 233.

173 "What makes Leonard Cohen": Columbia Records advertisement 1969.

"May I respectfully request": *Vancouver Province* (7 May 1969) 14.

"would not conform to": *Vancouver Province* (7 May 1969) 14. Also see "Quebec Writers Take Literary Lion's Share," *Montreal Star* (22 April 1969) 22.

174 "C'mere. I want to talk": Mordecai Richler in Alan Twigg, "The Gospel According to Leonard Cohen," *Georgia Straight* 12 (10-17 November 1978) 6; Sheldon Tietlbaum, "Leonard Cohen, Pain Free," *Los Angeles Times Magazine* (5 April 1992) 22.

"get behind Canada then": LC 12/29/94.

"I have no idea": JMCCL 7/23/94.

"MARITA": SP 239.

"Go your own way": Hugh Whitney Morrison, at one time married to Marita La Fleche, 11/14/ 93.

175 "a modern housewife's lament": *NYT* (29 September 1968) 21.

"Some were songs first": K. Murphy and G. Gross, "Leonard Cohen," *NYT* (13 April 1969) VI:36.

"When poetry strays": Ezra Pound quoted by LC in H. Kubernik and J. Pierce, "Cohen's New Skin," *Melody Maker* (1 March 1975) 41.

"Leonard Cohen: the poet as hero": *Saturday Night* (June 1969).

"He acts taller": Jack Batten, "The Poet as Hero Pt.1," *SN* (1969) 24.

176 "a betrayal of mankind": "Comme un Guerrier," *Throat Culture* 62.

"I swore by the sunlight": ES 11.

"Seig Heil!": LC 2/17/94.

177 "captivating self abasement": Canadian Press wire story, 13 May 1970.

"Word gets around": Tony Palmer, "A Modern Troubadour," *Observer* (7 June) 1970.

"Mr. Cohen sings": Michael Jahn, "Cohen and 'Army' Sing in Forest Hills," *NYT* (27 July 1970) 18.

178 "If you don't like": LC 2/17/94.

"did the damndest thing": Kris Kristofferson, *Take This Waltz* 104.

"Leonard Cohen is an old": LC, "Comme un Guerrier," *Throat Culture* 62.

"Cohen lays on": Farr in Jack Batten, "Cohen, the Genuine Article," *Globe and Mail* (5 December 1970) 33.

"I decided I": LC in Lumsden, *Weekend Magazine* (12 September 1970) 25.

179 "The book has been": LC in Lumsden, *Weekend Magazine* (12 September 1970) 25.

"a symbol of their own": Dorman 233-34.

180 "absolutely everything": LC, "Comme un Guerrier," *Throat Culture* 62.

"I began to believe": LC, "Comme un Guerrier," *Throat Culture* 62.

"I fell in love with": FR [91].

"familiar poison, dependence and love": LC, "Diary, Antigua, August 1973," LCA [1].

"Sometimes I feel": LC in Lumsden, *Weekend Magazine* (12 September 1970) 24.

"Suffering has led me": LC in Lumsden, *Weekend Magazine* (12 September 1970) 25.

"You've got to recreate": LC in Lumsden, *Weekend Magazine* (12 September 1970) 25.

Chapter 9

182 "I had, as the model": LC, *Goldmine* 17.

"thought I looked like": LC, "Notes," BLC.

"But the skylight is like skin": "Last Year's Man," SLH.

183 "with each": LC in H. Kibernick, "Cohen through the years," *Melody Maker* (6 March 1975) 13.

"the same old droning work": LC in Pirrie, "Cohen Regrets," *New Music Express* (10 March 1973) 66.

"European blues": LC in H. Kubernik and J. Pierce, "Cohen's New Skin," *Melody Maker* (1 March 1975) 41.

184 "the reason I need girls": LC in Paul Saltzman, "Famous Last Words from Leonard Cohen," *Maclean's* 85 (June 1972) 80.

"I'm just reeling": LC in Saltzman 78.

185 "Oh boy, we get to do": LC quoted by BJ 10/29/94.

"Once I was walking": LC in Burr Snider, "Leonard Cohen, Zooey Glass in Europe," *Leonard Cohen, The Artist and His Critics*, ed. Michael Gnarowski (Toronto: McGraw-Hill Ryerson, 1976) 61-62.

"One got the feeling": Roy Hollingworth, "Leonard Cohen," *Melody Maker* (1 April 1972) 14.

"I have no more songs": LC in Hollingworth 14.

186 "Should we not try some?": LC 10/24/95.

"Like the Eucharist": LC 10/24/95.

"Is this All?": LC 10/24/95.

"There are nights": LC in Dorman 259.

187 "Trying to maintain": LC in Dorman 242.

"life was art and God was music": Jennifer Warnes 5/13/94.

"to squeezing memory and vocabulary": FR 86-87.

"pious moods": FR 87; originally a journal entry dated 26 July 1972, LCA.

188 "You ask me how I write": FR 87.

"It took me eighty poems": Saltzman 79.

"because I have the feeling": Saltzman 80.

"what alone matters": IL, inscription in LC's copy of ES dated 4 December 1972.

189 "Partner in Spirit": LC, cancelled dedication, DLM, LCA.

"the Lion of our Youth": LC, cancelled dedication, DLM, LCA.

"To the late Robert Hershorn": "Dedication," RS.

"I can't seem to bring": LC, "Robert Appears Again," *Writing Away, The* PEN *Canada Travel Anthology*, ed. Constance Rooke (Toronto: McClelland & Stewart, 1994) 54.

"It was a tricky time": LC 5/12/94.

190 "It began": LC in Paul King, "Love, Zen and The Search for Self," *Vancouver Sun* (30 June 1983) L6.

"I can't get": LC 5/10/94.

"Bring friend": LC 5/10/94.

"It's going to hurt": LC 5/10/94.

"the revenge of World War II": LC 5/10/94.

"Even as we lie here": "O darling," ES 111.

191 "I dreamed about this": LC 5/11/94.

"How do you realize": LC 5/11/94.

"Where are the poems": "I'd like to read," ES 14.

"In many ways": LC *Goldmine* 18.

"welcome to this book": "How we loved you," ES 115-16.

192 "Come down to my room": "Come down," ES 84.

"Why don't you": "You are almost always," ES 82.

"the 15-year-old": "the fifteen-year-old," ES 97.

"I am no longer": "I am no longer," ES 24.

"write with compassion": "The silly girl," ES 39.

"Each man": "Each man," ES 122.

"I have no talent left:" "I have no talent," ES 112.

"It was like dipping": LC in Roy MacSkimming, "'New' Leonard Cohen opens up his thoughts," *Toronto Star* (22 January 1975) E16.

193 "I'm thirty-eight years": LC, autobiographical fragment (1973) LCA.

"While she suffers": FR 88.

"Listening to gypsy violins": FR 88.

"fighting over scraps": FR 89.

"the mad mystic hammering": Daphne Richardson, "Notes," LS.

194 "In the House of Honesty": "Seems So Long Ago, Nancy," LS

"I'm too old": LC in Twigg, *Georgia Straight* 24.

"I just cannot stand": LC to Roy Hollingworth in *Melody Maker* (14 February 1973) reported in "Leonard Cohen Quits his Musical Interests Will Stick to Writing," *Toronto Star* (15 February 1973) 32.

"no longer . . . to be tangled up": LC in *Toronto Star* (15 Feb 1973) 32.

195 "I never did retire": LC in "Leonard Cohen: A Sad Poet Gets Happy," *Toronto Star* (30 June 1973) 34.

"Bed–centered play": *Hamilton Spectator* (5 June 1973) [n.p.].

"musical journey": Clive Barnes, NYT reprinted in *Vancouver Sun* (28 September 1973) 24.

196 "to recover from": LC in Pike, *Zig Zag* 47.

"because it is so horrible": FR 5; DLM 54.

"to make my atonement": LC, *Vancouver Sun* (20 October 1973) 12.

"What a burden": FR 11.

"I never became a sign": FR 12.

"I won't fuck":FR 12.

"Nothing can stop me": FR 16.

"I could see": FR 20.

197 "I am in": FR 22.

"The war was": FR 24.

"long, stainless steel legs": FR 30.

"I went immediately to": FR 33.

"After I had showered": FR 33.

"You will only sing": FR 31.

"But I want her": FR 31.

198 "tanks are the only": FR 34.

"I manage to kill": FR 34.

"May I entertain": "My Life in Art," MCM. 40; this is a more polished section of *The Final Revision of My Life in Art*.

199 "It was very informal": LC in Pike, *Zig Zag* 47.

"but you get caught up": LC in Pike, *Zig Zag* 47.

"Feeling good in the desert": "My Life in Art," MCM. 41.

"the people stop me": "My Life in Art," MCM. 42.

"acid into diplomatic cocktail parties": "Field Commander Cohen," NS.

"passion and possession": "My Life in Art," MCM.43.

200 "It all breaks down": "Pulled out of bed," Prose Fragment, LCA [2].

"says I took away": "Pulled out of bed," LCA [2].

"make peace with the language of love": FR 95.

"It's no good": LC, journal fragment [1973] LCA.

"What unfreezes a man?": LC, ms. fragment, LCA, which continues with "By whose authority does he admit the Gulf Stream into his crystal? How does the humiliated spirit find its way out of the dead Kaballah?" cf. DLM 61.

Chapter 10

201 "I needed so much": "The Night Comes On," VP.

"If you want to see": Joshu Sasaki Roshi, *Buddha is the Center of Gravity* (San Cristobal, New Mexico: Lama Foundation, 1974) 46.

"You should sing sadder": Roshi to LC, "Comme un Guerrier," *Throat Culture* 62.

"I need to go deeper": LC, "Comme un Guerrier," *Throat Culture* 62.

202 "When I go there": LC, *People* 13 (14 January 1980) 57.

"the end of my life in art": DLM 190.

"Six-fifty [a.m.]": DLM 192.

"I swim in your love": DLM 62.

"I came so far for beauty": "Came So Far for Beauty," RS.

"Tibetan Desire": BL 10.

203 "I am growing sick": FR 26.
 "Once I walked": FR 30.
 "Goodnight once again": FR 95.
 "The man in chains": FR 97.
 "I lost that": FR 103.
204 "It's the least painful": FR 112.
 "Too early for the rainbow": "The Gypsy's Wife," RS.
 "So the Chinese girl": FR 103.
 "It will become clear": DLM 21.
 "You got old": "Is This What You Wanted?", NS.
 "I rise up from her arms": "There Is A War," NS.
205 "has the deepest understanding": LC in H. Kubernik, "Cohen Through the Years," *Melody Maker* (6 March 1975) 13.
206 "Thank you": LC in Pike, *Zig Zag* 50.
 "Maybe because": LC in Danny Fields, "Leonard Cohen Looks at Himself," *Soho News* 1 (5 December 1974) 8.
 "When I stand": LC in Fields, *Soho News* 9.
 "one of the strongest": H. Kubernik and J. Pierce, "Cohen, A True Craftsman," *Melody Maker* (28 December 1974) 12.
 "the first lover": FR 106.
 "There is a lot": John Rockwell, "Leonard Cohen Gives His Songs," NYT (9 February 1975) 16.
207 "he looks like an overworked": Andrew Weiner, "Poet on the Rack," *New Musical Express* (5 April 1975) 33.
 "It is not exactly": FR 36-37.
 "street father": FR 40.
 "to teach my son": FR 40.
208 "I am going": FR 43.
 "then the obscene silence": FR 44.
 "created so much tougher": FR 45.
 "I gave a woman": FR 45.
 "The moon is over": FR 46-47.
 "against Domestic Conversations": FR 48.
 "The first woman": FR48.
209 "Without the Name": FR 52.
 "My heart longs": DLM 63.
 "Names preserve": BL 40.
 "Leonard hasn't been": PH 33.
 "When it comes to": DLM 79.
 "I am almost": DLM 212.
 "We will go back": FR 53.
210 "I should have killed": FR 53.
 "who loves me": FR 57.
 "Did I know": FR 64.
 "Desire in Athens": FR 65.
211 "To see me you must": FR 81.
 "not been denied":FR 82.
 "We didn't get": LC 4/21/95.
 "I decided to worship": FR 85.
 "in the style of": FR 72.
212 "who lighted up": FR 73.
 "the song could not": FR 73.

"I don't know why": "Notes," BLC.

213 "Body important": LC 4/21/95.

"surprising how he sings": Rob Mackie, "Romance at the Broncoburger," *Street Life* (12-25 June 1976) 15.

"He told me about": LC, prose fragments (1 August 1976), LCA.

"When I'm not plotting": LC, prose fragments, LCA.

"life is not": LC in Mackie, *Street Life* 15.

"Bitterly": LC, prose fragments, (2 August 1976), LCA.

"I wanted to go": LC, *Matrix* 53.

214 "I came upon texts": LC, *Matrix* 53.

"How do you": LC reported by JM 8/26/94.

215 "As long as we": LC, "Comme un Guerrier," *Throat Culture* 63.

"very charming and hospitable": LC, *Songtalk* 3:2:30.

"I thought the songs": LC, *Goldmine* 19.

"He kept a lot of guns": LC, *Throat Culture* 63.

"I love you, Leonard": LC, *Throat Culture* 63.

216 "Dylan blew everybody's": Allen Ginsberg in *Songtalk* 3:2:1.

"It's direct and confessional": LC in Kubernik, "The greatest ones never just sit it out once," *Melody Maker* (26 November 1977) 9.

"the full flower": LC in Twigg, *Georgia Straight* 24.

217 "I know my work": LC 5/11/94.

"The listener could have been": LC in Hugh Seidman, "Unful'phil'ed: Cohen & Spector's Looney Tunes," *Crawdaddy* (February 1978) 20.

"capable of stunning": Seidman, *Crawdaddy* 20.

"I should get myself": LC, "Comme un Guerrier," *Throat Culture* 64.

"Leonard Cohen's doo-wop": *Rolling Stone* (9 February 1978) 93.

"Leonard Cohen is for": *Toronto Star* (19 November 1977) D5.

"Doyen of Doom meets": Roy Carr, "Doyen of Doom meets Teen Tycoon . . ." *Melody Maker* (November 1977) 32.

"most significant step": Ken Waxman, "Rebirth of a Ladies' Man," *Saturday Night* (March 1978) 61.

"either greatly flawed": *Rolling Stone* (9 February 1978) 95.

218 "She took his much admired": "Death of A Ladies' Man", DLM.

"every relationship": LC in Stephen Williams, "The confessions of Leonard Cohen," *Toronto Life* (February 1978) 49.

Chapter 11

219 "I must say": Anna Porter to JMCCL (10 November 1976), MCM.

"Leonard Cohen": Lily Miller, (? November 1976), MCM.

220 "I suggest": LM (? November 1976), MCM.

"because of language": anon., (? June? 1977), MCM.

"His drawings": LM, ? June 1977, MCM.

"He feels very excited": LM to JMCCL, 10 August 1977, MCM.

"This is a grim development": JMCCL to LM, 10 August 1977, MCM.

221 "pulled apart and uptight": JMCCL to LM, 11 August 1977, MCM.

"says he is re-writing": JMCCL to LM, 11 August 1977, MCM.

"He says he is writing": JMCCL to LM, 11 August 1977, MCM.

"I DOUBT THAT": LC to JMCCL, 18 August 1977, MCM.

"LEONARD THERE IS NO SWEAT": JMCCL to LC, 19 August 1977, MCM.

"where we are heading": JMCCL to LC, 11 October 1977, MCM.

222 "Christ, Leonard": JMCCL in Sandra Martin, "Don't be impatient: Leonard Cohen will let you see his new poems. Eventually," *Saturday Night* (November 1977) 30.

"If Leonard were": JMCCL in *Saturday Night* (November 1977) 35.

223 "bulk and elegance": LM to JMCCL, 7 July 1978, MCM. Miller had met with the elusive Cohen in Montreal on 6 July 1978 to solve many of the production issues.

"astonishing": Sam Ajzenstat, "The ploy's the thing," *Books in Canada* (October 1978) 10.

"coldly received in all circles": LC in *Goldmine* 19.

224 "marriage is a monastery": LC in Stephen Williams, "The Confessions of Leonard Cohen," *Toronto Life* (February 1978) 61. In DLM Cohen writes "This is the monastery of marriage" (153).

"the hottest furnace": LC in Williams, *Crawdaddy* (March 1975) 51.

"the quality of smoke": LC in Jeani Read, "Leonard Cohen: A Much Bigger Man than He Appears," *Vancouver Province* (27 October 1978) 15.

225 "Irving Layton": "Dedication," RS.

"I owe my thanks to": "Dedication," RS.

226 "the pasture of this world": Kakuan, "10 Bulls," tr. Nyogen Senzaki and Paul Reps in Paul Reps, *Zen Flesh, Zen Bones* (Rutland, Vt.: Charles E. Tuttle & Co., 1957) 168.

"forms of integration": *Zen Flesh, Zen Bones* 184.

"an ideal musical idiom": "Leonard Cohen — Reaching for the Right Idiom," Janet Maslin, NYT (18 November 1978) E30.

227 "everybody on tour": LC in Dorman 310.

"the confusion of seriousness": LC in Dorman 311.

"He has the same": LC in Stephen Godfrey, "A New Artistic Twist for Pied Piper Poet," *Globe and Mail* (1 March 1980) E1.

228 "I think it's a beautiful": LC, *Globe and Mail* E1.

"a classic, a grostesque masterpiece": LC, *Globe and Mail* E1.

"destined to be": John Monks in *The Australian*, Dorman 314-15.

"I never got out": LC in Dorman 316.

"it didn't seem": LC in *Globe and Mail* E1.

"The song seized me": LC in Harry Rasky, "The Song of Leonard Cohen," CBC-TV, 1980.

229 "a new spirit in my work": LC, "The Song of Leonard Cohen."

"Genius": IL, "The Song of Leonard Cohen."

"the gift of anxiety": IL, "The Song of Leonard Cohen."

"I wandered away from you": LC, tape (1980), LCA.

231 "a wandering monk": Steve Sanfield 10/3/94.

"Zero is activity": Joshu Sasaki Roshi, "Questions and Answers," *The Great Celebration* (Los Angeles: Rinzai-ji, Inc. 1992) 64-65.

"As long as we see": Roshi in Sanfield, *Zen and Hasidism* 227.

"through realizing oneself": Roshi, "The Nature of Zero," *Zero* III:12.

"everything is oneself": Roshi, *Zero* 13.

"is the possession of": Roshi, *Zero* 14.

232 "After you realize": Roshi quoted by LC 5/10/94.

"Roshi saw that I knew": LC 5/10/94.

"I am not a Buddhist": LC in Dorman 316.

"for the truly lost": NB 12/29/94.

"My father and mother": LC, *Hollywood Reporter* (25 October 1993), LCA.

233 "If you see": LC in Christof Graf, "Cohen in Nazi-Land," *Take This Waltz* 94.

"One more star": LC 11/14/94.
234 "dig in":LC 5/11/94.
"diligent application": LC 5/11/94.
"a combination of": LC in Stephen Holden, "Leonard Cohen Brings Back His Blues," *NYT* (3 May 1985) 22.
235 "reminiscent of the sixties": *Variety* (22 May 1985) 26.
237 "a kind of carousel": LC in Kate Daller, "I Am A Hotel," *Starweek* (5-12 May 1984) 4.
"My personal life is such": Daller, *Starweek* 4.
"must assume": LC 5/11/94.
"I like to get up": LC 5/11/94.
"get down": LC, [#13], BM, n.p.
"I was silenced": LC in Alan Twigg, "Leonard Cohen," *Strong Voices: Conversations with Fifty Canadian Writers* (Maderia Park, BC: Harbour Publishing, 1988) 45.
"the courage to write down": LC in Twigg, *Strong Voices* 46.
238 "inspired or it isn't": Mirolla, *Montreal Gazette* (12 May 1984) I 2.
"It came from an intense desire": LC, "Comme un Guerrier," *Throat Culture* 64.
"Broken in the unemployment": [#12], BM.
"It's a tricky thing": LC, *Quill and Quire* (May 1984) 5.
"Everyone is in some kind of fix": LC, Q & Q (May 1984) 5.
239 "We're such a hip age": LC in Twigg, *Strong Voices* 46.
"May it therefore": *Mahzor for Rosh Hashanah and Yom Kippur* (NY: Rabbinical Assembly, 1972) 407.
"I had no idea": LC, *Songtalk* 3:2:28.
"I bought": LC in Richard Guillatt, "Leonard Cohen" *The Magazine, Sunday Times* (12 December 1993) 64.
240 "I don't know why": LC, *Sunday Times* 64.
"The initial thing": Liam Lacey, "Leonard in Winter," *Globe and Mail* (27 November 1993) E1.
"I left everybody": "The Law," VP.
"We were locked": "The Night Comes On," VP.
241 "people who can't sing": LC, National Public Radio (1 May 1985).
"the tomb of the Unknown": LC in Ashley Collie, "Leonard Cohen, Old Skin for the New Ceremony," *Canadian Musician* VII (August 1985) 44.
"Sinner": LC, Pete Fornetell, "Mixed Bag," WNEW (NYC), 5 May 1985.
"an old veteran:" LC in Jeffrey Ressner, "Leonard Cohen," *Hollywood Reporter* (14 June 1985) 10.

Chapter 12

243 "deep rescue": Jennifer Warnes 5/13/94.
"Leonard made sure": JW 5/13/94.
"Leonard's tours": JW 5/13/94.
244 "This is horrible": JW 5/13/94.
"*I* knew": JW 5/13/94.
"And I thank you": "First We Take Manhattan," IYM.
245 "It has been": LC in Steve Lakes, "The Grocer of Despair, Leonard Cohen," *Münchner Stadt Zeitung* 14 (1987) 29.
"pry open": JW in, "Songs from the Life of Leonard Cohen," Omnibus, BBC TV 1988.
"the place where God and sex": JW in Paul Zollo, "Of Sunlight & Earthquakes,

Jennifer Warnes," *Songtalk* 3:1 (1992) 17.

"Your most particular answer": LC, *Songtalk* 3:2:26.

"Because of Leonard's facility": JW, *Songtalk* 3:1:18.

"Her voice": LC in JW, *Songtalk* 3:1:17.

"if you want to hear": LC in JW, *Songtalk* 3:1:17.

246 "Sharon showed it": LC in Gregg Quill, "Cohen Finds the Humor in Being Taken Seriously," *Toronto Star* (4 May 1988) 12.

"I thought we should do": LC, Howell Llewellyn, "Cohen Goes Surreal in Spain," *Toronto Star* (18 October 1986) G3.

247 "No, I'm a famous nobody": LC, "Cohen Goes Surreal," *Toronto Star* G3.

"holy condition": LC in Dorman 355.

"It broke down a lot": Rowland, *Musician Magazine* 102.

248 "I couldn't get behind": LC in Juan Rodriguez. "The Odd Couple, Leonard Cohen and Michel Pagliaro," *Montreal Magazine* (March 1990) 38.

"Everything is public": LC in Rowland, *Musician Magazine* 97.

"I have always been touched": LC at the CBS Records Crystal Globe ceremony, New York (9 March 1988) LCA.

"total commitment": LC, Norwegian Radio, Oslo, 13 February 1988.

"demented manifesto": LC in Siemerling, "A Political Constituency," *Take This Waltz* 164.

249 "First we take Manhattan": LC in Siemerling, *Take This Waltz* 165.

"This waltz, this waltz": "Take This Waltz," IYM.

"to get at the dramatic depths": Lorca, *Collected Poetry,* xl.

"ought to be": Lorca, *Collected Poetry,* xl.

"it caught the mood": LC in Rowland, *Musician Magazine* 104.

"started off as a song": LC in Rowland, *Musician Magazine* 102.

"What is my life?": LC in Rowland, *Musician Magazine* 102.

"make a definite statement": LC in Rowland, *Musician Magazine* 104.

"necessity to transcend": LC 5/11/94.

250 "really placed it": LC 5/11/94.

"Well, my friends are gone": "Tower of Song," IYM.

"I never thought I *was*": LC in Rowland, *Musician Magazine* 119.

"Now I know what I am": LC in Rowland, *Musician Magazine* 100.

"They say the Torah": LC in *Songtalk* 3:2:27.

"I don't really know": LC in Brian Cullman, "Sincerely, L. Cohen," *Details* (January 1993) 105.

"a sardonic last call": Liam Lacey, *Globe and Mail* (27 November 1993) E1.

251 "it doesn't sound like music": LC quoted by Perla Batalla, 5/11/94.

"what you have to go for": LC quoted by Perla Batalla, 5/11/94.

"make it like": LC in *Vancouver Province* (16 October 1988) 67.

"Orbisize": LC in *Vancouver Province* (16 October 1988) 67.

252 "what you have to do": LC in Rodriguez, "The Odd Couple," *Montreal Magazine* (March 1990) 38.

"I was born like this": "Tower of Song," IYM.

"I think if": LC in Rowland, *Musician Magazine* 95.

"I've come a long way": LC in *Songtalk* 3:2:31.

253 "as a tribute to": Lorna Knight, *Let Us Compare Mythologies, Half a Century of Canadian Poetry in English* (Ottawa: National Library of Canada, 1989) 5.

"links two vital periods": Knight 5.

"poetic voices became": Knight 5.

"romantic lyricism": Knight 39.

254 "That's what it's all about": LC 5/14/94.

"he has no psychic skin": Sean Dixon 5/11/94.

"We would go": SD 5/11/94.

"It's hell, darling": LC quoted by SD 5/11/94.

"Leonard, you just": SD 5/11/94.

"You can't say": SD 5/11/94.

"Things are going to slide": "The Future," TF.

"If you're pressed": "Waiting for the Miracle," TF.

255 "Leonard is one of": Rebecca De Mornay in David Browne, "7 Reasons Leonard Cohen is the Next-Best Thing to God," *Entertainment Weekly* (8 January 1993) 31.

256 "Do you want to know": "Knowing Rebecca De Mornay like only Leonard Cohen Can," *Interview* (June 1993) 81.

"Solid gold artists": LC in *Entertainment Weekly*(8 January 1993) 31.

"Rebecca got wise": LC in *RTE Weekly* (20-26 August 1993) 6.

258 "I am trying": LC in Ian Pearson, "Growing Old Disgracefully," *Saturday Night* (March 1993) 49.

"one of the most popular": Citation, Order of Canada, Governor General's Office, Rideau Hall, Ottawa (16 August 1993).

"exposure to [Layton's] work": LC, *Globe and Mail* (25 October 1991) 18.

"has never been disloyal": IL 7/25/94.

Chapter 13

259 "From my balcony": John Walsh, "Melancholy Baby," *Independent Magazine* (8 May 1993) 40.

"those soft California stars": Jack Kerouac, "The Mexican Girl," *The Portable Jack Kerouac* 177.

260 "a training in self-reform": LC 5/11/94; also see LC in Alan Twigg, *Georgia Straight* 20.

"It's very dangerous": LC in *MOJO* (September 1994) 61.

"When you rose out": "The Mist of Pornography," LCA.

"My Life in Art": DLM 192.

261 "to the painful decision": LC 12/29/94.

"but when I listened": LC, *Songtalk* 3:2:27.

"the way I do things": LC 5/11/94.

262 "And the whole damn place": "Closing Time," TF.

"A pessimist": LC in Reuter's, "Leonard Cohen enjoying the spotlight," *Vancouver Province* (28 December 1993) B7.

"Only in a country": acceptance speech, JUNO Awards, CBC TV 21 March 1993.

"gritty realistic voice": Allen Ginsberg, "Leonard Cohen" *Take This Waltz* 93.

263 "there is nothing like": LC in *Georgia Straight* (9 July 1993) 41.

"Leonard Cohen wrapped": *Boston Globe* (26 December 1993) A10.

"I feel like a soldier": LC in Paul Cantin, "Citizen Cohen," *Ottawa Sun* (28 November 1993) 34.

"The implication is": *Ottawa Sun* 34.

264 "primitivist, protuberant": LC in *Toronto Star* (21 November 1993) B1.

"came up with": LC in Siemerling, *Take This Waltz* 154.

"could never get around to": LC in Dev Sherlock, "Leonard Cohen," *Musician Magazine* (November 1993) 7.

"select the pieces": LC quoted by NB 2/18/94; 12/29/94.

265 "a book that was good": J. Lozaw, "Leonard Cohen," *Boston Rock* #141 (June 1994) 20.

"coherent": LC 5/11/94.

266 "I'm glad we ran off": ES 111.

"I'm glad we got over": SM 161.

"major new book": Doug Gibson to JMCCL, 11 December 1989, MCM.

"reflections on his career": DG to JMCCL, 5 October 1991, MCM.

"I tried to eliminate": LC in Lacey, *Globe and Mail* (12 November 1993) E1.

267 "it's very agreeable": LC in *Goldmine* 56.

"I'm really not": LC in Lozaw, *Boston Rock* 20.

268 "the final pages": LC *RTE Guide* 6.

"the voice": LC, *RTE Guide* 6.

"This glum": David Hiltbrand, "Cohen Live," *People* 42 (4 July 1994) [19].

"I only drink professionally": LC, *RTE Guide* 6.

"a Tibetan fairy tale": LC 12/29/94.

"I respect the book": LC, "Morningside," CBC Radio, 13 December 1994.

"the event itself": LC, "Morningside," 13 December 1994.

269 "I was ready": LC 12/29/94.

"I remember when": LC 12/29/94.

270 "On the path of loneliness": LC, *Globe and Mail* (4 June 1994) C10; PEN *Canadian Travel Anthology*, ed. Rooke 55.

"a ponderous mind": LC in James Adams, "Dancing in the Tower of Song," *Globe and Mail* (3 August 1995) A9.

"I am very happy": LC, "Press Release," A&M Records, August 1995.

271 "A quill in his teeth": Tom Robbins, "Tom Robbins Considers the Man in the Tower," TS [1] [3],[5] [10].

"In Search of Optimism": Rod Usher, "In Search of Optimism," *Time* (25 September 1995) 72.

"there is a crack": "Anthem," TF.

"when [love] can be assimilated": LC in Anjelica Huston, "Leonard Cohen," *Interview* (November 1995) 92, 90.

272 "Nowadays my only need": LC in Merja Asikainen, "Leonard Cohen," *Ilta-Sanomat* (14 October 1995) 14, in Finnish; for English summary see Jarkko Arjatsalo, "Everybody Knows," *Intensity* 9 (December 1995) [15].

"With him there's no sense": LC in James Adams, "Dancing to the Tower of Song," *Globe and Mail* (3 August 1995) A 10.

"I love it, Man": LC in *MOJO* (September 1994) 59.

"survival": LC 5/11/94.

"For me": LC 5/11/94.

"[Zen] has a kind of": LC, "Morningside," 13 December 1994.

274 "the crumbs of love": "Avalanche," SLH.

"I'll rise up": "My Honour," SM 394.

"I find that my life": LC, BRAVO TV, 31 August 1995.

INDEX

PERMISSIONS